中英对照

青草中英双语分级读物

那些给我爱与温暖的人

第3级

总主编 林 梅

本书主编 张晓红 吴秀秀 何敏

生命中总会有一些人一些事
陪伴着我们，温暖着我们

北京航空航天大学出版社
BEIHANG UNIVERSITY PRESS

图书在版编目（CIP）数据

那些给我爱与温暖的人：汉英对照 / 林梅等主编
. -- 北京：北京航空航天大学出版社，2016.4
（青青草中英双语分级读物 / 林梅主编 . 第3级）
ISBN 978-7-5124-2087-8

Ⅰ.① 那… Ⅱ.① 林… Ⅲ.①英语 – 汉语 – 对照读物
②名人 – 生平事迹 – 世界 Ⅳ.① H319.4：K

中国版本图书馆 CIP 数据核字（2016）056345 号

青青草中英双语分级读物
——那些给我爱与温暖的人（第3级）

总主编 林 梅

本书主编 张晓红 吴秀秀 何 敏

责任编辑 秦 莹

*

北京航空航天大学出版社出版发行

北京市海淀区学院路 37 号（邮编 100191） http://www.buaapress.com.cn
发行部电话：（010）82317024 传真：（010）82328026
读者信箱：bhwaiyu@163.com 邮购电话：（010）82316936
涿州市星河印刷有限公司印装 各地书店经销

*

开本：787×1092 1/32 印张：7.875 字数：258 千字
2016 年 9 月第 1 版 2016 年 9 月第 1 次印刷
ISBN 978-7-5124-2087-8 定价：23.80 元

编委会

前　言

　　语言表达能力的好坏主要靠词汇量的积累，而词汇量的积累最主要的途径是阅读。研究表明：美国儿童的阅读量是中国儿童的六倍。所以想要英语好，阅读是不可忽略的关键因素。

　　《青青草中英双语分级读物》是一套适合小学到大学的分级阅读材料，整个套系选材考究、内容丰富多样，涵盖了童话、寓言、歌曲、电影、小说、演讲等题材，能帮助您从培养兴趣开始，循序渐进，一步一步地把您带入英语的殿堂。

　　配有外教真人原声录制的音频，可让您在阅读之余练习听力和跟读，也可让您进行复述、提炼和总结。这是一套能帮助您提高语言发展、阅读能力、写作能力等综合训练的工具。

　　这套读物的教育意义不靠说教，不靠灌输，而是渗透式、启发式的，让您在愉悦的阅读过程中学习语言、爱上阅读，并为将来的写作奠定基础。

编者

2016 年于北京

目 录

Chapter 1 亲人至爱，心灵最大的港湾

Chapter 2 谢谢你给我的温暖

Chapter 3 爱是永恒的主题

Chapter 1

亲人至爱，心灵最大的港湾

A Daughter Thanks Her Mother 女儿对母亲的感谢

带着问题去阅读

1. 你经常给你的母亲写信吗？
2. 每年你能陪伴母亲多少天？
3. 你内心最想跟妈妈说的话是什么？

 美文欣赏

1 Dear Mum,

2 I haven't written many letters to you before, as we've almost always been able to just pick up the phone and have a chat, so it's hard to know how to start.

3 Of course, all the usual things apply—we all miss you and hope you're all right wherever you are.

4 When you left us, it took a little while for it to sink in thinking that I would never see you again. I guess it was a bit like you being away on a trip or those times when we didn't find the time to even speak on the phone for a week or so.

 译文

1 亲爱的妈妈：

2 以前我没有给您写过多少信，因为我们几乎总能拿起电话，聊上一会儿，所以真的不知道如何下笔。

3 当然，可以说些常说的套话——我们都想念您，无论您身在何方，愿您一切安好。

4 在您离开我们的时候，我曾陷入永远不能再见到您的痛苦中，好一阵才缓过来。有时会感觉就像您离开我们去旅行了，或者我们有一个星期左右没有时间通电话一样。

5 I realize now there are too many things left unsaid—as everyone always says—and too many questions unasked. Silly thing really, like yesterday, when I was doing my washing, I wondered how you felt when you got your first automatic washing machine. I can still remember the old machine you had when I was a child. Though, I guess I know the answers to most of the important things about you.

6 Dad finds life difficult without you and his loneliness is almost unbearable to me, as there's so little I can do to help him. I think in time he'll find some interests and make a new kind of life. But at the moment he seems only to look forward to the time when he can join you again.

7 Emily and I are feeling a little better each day and, in a way, your death has brought us closer together. We seem to understand each other better at the moment and maybe eventually we'll have the sort of relationship that really close sisters enjoy.

8 We've both found strengths in each other over the past weeks, and these are a huge of comfort. Perhaps we never needed to look for them before, because we had you to be strong for us.

9 I guess I'm lucky to have my own children to keep me so busy. I don't have much time to dwell on my sadness but

5 我现在意识到有太多的话还没有说（就像大家常说的那样），还有太多的问题没来得及问。其实尽是些愚蠢的问题，比如昨天，在我洗衣服的时候，我想知道您买来第一台自动洗衣机时心情如何。我还记得我小时候您用的那台旧洗衣机。然而我想有关您的故事，我大多数都了解。

6 没有了您，爸爸觉得日子很难熬，他的孤独让我很难受，因为我帮不了他多少忙。我想早晚他会找到些感兴趣的事，开始一种新的生活。但是眼下他似乎只是在期待着再次与您相聚。

7 我和埃米莉的心情日渐平复。从某种意义上讲，您的过世使我们关系更加密切了。此时此刻，我们似乎对彼此更加了解，也许最终我们会像亲姐妹一样。

8 在过去的几周里，我们从彼此的身上找到了力量，这真是莫大的安慰。也许我们以前从不需要寻求这种力量，因为有您作为我们的坚强后盾。

9 我想幸运的是我自己有了孩子，使我忙忙碌碌，因此没有多少时间沉湎在悲伤之

sometimes I crave the peace to just have a private think about you.

10　For a couple of weeks after you died, my brain seemed to go crazy, searching through its memory banks for something I could keep in my heart which was special to you and me. One day it came to me—the tour we made of some special garden.

11　Remember the day it poured with rain the whole time but we were determined to make the most of it? I enjoyed just being with you by myself, without the children clamoring for your attention. The gardens were beautiful despite the rain and you bought me a rose I'd admired for my own garden.

12　For a while after your death, I expected to feel your presence around me as Dad and Emily seem to do with such ease. When I was out walking, I would look at the sky and wonder whether you could see me, or whether you were with me. At night I wondered whether you'd become a star, as some people believe.

13　But as time passes, I think I'm closer to finding the truth. You're with me every time I comfort one of the children or try to find the right word to gently chastise

中，但有时我渴望有安静的一刻，可以私下思念您。

10　在您去世的好几周里，我的大脑好像发了疯一样，拼命地在我脑海的记忆库中寻找珍藏在我心中的某件事情——某件对你我二人都具有特殊意义的事情。有一天我突然想起了一件——我们曾去过一个秘密花园。

11　您还记得吗？那天一直下着倾盆大雨，但是我们打定主意，要充分利用这次机会好好玩一玩。我很高兴能和您单独一起，没有孩子们的吵闹使您分神。尽管下着雨，花园还是很美。您给我买了一支玫瑰，我一直希望自己的花园也有这种玫瑰。

12　您去世后的一段时间里，我期望能感到您就在我身边，爸爸和埃米莉似乎毫不费力就能感到您的存在。当我外出散步时，我常常仰望天空，想知道您是否看着我，或者您是否和我在一起。在夜晚，我会想，您是否像人们认为的那样变成一颗星星。

13　但是随着时间的流逝，我想我差不多找到了真实的感觉。每当我安慰一个孩子的时候，或者要找出合适的语

them. I listen for your words of wisdom and they come from within me because your greatest gift to me was teaching me how to be a good mother to my own children.

14 And although you're no longer here with us, I know in times of sadness or pain the children feel their mother's arms are around them just as I *sense* that I feel your arms are around me, too. In years to come I hope your gift to me will be passed to my own children's children. And I know it's your voice telling me in these changing times the thing we can give our children is love, because love is *eternal* and love doesn't die. So long for now, and thank you from all of us.

15 Happy Mother's Day, Mum

16 —Love Carol

言来轻轻地责备他们的时候，您都同我在一起。我留神倾听您充满智慧的语言，并留心记下，因为您给我最宝贵的礼物，就是教会了我如何成为自己孩子的好妈妈。

14 虽然您已经不再和我们一起生活了，但我知道在痛苦和悲伤的时候，孩子们总能感到母亲的臂膀拥抱着他们，就像我感到您的臂膀也在拥抱着我一样。在未来的岁月中，我希望把您留给我的礼物传给我的子孙。我知道那是您的声音在告诉我，在这个不断变化的时代，我们能留给我们的孩子的最好的东西就是爱，因为爱是永恒的，爱是不朽的。再见，我们都衷心地感谢您。

15 祝您母亲节快乐，妈妈！

16 爱您的卡罗尔

 阅读无障碍

chat [tʃæt] n. 聊天，谈话
apply [ə'plaɪ] v. 适合，适用
sink [sɪŋk] v. 沉下，陷入
realize ['riːəlaɪz] v. 认识到
wonder ['wʌndə(r)] v. 想知道

washing machine 洗衣机
unbearable [ʌn'beərəbl] adj. 无法忍受的，承受不住的
eventually [ɪ'ventʃuəlɪ] adv. 最后，最终

5

relationship [rɪˈleɪʃnʃɪp] *n.* 关系

strength [streŋθ] *n.* 力量

crave [kreɪv] *v.* 渴望，需要

private [ˈpraɪvət] *adj.* 私人的，个人的

memory [ˈmemərɪ] *n.* 记忆，回忆

pour [pɔ:(r)] *v.* 倾，倒，涌流

clamor [ˈklæmə] *v.* 喧哗，吵闹

presence [ˈprezns] *n.* 存在，在场

comfort [ˈkʌmfət] *v.* 安慰，使（痛苦等）缓和

chastise [tʃæˈstaɪz] *v.* 严惩

sense [sens] *v.* 感觉，感到

eternal [ɪˈtɜ:nl] *adj.* 永恒的，永久的

 **极品佳句背诵**

1. When I was out walking, I would look at the sky and wonder whether you could see me, or whether you were with me.
   当我外出散步时，我常常仰望天空，想知道您是否看着我，或者您是否和我在一起。

2. And although you're no longer here with us, I know in times of sadness or pain the children feel their mother's arms around them just as I sense that I feel your arms around me, too.
   虽然您已经不再和我们一起生活了，但我知道在痛苦和悲伤的时候，孩子们总能感到母亲的臂膀拥抱着他们，就像我能感到您的臂膀也在拥抱着我一样。

3. And I know it's your voice telling me in these changing times the thing we can give our children is love, because love is eternal and love doesn't die.
   我知道那是您的声音在告诉我，在这个不断变化的时代，我们能留给我们的孩子的最好的东西就是爱，因为爱是永恒的，爱是不朽的。

A Father and a Son
父与子

带着问题去阅读

1. 小时候你的父亲经常陪你玩吗？
2. 你和父亲周六通常会哪里玩？
3. 你和父亲之间的关系是怎样的？

美文欣赏

1 Passing through the Atlanta airport one morning, I caught one of those trains that take travelers from the main terminal to their boarding gates.

2 Free, sterile and impersonal, the trains run back and forth all day long. Not many people consider them fun, but on this Saturday I heard laughter.

3 At the front of the first car, looking out the window at the track that lay ahead, were a man and his son. They had just stopped to let off passengers, and the doors were closing again.

译文

1 一天早晨途经亚特兰大机场时，我看见一辆轻轨车载着旅客从主航站楼驶向登机口。

2 这些免费的经过消毒的轻轨车每天单调、无味地往返于主航站楼和登机口之间，没人觉得有趣。但这个周六我却听到了笑声。

3 在头节车厢的最前面，坐着一个男人和他的儿子。他们正透过窗户观赏着一直往前延伸的轨道。他们停下来等候旅客下车，之后，车门关上了。

4 "Here we go! Hold on to me *tightly*!" the father said.

5 The boy, about five years old, made sounds of *sheer* delight.

6 I know we're supposed to avoid making *racial* distinctions these days, so I hope no one will mind if I mention that most people on the train were white, dressed for business trips or vacations – and that the father and son were black, dressed in clothes that were just about as inexpensive as you can buy.

7 "Look out there," the father said to his son." See that *pilot*? I bet he's walking to his plane." The son *craned* his neck to look.

8 As I got off, I remembered something I'd wanted to buy in the terminal. I was early for my flight, so I decided to go back.

9 I did and just as I was about to re-board the train for my gate, I saw that the man and his son had returned too. I realized then that they hadn't been heading for a *flight*, but had just been riding the *shuttle*.

10 "You want to go home now?" the father asked.

11 "I want to ride some more!"

12 "More?" the father said, mocking *exasperation* but clearly pleased. "you're

4 "走吧。拉紧我！"父亲说。

5 儿子大约5岁吧，一路喜不自禁。

6 车上坐的多半是衣冠楚楚，或公差或度假的白人，只有这对黑人父子穿着朴素简单。我知道如今我们不该有种族歧视的看法，我希望我这样描述没人介意。

7 "快看！"父亲对儿子说："看见那位飞行员了吗？我敢肯定是去开飞机的。"儿子伸长脖子看。

8 下了车后我突然想起还得在航站楼买点东西。离起飞时间还早，于是我决定再乘车回去。

9 正准备上车的时候，我看到那对父子也来了。我意识到他们不是来乘飞机的，而是特意来坐区间轻轨车的。

10 "现在回家吧？"父亲问。

11 "我还想再坐一会儿！"

12 "再坐一会儿！"父亲嗔怪模仿着儿子的语调，"你

not tired?"

13 "This is fun!!" his son said.

14 "All right," the father replied, and when a door opened, we all got on.

15 There are parents who can afford to send their children to Europe or Disneyland, and the children turn out rotten.

16 There are parents who live in million-dollar houses and give children cars and swimming pools, yet something goes wrong.

17 "Where are all these people going, daddy?" the son asked.

18 "All over the world," came the reply.

19 The other people in the airport were leaving for distant destination or arriving at the ends of their journeys.

20 The father and son though were just riding this shuttle together, making it exciting, sharing each other's company.

21 He was a father who cared about the day with his son and who had come up with this plan on a Saturday morning.

22 Parents who care enough to spend time, and to pay attention and to try their best. It doesn't cost a cent, yet it is the most valuable thing in the world.

23 The train picked up speed, and the

还不累？"

13 "真好玩！"儿子说。

14 "好吧，"父亲说。车门开了，我们都上了车。

15 很多家长有钱带孩子去欧洲，去迪斯尼乐园，可他们的孩子却堕落了。

16 很多家长住豪华别墅，孩子有车有游泳池，可孩子还是学坏了。

17 "爸爸，这些人去哪？"儿子问。

18 "世界各地。"父亲回答。

19 机场来来往往的人流或准备远行，或刚刚归来。

20 这对父子却在乘坐区间轻轨车，享受着父子间的亲情与陪伴。

21 这位父亲很在意花上一天陪伴儿子，并在这样一个星期六的早上，提出这样一个点子。

22 父母愿意花时间，愿意关注，愿意尽心尽职。这不要花一分钱，可这却是世间无价之宝。

23 火车加速了，父亲指

father pointed something out, and the boy laughed again.

着窗外说着什么，儿子又笑了起来。

阅读无障碍

Atlanta [æt'læntə] n. 亚特兰大 [美国佐治亚州首府]

terminal ['tɜːmɪn(ə)l] n. 终点站

sterile ['steraɪl] adj. 枯燥乏味的

passenger ['pæsɪndʒə] n. 乘客，旅客

tight [taɪt] adv. 紧紧地

sheer [ʃɪə] adj. 纯粹的

racial ['reɪʃ(ə)l] adj. 种族的，人种的

pilot ['paɪlət] n. 飞行员

crane [kreɪn] v. 伸长脖子，探头

flight [flaɪt] n. 飞机，航班

shuttle ['ʃʌt(ə)l] n. 短程穿梭运行的轻轨列车、飞机等

exasperation [ɪɡˌzæspə'reɪʃn] n. 恼怒

Disneyland ['dɪznɪlænd] n. 迪斯尼乐园

rotten ['rɒtn] adj. 堕落的

pool [puːl] n. 池塘，水池

distant ['dɪstənt] adj. 遥远的

cent [sent] n. 分 (货币单位)

point [pɔɪnt] v. 指向

极品佳句背诵

1. There are parents who can afford to send their children to Europe or Disneyland, and the children turn out rotten.
   很多家长有钱带孩子去欧洲，去迪斯尼乐园，可他们的孩子却堕落了。

2. It doesn't cost a cent, yet it is the most valuable thing in the world.
   这不要花一分钱，可这却是世间无价之宝。

3. The train picked up speed, and the father pointed something out, and the boy laughed again.
   火车加速了，父亲指着窗外说着什么，儿子又笑了起来。

Flowery Love
鲜花般的爱

带着问题去阅读

1. 你爸爸送过你鲜花吗?
2. 在你人生的重要时刻你爸爸通常会送给你什么礼物?
3. 在节日或者人生的重要时刻你希望收到什么礼物?

 美文欣赏

 译文

1　I was nine when my father first sent me flowers. I had been taking tap-dancing lessons for six months, and the school was giving its yearly recital. As an excited member of the beginners' chorus line, I was aware of my lowly status.

2　So it was a surprise to have my name called at the end of the show along with the lead dancers and to find my arms full of long-stemmed red roses. I can still feel myself standing on that stage, blushing furiously and gazing over the footlights to see my father grin as he applauded loudly.

1　父亲第一次给我送花是在我九岁那年。当时,我在学校踢踏舞班才学了六个月,恰逢学校举办一年一度的演出。我只能编入新学员合唱队,却依然兴致勃勃,不过我清楚自己只是个不起眼的小角色。

2　可演出一结束,我竟与领舞一起被叫到台前,双手捧着一束枝繁叶茂的红玫瑰。我至今还感觉得到自己站在舞台上,双颊绯红,越过绚丽的脚光灯光线向下张望,看见的竟是父亲的笑脸,他一边使劲地鼓掌,一边高兴地笑着。

3 Those roses were the first in a series of large bouquets that accompanied all the milestones in my life. They brought a sense of embarrassment. I enjoyed them, but was flustered by the extravagance.

4 Not my father. He did everything in a big way. If you sent him to the bakery for a cake, he came back with three. Once, when Mother told him I needed a new party dress, he brought home a dozen.

5 His behavior often left us without funds for other more important things. After the dress incident, there was no money for the winter coat I really needed-- or the new ice skates I wanted.

6 Sometimes I would be angry with him, but not for long. Inevitably he would buy me something to make up with me. The gift was so apparently an offering of love he could not verbalize that I would throw my arms around him and kiss him an act that undoubtedly perpetuated his behavior.

7 Then came my 16th birthday. It was not a happy occasion. I was fat and had no boyfriend. And my well-meaning parents furthered my misery by giving me a party. As I entered the dining room, there on the

3 这束鲜花是第一束，往后，每逢我人生的里程碑，父亲都要送我一大束鲜花。可收到那些鲜花时，我的心情总是很矛盾：既高兴，又有些不自在。我喜爱鲜花，可又为这种奢侈而不安。

4 父亲却从不会觉得不安，他做什么事都大方得很。你若让他去糕点铺买一块蛋糕，他定会买来三块。一次，母亲对他说我需要一条新舞裙，他竟买回一打。

5 他这么做常常使我们没有钱再去添置其它更需要的东西。那次他买回一打舞裙后，就再也没钱去买我真正急需的冬大衣和我一直向往的新溜冰鞋。

6 有时我会为这些事跟父亲赌气，但时间都不会长。每次他必定会给我买些礼物与我和好。这礼物显然传达着他不善用言辞表达的爱，这时我便会搂住父亲，吻他 ---- 这亲昵的行为无疑会使他再度大方。

7 后来我迎来了16岁生日，可我并不快乐。我长得胖，那时还没有男朋友。好心的父母为我准备了个生日晚会，可这更让我觉得难受。我

table next to my cake was a huge bouquet of flowers, bigger than any before.

8　I wanted to hide. Now everyone would think my father had sent flowers because I had no boyfriend to do it. Sweet 16, and I felt like crying. I probably would have, but my best friend, Phyllis, whispered, "Boy, you're lucky to have a father like that."

9　As the years passed, other occasions-birthdays, recitals, awards, graduations-were marked with Dad's flowers. My emotions continued to see between pleasure and embarrassment.

10　When I graduated from college, though, my days of ambivalence were over. I was embarking on a new career and was engaged to be married. Dad's flowers symbolized his pride, and my triumph. They evoked only great pleasure.

11　Now there were bright-orange mums for Thanksgiving and a huge pink poinsettia at Christmas. White lilies at Easter, and velvety red roses for birthdays. Seasonal flowers in mixed bouquets celebrated the births of my children and the move to our first house.

12　As my fortunes grew, my father waned, but his gifts of flowers continued

走进餐厅，看见餐桌上生日蛋糕旁边，摆着很大一束鲜花，比以往的都要大。

8　我真想找个地缝钻进去，这下谁都会以为我没有男朋友送花，只好由父亲来送了。16岁该是最甜蜜的，我却只想哭。或许当时我的确哭了，但我最好的朋友菲利斯在我耳边小声说："嘿，你有这样的父亲可真幸运。"

9　随着光阴流逝，许多特别的日子，像生日、演出、获奖、毕业都会伴有父亲的鲜花。我也依然时而高兴，时而感觉不自在。

10　可我到大学毕业时，那种矛盾的心情消失了。我开始了新的工作，也订了婚。父亲的鲜花代表了他的骄傲、我的胜利。它们带来的全是极大的喜悦。

11　后来每逢感恩节我们都会收到父亲的一捧黄灿灿的菊花；圣诞节会有一大束粉红的一品红；复活节是洁白的百合花；生日里会有天鹅绒般的红玫瑰；孩子出世或逢乔迁之喜，父亲会送来那个季节里盛开的许多种鲜花扎成的花束。

12　随着我不断取得成功，父亲却日渐衰老，但他依

until he died of a heart attack a few months before his 70th birthday. Without embarrassment, I covered his coffin with the largest, reddest roses I could find.

13　Then one birthday, the doorbell rang. I was feeling blue because I was alone. My husband was playing golf, and my two daughters were away. My 13-year-old son, Matt, had run out earlier with a "see you later," never mentioning my birthday. So I was surprised to see his large frame at the door. "Forgot my key," he said, shrugging. "Forgot your birthday too. Well, I hope you like flowers, Mum." He pulled a bunch of daisies from behind his back.

14　"Oh, Matt," I cried, hugging him hard. "I love flowers!"

然坚持给我送花，直到他70岁生日的前几个月，因心脏病发作而瘁然逝去。我在他的棺木上铺满了我所能寻得的最红最艳最大的玫瑰花，而且，没有一丝不自在。

13　后来有一天我生日，我听见门铃响了。那天，我本来很沮丧，因为只有我一人待在家中。丈夫打高尔夫球去了，两个女儿出远门了，13岁的儿子马特也走得格外早，只道了声"再见"，只字未提我的生日。所以开门看见马特胖胖的身体站在门边时，我有几分惊讶，他耸耸肩，说道："忘带钥匙了，也忘了今天是你生日，嗯，我希望你喜欢鲜花，妈妈。"说着，他从背后抽出一束雏菊。

14　"哦，马特，"我大叫一声，紧紧搂住他，"我爱鲜花。"

 阅读无障碍

tap-dancing 踢踏舞
recital [rɪˈsaɪtl] n. 舞蹈表演会，小型音乐会
lowly [ˈləʊlɪ] adj. 地位低的，卑微的

long-stemmed [ˈlɒŋ-stemd] adj. 长茎的
blush [blʌʃ] v. 脸红，害羞
footlight [ˈfʊtlaɪt] n. 舞台脚灯
applaud [əˈplɔːd] v. 鼓掌

bouquet [bu'keɪ] *n.* 花束

milestone ['maɪlstəʊn] *n.* 里程碑，重要事件

embarrassment [ɪm'bærəsmənt] *n.* 窘迫，难堪

extravagance [ɪk'strævəgəns] *n.* 奢侈

make up with 和某人和解，重归于好

verbalize ['vɜːbəlaɪz] *v.* 用言语表达，描述

perpetuate [pə'petʃʊeɪt] *v.* 使永存，使不休

probably ['prɒbəblɪ] *adv.* 大概，或许

graduation [ˌgrædʒʊ'eɪʃn] *n.* 毕业，毕业典礼

emotion [ɪ'məʊʃn] *n.* 情绪，情感

symbolize ['sɪmbəlaɪz] *v.* 象征

triumph ['traɪʌmf] *n.* 胜利

daisy ['deɪzɪ] *n.* 雏菊

🐰 极品佳句背诵

1. I can still feel myself standing on that stage, blushing furiously and gazing over the footlights to see my father's grin as he applauded loudly.

   我至今还能觉得到自己站在舞台上，双颊绯红，越过绚丽的脚光灯光线向下张望，看见的竟是父亲的笑脸，他一边使劲地鼓掌，一边高兴地笑着。

2. As the years passed, other occasions-birthdays, recitals, awards, graduations-were marked with Dad's flowers.

   随着光阴流逝，许多特别的日子，像生日、演出、获奖、毕业都会伴有父亲的鲜花。

3. As my fortunes grew, my father waned, but his gifts of flowers continued until he died of a heart attack a few months before his 70th birthday.

   随着我不断取得成功，父亲却日渐衰老，但他依然坚持给我送花，直到他 70 岁生日的前几个月，因心脏病发作而瘁然逝去。

Love Is Like a Broken Arm
爱如断臂

 美文欣赏

1　"But what if I break my arm again?" my five-year-old daughter asked, her lower lip trembling. I knelt holding onto her bike and looked her right in the eyes. I knew how much she wanted to learn to ride. How often she felt left out when her friends pedaled by our house. Yet ever since she'd fallen off her bike and broken her arm, she'd been afraid.

2　"Oh honey," I said. "I don't think you'll break another arm."

 译文

1　"但如果我再把胳膊摔断了怎么办？"我五岁的女儿下唇颤抖着问道。我跪着抓稳她的自行车，直视着她的眼睛。我明白她很想学会骑车。多少次了，她的朋友们骑车经过我们家时，她感到自己被抛下了。可自从上次她从自行车上摔下来，把胳膊摔断之后，她就对骑车敬而远之了。

2　"噢，亲爱的。"我说，"我相信你不会把另一只胳膊给摔断的。"

3 "But I could, couldn't I?"

4 "Yes," I admitted, and found myself struggling for the right thing to say. At times like this, I wished I had a partner to turn to. Someone who might help find the right words to make my little girl's problems disappear. But after a disastrous marriage and a painful divorce, I'd welcomed the hardships of being a single parent and had been adamant in telling anyone who tried to fix me up that I was terminally single.

5 "I don't think I want to ride," she said and got off her bike.

6 We walked away and sat down beside a tree.

7 "Don't you want to ride with your friends?" I asked.

8 "Yes," she admitted.

9 "And I thought you were hoping to start riding your bike school next year," I added.

10 "I was," she said, her voice almost quivered.

11 "You know, honey," I said. "Almost everything you do comes with risks. You could get a broken arm in a car wreck and then be afraid to ever ride in a car again. You could break your arm jumping rope. You could break your arm at gymnastics. Do you want to stop going to gymnastics?"

3 "但有可能，不是吗？"

4 "是的，"我承认道，努力想找出些道理来说。每逢此时，我便希望自己有人可依靠。一个可以说出正确道理、帮我小女儿解决难题的人。可经过一场可悲的婚姻和痛苦的离婚后，我更倾向于当个单身母亲，并且我还态度坚决地告诉每个要给我介绍对象的人说我决定终身不再嫁。

5 "我不想学了。"她说着，下了自行车。

6 我们走到一边，在一棵树旁坐下。

7 "难道你不想和朋友们一起骑车吗？"我问。

8 "想。"她承认。

9 "而且我原以为你希望明年可以骑着车去上学呢。"我补充道。

10 "我是希望。"她说，声音有点颤。

11 "知道吗，亲爱的。"我说，"很多要做的事情都是有风险的。汽车失事也会折断胳膊，那么你会因害怕而不坐车。跳绳也有可能折断胳膊，做体操也有可能折断胳膊。那你连体操也想不练了吗？"

12 "No," she said. And with a determined spirit, she stood up and agreed to try again. I held on to the back of her bike until she found the courage to say, "Let's go!"

13 I spent the rest of the afternoon at the park watching a very brave little girl overcome a fear, and congratulating myself for being a self-sufficient single parent.

14 Pushing the bike, we made our way home along the sidewalk, she asked me about a conversation she'd overheard me having with my mother the night before.

15 "Why were you and grandma arguing last night?"

16 My mother was one of the many people who constantly tried to fix me up. How many times had I told her "no" to meeting the Mr. Perfect she picked out for me. She just knew Steve was the man for me.

17 "It's nothing," I told her.

18 She shrugged. "Grandma said she just wanted you to find someone to love."

19 "What grandma wants is for some guy to break my heart again," I snapped and was angry that my mother had said anything about this to my daughter.

20 "But Mom."

12 "想。"她说。然后她毅然站起，同意再试试。我扶着车尾，直到她有勇气说："开始吧！"

13 后来的那个下午，我就在公园里看着这个充满勇气的小女孩克服了恐惧，我恭喜自己成了可以独当一面的单身家长。

14 回家时，我们推着自行车顺着人行道走，她问起昨天晚上无意中听到的我和我妈妈的谈话。

15 "你昨晚为什么和姥姥争吵？"

16 我妈妈也总想安排我去相亲。我多次拒绝去和她给我找的合适对象相亲。她总认为史蒂文和我会合得来。

17 "没什么事。"我告诉她。

18 她耸耸肩。"姥姥说她只不过想让你找个人来爱。"

19 "姥姥想再找个人来伤我的心。"我厉声说道，并且很生气我妈妈把这件事跟我的女儿说了。

20 "可妈妈。"

21 "You're too young to understand," I told her.

22 She was quiet for the next few minutes. Then she looked up and in a small voice gave me something to think about.

23 "So I guess love isn't like a broken arm."

24 Unable to answer, we walked the rest of the way in silence. When I got home, I called my mother and scolded her for talking about this to my daughter. Then I did what I'd seen my brave little girl do that every afternoon. I let go and agreed to meet Steve.

25 Steve was the man for me. We married less than a year later. It turned out mother and my daughter were right.

21 "你还太小，不明白。"我对她说。

22 接下来好几分钟她都很安静。然后她抬起头，小声地说了句令我深思不已的话。

23 "那么我猜爱情和断胳膊不是一回事了。"

24 我无言以对，沉默着走完了余下的路。回到家后，我给妈妈打了个电话，责备她不该和我女儿谈论这个话题。接着我做了一件那个下午看到我那勇敢的小女儿所做过的事。我松口答应和史蒂文见面。

25 史蒂文正是我的合适人选。不到一年我们就结了婚。结果证明我的妈妈和女儿是正确的。

阅读无障碍

trembling ['tremblɪŋ] adj. 发抖的

pedal ['pedl] v. 踩自行车的踏板

afraid [ə'freɪd] adj. 害怕的，担心的

admit [əd'mɪt] v. 承认

disappear [ˌdɪsə'pɪə(r)] v. 消失，不见

disastrous [dɪ'zɑːstrəs] adj. 悲惨的

divorce [dɪ'vɔːs] n. 离婚

adamant ['ædəmənt] adj. 坚决的，坚定不移的

terminally ['tɜːmɪnəli] adv. 最后地，结尾地

quiver ['kwɪvə(r)] v. 微颤，抖动

gymnastics [dʒɪm'næstɪks] n. 体操，

体操运动

determined [dɪˈtɜːmɪnd] *adj.* 坚定的

the rest of 其余的，剩下的

self-sufficient [self səˈfɪʃnt] *adj.* 自
给自足的，自立的

parent [ˈpeərənt] *n.* 母亲（或父亲）

sidewalk [ˈsaɪdwɔːk] *n.* 人行道

constantly [ˈkɒnstəntlɪ] *adv.* 不断地，
时常地

shrug [ʃrʌg] *v.* 耸肩（以表示冷淡、
怀疑等）

unable [ʌnˈeɪbl] *adj.* 不会的，不能
的

et go 放开，放手

🐰 极品佳句背诵

1. I wished I had a partner to turn to. Someone who might help find the right words to make my little girl's problems disappear.

   每逢此时，我便希望自己有人可依靠。一个可以说出正确道理、帮我小女儿解决难题的人。

2. I spent the rest of the afternoon at the park watching a very brave little girl overcome a fear, and congratulating myself for being a self-sufficient single parent.

   后来一个下午，我就在公园里看着这个充满勇气的小女孩克服了恐惧，我恭喜自己成了可以独当一面的单身家长。

3. So I guess love isn't like a broken arm.

   那么我猜爱情和断胳膊不是一回事了。

When You Are Becoming a Mother 当你要成为母亲

带着问题去阅读

1. 你对母爱的理解是什么？
2. 做母亲的伟大之处是什么？
3. 你对丁克家庭有着怎样的理解？

美文欣赏

 译文

1 Time is running out for my friend. While we are sitting at lunch she casually mentions she and her husband are thinking of starting a family.

2 "We're taking a survey," she says, half-joking. "Do you think I should have a baby?"

3 "It will change your life," I say, carefully keeping my tone neutral.

4 "I know," she says, "no more sleeping in on weekends, no more spontaneous holidays..."

1 我的朋友已经不再年轻了。我们坐在一起吃饭的时候，她漫不经心地提到她和她的丈夫正考虑要小孩。

2 "我们正在做一项调查，"她半开玩笑地说。"你觉得我应该要个小孩吗？"

3 "他将改变你的生活。"我小心翼翼地说道，尽量使语气保持客观。

4 "这我知道。"她答道，"周末睡不成懒觉，再也不能随心所欲休假了……"

5 But that's not what I mean at all. I look at my friend, trying to decide what to tell her. I want her to know what she will never learn in childbirth classes. I want to tell her that the physical wounds of child bearing will heal, but becoming a mother will leave her with an emotional wound so raw that she will be vulnerable forever.

6 I consider warning her that she will never again read a newspaper without thinking: "What if that had been MY child?" That every plane crash, every house fire will haunt her. That when she sees pictures of starving children, she will wonder if anything could be worse than watching your child die. I look at her carefully manicured nails and stylish suit and think that no matter how sophisticated she is, becoming a mother will reduce her to the primitive level of a bear protecting her cub.

7 I feel I should warn her that no matter how many years she has invested in her career, she will be professionally derailed by motherhood. She might arrange for child care, but one day she will be going into an important business meeting, and she will think her baby's sweet smell. She will have to use every ounce of discipline to keep from running home, just to make sure her child is all right.

5 但我说的绝非这些。我注视着朋友，思索着该告诉她什么。我想让她知道她永远不可能在分娩课上学到的东西。我想让她知道：分娩时身体上的伤疤可以愈合，但是做母亲会给她带来感情创伤，以至于她将永远脆弱。

6 我想告诫她：做了母亲后，每当她看报纸时都会思索一番："如果那是我的孩子将会怎样啊！"每一次飞机失事、每一场住宅火灾都会让她提心吊胆。看到那些忍饥挨饿的孩子们的照片时，她会思索：世界上还有什么比眼睁睁地看着自己的孩子饿死更惨的事情呢？我打量着她精修细剪的指甲和时尚前卫的衣服，心里想到：不管她打扮多么考究，做了母亲后，她会变得像护崽的母熊那样原始和传统。

7 我觉得自己应该提醒她，不管她在工作上投入了多少年，一旦做了母亲，工作就会脱离常规。她自然可以安排他人照顾孩子，但说不定哪天她要去参加一个非常重要的商务会议，却忍不住想起宝宝身上散发的甜甜乳香。她必须得拼命克制自己，才不致于为了看看孩子是否安然无恙而中途

8　I want my friend to know that every decision will no longer be routine. That a five-year-old boy's desire to go to the men's room rather the women's at a restaurant will become a major dilemma.

9　The issues of independence and gender identity will be weighed against the prospect that a child molester may be lurking in the lavatory. However decisive she may be at the office, she will second-guess herself constantly as a mother.

10　Looking at my attractive friend, I want to assure her that eventually she will shed the added weight of pregnancy, but she will never feel the same about herself. That her own life, now so important, will be of less value to her once she has a child. She would give it up in a moment to save her offspring, but will also begin to hope for more years—not to accomplish her own dreams—but to watch her children accomplish theirs.

11　I want to describe to my friend the exhilaration of seeing your child learn to hit a ball. I want to capture for her the belly laugh of a baby who is touching the soft fur of a dog for the first time. I want her to taste the joy that is so real it hurts.

12　My friend's look makes me realize

8　我想告诉朋友，有了孩子后，每一个决定都不再是惯例。在餐馆，5 岁的儿子想进男厕而不愿进女厕，这将成为摆在她眼前的一大难题。

9　是尊重孩子的独立和性别意识，还是让他进男厕所冒险被潜在的儿童性骚扰者侵害都需要她费心思量一番？任凭她在办公室多么果断，作为母亲，她仍会经常事后后悔自己当时的决定。

10　注视着我这位漂亮的朋友，我想让她明确地知道，她最终会恢复到怀孕前的体重，但是她会觉得自己和以前不一样了。她现在视为珍贵的生命将随着孩子的诞生而变得不那么宝贵。为了救自己的孩子，她时刻愿意献出自己的生命。但她也开始希望多活一些年头，不是为了实现自己的梦想，而是为了看着孩子们美梦成真。

11　我想向朋友形容自己看到孩子学会击球时的喜悦之情。我想让她留意宝宝第一次触摸狗的绒毛时的捧腹大笑。我想让她品尝快乐，这快乐真实得令人心痛。

12　朋友的表情让我意识

that tears have formed in my eyes. "You'll never regret it," I say finally.

13　Then, squeezing my friend's hand, I offer a prayer for her and me and all of the mere mortal women who stumble their way into this holiest callings.

到自己已经是热泪盈眶。"你永远不会后悔"我最后说。

13　然后我紧紧地握住朋友的手，为她、为自己，也为每一位艰难跋涉、准备响应母亲神圣职业的召唤的平凡女性献上自己的祈祷。

阅读无障碍

casually ['kæʒjʊəli] adv. 偶然地，随便地

half-joking 半开玩笑地

neutral ['nju:tr(ə)l] adj. 中立的

spontaneous [spɒn'teɪnɪəs] adj. 自发的

childbirth ['tʃaɪl(d)bɜ:θ] n. 分娩

heal [hi:l] v. 治愈，痊愈

vulnerable ['vʌln(ə)rəb(ə)l] adj. 脆弱的，易受伤害的

starving ['sta:vɪŋ] adj. 饥饿的

manicured ['mænɪkjʊrd] adj. 修剪整齐的

stylish ['staɪlɪʃ] adj. 时髦的

primitive ['prɪmɪtɪv] adj. 原始的

derail [dɪ'reɪl] v. 出轨

independence [ɪndɪ'pend(ə)ns] n. 独立

molester [mə'lestə] n. 性骚扰者，猥亵者

eventually [ɪ'ventʃuəli] adv. 终于，最后

pregnancy ['pregnənsi] n. 怀孕

offspring ['ɒfsprɪŋ] n. 后代，子孙

exhilaration [ɪgzɪlə'reɪʃn] n. 愉快，令人高兴

mortal ['mɔ:tl] adj. 凡人的

stumble ['stʌmbl] v. 蹒跚

极品佳句背诵

1. I want to tell her that the physical wounds of child bearing will heal, but becoming a mother will leave her with an emotional wound so raw that she will be vulnerable forever.
我想让她知道：分娩时身体上的伤疤可以愈合，但是做母亲会给她带来感情创伤，以至于她将永远脆弱。

2. Looking at my attractive friend, I want to assure her that eventually she will shed the added weight of pregnancy, but she will never feel the same about herself.

注视着我的这位漂亮的朋友，我想让她明确地知道，她最终会恢复到怀孕前的体重，但是她对自己的感觉会全然不同。

3. Then, squeezing my friend's hand, I offer a prayer for her and me and all of the mere mortal women who stumble their way into this holiest of callings.

然后我紧紧地握住朋友的手，为她、为自己、也为每一位艰难跋涉、准备响应母亲神圣职业的召唤的平凡女性献上自己的祈祷。

Mother's Hands
妈妈的手

带着问题去阅读

1. 妈妈的双手是怎样的?
2. 你还记得妈妈手掌的温度吗?
3. 妈妈的手为什么变得粗糙?

美文欣赏

1 Night after night, she came to tuck me in, even long after my childhood years. Following her longstanding custom, she'd lean down and push my long hair out of the way, then kiss my forehead.

2 I don't remember when it first started annoying me — her hands pushing my hair that way. But it did annoy me, for they felt work-worn and rough against my young skin. Finally, one night, I shouted out at her, "Don't do that anymore — your hands are too rough!" She didn't say anything in reply. But never again did my

译文

1 夜复一夜,她总是来帮我来盖被子,即使我早已长大。这是妈妈长期的习惯,她总是弯下身来,拨开我的长发,温柔地亲吻一下我的额头。

2 我不记得从何时起,她拨开我的头发令我非常不耐烦。但的确,我讨厌她长期操劳、粗糙的手摩擦我细嫩的皮肤。终于在一天晚上,我冲她叫道:"别再这样了——你的手太粗糙了!"回应我的是妈妈的沉默。但是从那以后,妈

mother close out my day with that familiar expression of her love. Lying awake long afterward, my words haunted me. But pride stifled my conscience, and I didn't tell her I was sorry.

3　Time after time, with the passing years, my thoughts returned to that night. By then I missed my mother's hands, missed her goodnight kiss upon my forehead. Sometimes the incident seemed very close, sometimes far away. But always it lurked, in the back of my mind.

4　Well, the years have passed, and I'm not a little girl anymore. Mom is in her mid-seventies, and those hands I once thought to be so rough are still doing things for me and my family. She's been our doctor, reaching into a medicine cabinet for the remedy to calm a young girl's stomach or soothe the boy's scraped knee. She cooks the best fried chicken in the world... gets stains out of blue jeans like I never could... and still insist on dishing out ice cream at any hour of the day or night.

5　Now, my own children are grown and gone. Mom no longer has Dad, and on special occasions, I find myself drawn next door to spend the night with her. So it was late on Thanksgiving Eve, as I slept in the bedroom of my youth, a familiar hand hesitantly run across my face to brush the hair from my forehead. Then a kiss, ever so

妈再也没有用那种我熟悉的方式来表达她的爱了。那之后我很久未能入眠，我说过的话一直萦绕在耳边。但是，自尊心战胜了我的内疚，我没有向她道歉。

3　时光流逝，我又想到那个晚上。这时我总会想念妈妈的手，想念她晚上在我额上的一吻。有时这幕情景似乎很近，有时又似乎很遥远。但它总是潜伏在我的脑海中。

4　一年年过去，我不再是一个小女孩，妈妈也有 70 多岁了。那双我曾经认为很粗糙的手依然在为我和我的家庭忙碌着。她是我家的医生，为我女儿在药橱里找胃药或在我儿子擦伤的膝盖上敷药。她能做出世界上最美味的炸鸡……能帮我清理掉我从来不能够清理的牛仔裤上的污渍……而且可以在任何时候盛出冰激凌。

5　现在，我的孩子都已经长大，离开了家。爸爸也去世了，在一些特殊的日子，我睡在妈妈的隔壁房间陪伴她。一次感恩节前夕的深夜，我睡在年轻时的卧室里，一只熟悉的手有些犹豫地、悄悄地略过我的脸，从我额头上拨开头

gently, touched my brow.

6　In my memory, for the thousandth time, I recalled the night my young surly voice complained, "Don't do that anymore — your hands are too rough!" Catching Mom's hand in hand, I blurted out how sorry I was for that night. I thought she'd remember as I did. But Mom didn't know what I was talking about. She had forgotten — and forgiven — long ago.

7　That night, I fell asleep with a new appreciation for my gentle mother and her caring hands. And the guilt that I had carried around for so long was nowhere to be found.

发，然后轻轻地吻了吻我的眉毛。

6　在我的记忆中，我曾无数次想起那晚，年轻的我粗暴地抱怨："别再这样了——你的手太粗糙了！"这次，我紧紧握住妈妈的手，毫不犹豫地告诉她我对那天晚上的事情感到多么地抱歉。我以为她和我一样都记着那天的事，但妈妈不知道我在说些什么。她已经在很久以前就忘了这事，早就原谅了我。

7　那晚，我带着对温柔的母亲和她温暖的双手的感激入睡。这些年来，埋藏在我心里的愧疚感也随之消失。

🐱 **阅读无障碍**

longstanding [lɒŋˈstændɪŋ] adj. 长时间的，为时甚久的

lean [liːn] v. 倾斜，屈身

forehead [ˈfɔːhed] n. 额头，前额

annoy [əˈnɔɪ] v. 使烦恼，打搅

rk-worn 被工作磨坏了的

rough [rʌf] adj. 粗糙的

familiar [fəˈmɪljə] adj. 熟悉的，常见的，亲密的

expression [ɪksˈpreʃən] n. 表达，表示

incident [ˈɪnsɪdənt] n. 附带事件，小事件

lurk [lɜːk] v. 潜藏，潜伏

cabinet [ˈkæbɪnɪt] n. 柜子，橱子，箱子

remedy [ˈremɪdɪ] n. 药物，治疗法

soothe [suːð] v. 缓和，安慰

scrape [skreɪp] v. 刮，擦，擦伤

stain [steɪn] n. 污染，污点

jeans [dʒiːnz] n. 牛仔裤

hesitantly [ˈhezɪtəntlɪ] adv. 迟疑地；

踟躇地

brow[braʊ] *n.* 眉毛

blurt [blɜːt] *v.* 冲口说出，突然说出

appreciation [əˌpriːʃɪˈeɪʃən] *n.* 感激

极品佳句背诵

1. Time after time, with the passing years, my thoughts returned to that night. By then I missed my mother's hands, missed her goodnight kiss upon my forehead.

   时光流逝，我又想到那个晚上。这时我总会想念妈妈的手，想念她晚上在我额上的一吻。

2. She's been our doctor, reaching into a medicine cabinet for the remedy to calm a young girl's stomach or soothe the boy's scraped knee.

   她是我家的医生，为我女儿在药橱里找胃药或在我儿子擦伤的膝盖上敷药。

3. That night, I fell asleep with a new appreciation for my gentle mother and her caring hands. And the guilt that I had carried around for so long was nowhere to be found.

   那晚，我带着对温柔的母亲和她温暖的双手的感激入睡。这些年来，埋藏在我心里的愧疚感也随之消失。

The First Mother Lord Made
上帝创造的第一位母亲

带着问题去阅读

1. 母亲对家庭意味着什么？
2. 你对母爱有怎样的理解？
3. 母亲为什么会创造出眼泪？

 美文欣赏

1　By the time the Lord made the first mother, he was into the sixth day working overtime. An Angel appeared and said, "Why are you spending so much time on this one!"

2　And the Lord answered and said, "Have you read the spec sheet on her! She has to be completely washable, but not elastic; has 200 movable parts, all replaceable; runs on black coffee and leftovers; has a lap that can hold three children at one time and that disappears

 译文

1　等到上帝创造第一位母亲时，他已经超时工作到第六天。一位天使出现了，问道："您为什么花这么长时间造这个人？"

2　上帝回答说："你读说明书了吗？她必须是耐水洗的，但不是橡胶的；她有200个可活动的零件，而且全部可以更换；她工作废寝忘食，以至于拿剩饭菜填充饥饿，用黑咖啡提振精神；她的腿上可以

when she stands up; has a kiss that can cure anything from a scraped knee to a broken heart and has six pairs of hands."

3 The Angel was astounded at the requirements for this one. "Six pairs of hands? No way" said the Angel.

4 The Lord replied, "Oh, it's not the hands that are the problem. It's the three pairs of eyes that mothers must have"

5 "And that's on the standard model!" the Angel asked.

6 The Lord nodded in agreement, "Yep, one pair of eyes are to see through the closed door as they asks her children what they are doing even though she already knows. Another pair in the back of her head are to see what she needs to know even though no one thinks she can. And the third pair are here in the front of her head. They are for looking at an errant child and saying that she understands and loves him or her without even saying a single word."

7 The Angel tried to stop the Lord. "This is too much work for one day. Wait until tomorrow to finish."

8 "But I can't" the Lord protested, "I am so close to finishing this creation that is

同时坐上 3 个孩子，而她站起身后，这腿又得恢复正常；她的吻可以抚平一切伤痛，不论是皮肉的擦伤，还是心碎的痛楚；她还有 6 双手。"

3 天使听了大为吃惊。"6 双手！不可能！"

4 上帝回答："哦，手并不是难题。母亲必须有 3 双眼睛，这才是最难做的！"

5 "标准模型上是这样的吗？"天使问。

6 上帝点点头表示同意，"是的。一双是能看穿紧闭房门的眼睛，这样母亲就可以询问她的孩子独自在家的时候都做了什么，有没有淘气，尽管她早已知道答案。另一双眼睛长在后脑勺儿上面，能使她能看到想要看到的东西，尽管没有人认为她能看得见。第三双眼睛长在头部前方，它们是用来关注那些犯错误的孩子，尽管她默默无语，但那目光中早已充满了她对这个孩子的理解与关爱。"

7 天使试图让上帝停下手中的活。"一天怎么能干这么多活儿？等明天再完成吧。"

8 "我不能！"上帝拒绝道，"我这就要完成这件创造

so close to my own heart. She always heals herself when she is sick and can feed a family of six on a pound of hamburger and can get a nine-year-old boy to stand in the shower."

9　The Angel moved closer and touched the woman, "But you have made her so soft, Lord."

10　"She is soft," the Lord agreed, "but I have also made her tough. You have no idea what she can endure or accomplish."

11　"Will she be able to think!" asked the Angel.

12　The Lord replied, "Not only will she be able to think, she will be able to reason, and negotiate."

13　The Angel then noticed something and reached out and touched the woman's cheek. "Oops, it looks like there's a leak in her face. You were trying to put too much into this one."

14　"That's not a leak," the Lord objected. "That's a tear."

15　"What's the tear for!" the Angel asked.

16　The Lord said, "The tear is her way of expressing her joy, her sorrow, her disappointment, her pain, her loneliness, her grief, and her pride."

17　The Angel was impressed. "You are a genius, Lord. You thought of

了，它是那么贴合我的心意。她生病的时候总能不药而愈，而且，她能为一家6口人准备好丰富的饭菜，还能让一个9岁男孩子乖乖地站在莲蓬头下淋浴。"

9　天使走近了些，抚摸着那女人，"但是，上帝，您把她做得如此柔软。"

10　"她确实柔软，"上帝说到，"但是也坚强。你想象不出来她是多么的坚韧，多么的能干。"

11　"她能够思考吗？"天使问。

12　上帝回答："她不仅能思考，还能判断，能与人协商。"

13　这时天使注意到什么，伸出手触摸女人的面颊。"哎呀，她脸上好像有一处缺憾。您试图在这件作品中注入太多的东西。"

14　"那不是什么缺憾，"上帝反驳，"那是一滴眼泪！"

15　"这眼泪是干什么的！"天使问。

16　上帝说："眼泪是她表达喜悦、悲伤、失望、痛苦、孤独、哀伤和骄傲的方式。"

17　天使深受感动。"上帝，您真是天才。您为这作品

everything for this one. You even created the tear."

18 The Lord looked at the Angel and smiled and said, "I'm afraid you are wrong again. I created the woman, but she created the tear."

考虑的真是无微不至。您甚至造出了眼泪。"

18 上帝看看天使，露出微笑，说："你又错了。是我造了女人，但却是女人自己创造的眼泪。"

阅读无障碍

overtime ['əuvətaim] *adv.* 超时地，加班

appear [ə'piə] *v.* 出现

washable ['wɒʃəbl] *adj.* 可洗的

elastic [ı'læstık] *n.* 橡胶制品

replaceable [rı'pleisəbl] *adj.* 可代替的

leftover ['leftəuvə] *n.* 残羹剩菜

scrape [skreip] *v.* 擦，刮

astound [əs'taund] *v.* 使震惊

requirement [rı'kwaiəmənt] *n.* 要求

agreement [ə'gri:mənt] *n.* 同意，协定

in the front of 在最前面

single ['sıŋgl] *adj.* 单独的、单一的

protest [prə'test] *v.* 反对，抗议

endure [ın'djuə] *v.* 忍耐

accomplish [ə'kɒmplıʃ] *v.* 实现

negotiate [nı'gəuʃieıt] *v.* 谈判

cheek [tʃi:k] *n.* 脸颊

express [ıks'pres] *v.* 表达

loneliness ['ləunlınıs] *n.* 孤独

impress [ım'pres] *v.* 给…以深刻印象

极品佳句背诵

1. And the third pair are here in the front of her head. They are for looking at an errant child and saying that she understands and loves him or her without even saying a single word.
   第三双眼睛长在头部前方，它们是用来关注那些犯错误的孩子，尽管她默默无语，但那目光中早已充满了她对这个孩子的理解与关爱。

2. The tear is her way of expressing her joy, her sorrow, her disappointment, her pain, her loneliness, her grief, and her pride.
   眼泪是她表达喜悦、悲伤、失望、痛苦、孤独、哀伤和骄傲的方式。

3. The Lord looked at the Angel and smiled and said, "I'm afraid you are wrong again. I created the woman, but she created the tear."
   上帝看着天使，露出微笑，说："你又错了。是我造了女人，但却是女人自己创造的眼泪。"

Love Your Mother
深爱你的母亲

带着问题去阅读

1. 你知道母亲为你付出了些什么吗？
2. 母爱是最无私的爱吗？
3. 你为母亲做过些什么？

 美文欣赏

 译文

1 When you came into the world, she held you in her arms. You thanked her by wailing like a banshee.

2 When you were 13, she suggested a haircut that was becoming. You thanked her by telling her she had no taste.

3 When you were 14, she paid for a month away at summer camp. You thanked her by forgetting to write a single letter.

4 When you were 15, she came home from work, expecting a hug. You thanked

1 你来到人世时，她把你抱在怀里。而你对她的感恩回报，就是像报丧女妖一样哭得天昏地暗。

2 你 13 岁时，她建议你把发型修剪得体。而你对她的感恩回报，就是说她一点品味都没有。

3 你 14 岁时，她花钱让你参加一个月的夏令营。而你对她的感恩回报，就是连一封信都不记得给她写。

4 你 15 岁时，她下班回到家，期望你能给她一个拥

her by having your bedroom door locked.

5　When you were 16, she taught you how to drive her car. You thanked her by taking it every chance you could.

6　When you were 17, she was expecting an important call. You thanked her by being on the phone all night.

7　When you were 18, she cried at your high school graduation. You thanked her by staying out partying until dawn.

8　When you were 19, she paid for your college tuition, drove you to campus, and carried your bags. You thanked her by saying good-bye outside the dorm so you wouldn't be embarrassed in front of your friends.

9　When you were 20, she asked whether you were dating anyone. You thanked her by saying, "It's none of your business."

10　When you were 21, she suggested certain careers for your future. You thanked her by saying, "I don't want to be like you."

11　When you were 22, she hugged you at your college graduation. You thanked her by asking whether she could pay for a trip to Europe.

抱。而你对她的感恩回报，就是呆在卧室中将房门紧锁。

5　你16岁时，她教你学开车。而你对她的感恩回报，就是逮着机会就把车开走。

6　你17岁时，她在等一个重要电话。而你对她的感恩回报，就是煲了一个通宵的电话粥。

7　你18岁时，她为你高中毕业喜极而泣。而你对她的感恩回报，就是在外面参加聚会通宵不回家。

8　你19岁时，她为你支付大学的学费，开车送你去学校，帮你提包裹行李。而你对她的感恩回报，就是在宿舍门外匆匆说再见，为的是不要在朋友面前丢人。

9　你20岁时，她问你是否在和别人约会。而你对她的感恩回报，就是对她说："这不关你的事！"

10　你21岁时，她为你将来从事什么职业提出一些建议。而你对她的感恩回报，就是对她说："我才不愿像你那样！"

11　你22岁时，她在你大学毕业典礼上紧紧抱抱你。而你对她的感恩回报，就是问她能否掏钱让你去欧洲旅行。

12 When you were 23, she gave you furniture for your first apartment. You thanked her by telling your friends it was ugly.

13 When you were 24, she met your fiancé and asked about your plans for the future. You thanked her by glaring and growling, "Muuhh-ther, please!"

14 When you were 25, she helped to pay for your wedding, and she cried and told you how deeply she loved you. You thanked her by moving halfway across the country.

15 When you were 30, she called with some advice on the baby. You thanked her by telling her, "Things are different now."

16 When you were 40, she called to remind you of a relative's birthday. You thanked her by saying you were "really busy right now".

17 When you were 50, she fell ill and needed you to take care of her. You thanked her by talking about the burden parents become to their children.

18 And then, one day, she quietly died. And everything you never did came crashing down like thunder. "Rock me baby, rock me all night long." "The hand

12 你23岁时，她为你的第一套公寓置办家具。而你对她的感恩回报，就是告诉朋友说这些家具非常难看。

13 你24岁时，她见到了你的未婚夫，问你们将来有什么打算。而你对她的感恩回报，就是对她怒目而视，大声吼叫："妈……，求求你别烦了！"

14 你25岁时，她花钱帮你筹办婚礼，含泪对你说她是多么地深爱着你。而你对她的感恩回报，就是把家安得离她远远的。

15 你30岁时，她打来电话为宝宝抚养提出忠告。而你对她的感恩回报，就是告诉她："现在情况和以前不同了！"

16 你40岁时，她打电话提醒你别忘了一个亲戚的生日。而你对她的感恩回报，就是说你"现在忙得不可开交"。

17 你50岁时，她生病了需要你照顾。而你对她的感恩回报，就是念叨着父母成了子女的负担。

18 后来，有一天，她静悄悄地去了。所有那些你该做而未做的事，仿佛炸雷般在你耳边轰隆而过。"摇啊摇，小

who rocks the cradle... may rock the world". Let us take a moment of the time just to pay tribute and show appreciation to the person called MOM though some may not say it openly to their mother. There's no substitute for her. Cherish every single moment. Though at times she may not be the best of friends, may not agree to our thoughts, she is still your mother! Your mother will be there for you; to listen to your woes, your brags, your frustrations, etc. Ask yourself "Have you put aside enough time for her, to listen to her 'blues' of working in the kitchen, her tiredness?" Be tactful, loving and still show her due respect, though you may have a different view from hers. Once gone, only fond memories of the past and also regrets will be left. Do not take for granted the things closest to your heart. Love her more than you love yourself. Life is meaningless without her.

宝宝，一摇摇到大天亮。""摇摇篮的手啊……可以摇世界。"让我们花一点点时间，对那个被我们叫做"妈妈"的人表达敬意和感激之情，虽然有些人当着面说不出口。她是不可替代的。珍惜与她在一起的每一时刻吧。虽然有时候，她可能不是我们最好的朋友，可能不同意我们的想法，但她依然是你的妈妈！你的妈妈始终陪伴你身边，听你倾诉伤心事，你神吹海侃，听你诉说受挫的沮丧……扪心自问，"你是否曾经抽出过足够的时间陪伴她，听听她讲围着灶台转的'烦心事'，听听她讲她有多疲惫？"即使你与她意见不一，也要委婉一些，充满爱心，对她表示出应有的尊敬。一旦她去了，剩下的就只有对过去岁月的美好回忆和无尽的遗憾。不要对内心深处的东西漠然视之。爱她要甚于爱你自己。没有了她，生命将毫无意义。

阅读无障碍

banshee ['bænʃiː] n. (英国古代民间传说中的) 报丧女妖

hug[hʌg] n. 拥抱

expect[ɪks'pekt] v. 期盼

graduation[grædʒu'eɪʃən] n. 毕业典礼

dawn[dɔ:n] n. 黎明

tuition [tju:ˈɪʃən] n. 学费

embarrass[ɪmˈbærəs] v. 使窘迫

fiancé n. 〔法语〕未婚夫

glare [ɡleər] v. 瞪视

growl [ɡraʊl] v. 咆哮

remind[rɪˈmaɪnd] v. 使想起，提醒

burden[ˈbɜ:dn] n. 负担

cradle [ˈkreɪd] n. 摇篮

tribute [ˈtrɪbju:t] n. 称赞

substitute[ˈsʌbstɪtju:t] n. 替代者，替代物

woe [wəʊ] n. 苦恼，悲痛

brag [bræɡ] n. 自夸，夸耀之词

tactful[ˈtæktful] adj. 委婉的

regret [rɪˈɡret] n. 遗憾

meaningless [ˈmi:nɪŋlɪs] adj. 无意义的

🐰 极品佳句背诵

1. Let us take a moment of the time just to pay tribute and show appreciation to the person called MOM though some may not say it openly to their mother.
   让我们花一点点时间，对那个被我们叫做"妈妈"的人表达敬意和感激之情，虽然有些人当着面说不出口。

2. "Have you put aside enough time for her, to listen to her 'blues' of working in the kitchen, her tiredness?"
   扪心自问，"你是否曾经抽出过足够的时间陪伴她，听听她讲围着灶台转的'烦心事'，听听她讲她有多疲惫？"

3. Do not take for granted the things closest to your heart. Love her more than you love yourself. Life is meaningless without her.
   不要对内心深处的东西漠然视之。爱她要甚于爱你自己。没有了她，生命将毫无意义。

To Buy an Hour from Father
向爸爸买一个小时

带着问题去阅读

1. 小男孩为什么要攒钱？
2. 男孩的父亲是否后悔未能陪伴孩子？
3. 工作和孩子哪个更重要？

美文欣赏

译文

1 A man came home from work late, tired and *irritated*, only to find his five-year-old son waiting for him at the door.

2 "Daddy, may I ask you a question?"

3 "Yeah, sure, what is it?" *replied* the man.

4 "Daddy, how much do you make an hour?"

5 "That's *none of your business*. Why do you ask such a thing?" the man said *angrily*. " I just want to know. Please tell

1 男人带着一身的疲倦，恼火地回到家，这时天色已晚，他发现五岁的儿子在门口等他。

2 "爸爸，可以问你个问题吗？"

3 "当然可以，想问什么？"男人回答道。

4 "你一个小时能赚多少钱？"

5 "那和你没关系。为什么问这个？"男人生气了。"我想知道。请你告诉我，你一个

me, how much do you make an hour?" pleaded the little boy.

6 "If you must know, I make $20 an hour."

7 "Oh" the little boy replied with his head down. Looking up he said, " Daddy, may I please borrow $10?"

8 The father was furious, "If the only reason you asked that is so you can borrow some money to buy a silly toy or some other nonsense, then you march yourself straight to your room and go to bed. Think about why you are being so selfish. I work hard everyday for this childish behaviour."

9 The little boy quietly went to his room and shut the door. The man sat down and started to get even angrier about the little boy's questions. How dare he ask such questions only to get some money? After about an hour or so, the man had calmed down, and started to think, maybe there was something he really needed to buy with that $10 and he really didn't ask for money very often. The man went to the door of the little boy's room and opened the door.

10 "Are you sleep, son?" he asked.

11 "No, daddy, I'm awake." replied the boy.

小时能赚多少钱？"小男孩哀求道。

6 "如果非要知道的话，告诉你，我一小时赚20美元。"

7 "哦，"小男孩的头低下了，然后，又抬起头说道："爸爸，我可以向你借10美元吗？"

8 男人暴怒，"如果你问这个问题，只是为了借钱买个愚蠢的玩具或一些废品，那你马上回到房间睡觉去。好好想想你这种自私的行为！我每天辛辛苦苦地工作，难道就是为了你这种幼稚行为？"

9 小男孩默默地回到房间，关上门。这时男人坐下来，更加恼怒。为什么他仅仅为了借钱就要问这个问题？大约一个小时后，男人平静下来，开始想："或许他真的需要10美元买东西呢？他很少要钱。"男人走到小男孩房门前，打开了门。

10 "睡了吗，儿子？"男人问道。

11 "没有呢，爸爸。"男孩回答说。

12 "I've been thinking, maybe I was too hard on you earlier," said the man, "it's been a long day and I took out my aggravation on you. Here is the $10 you asked for."

13 The little boy sat straight up, smiling. " Oh, thank you daddy!" he yelled. Then reaching under his pillow he pulled out some crumpled bills. The man seeing that the boy already had money, started to get angry again. The little boy slowly counted out his money, then looked up at his father.

14 "Why do you want more money if you already have some?" the father grumbled.

15 "Because I didn't have enough, but now I do." the little boy replied. "Daddy, I have $20 now. Can I buy an hour of your time? Please come home early tomorrow. I would like to have dinner with you."

12 "我一直在想，可能我刚才对你太过分了，"男人说，"我把一天的火都撒在你身上了。这是你要的 10 美元。"

13 小男孩顿时坐了起来，兴奋地叫道："谢谢，老爸！"然后，他把手伸到枕头底下，摸出几张皱巴巴的钞票。男人看到男孩手里的钱，又生气了。小男孩慢慢数着钱，然后抬头望着父亲。

14 "你自己有钱，为什么还要钱？"父亲抱怨道。

15 "因为我的钱不够，但现在够了。"小男孩答道。"爸爸，我现在有 20 美元。我能买您一个小时的时间吗？明天请早点回家，我想和您一起吃晚饭。"

阅读无障碍

irritated['ɪrɪ'teɪtɪd] adj. 恼火的，生气的
reply[rɪ'plaɪ] v. 答覆，回答
none of your business 与你无关
angrily['æŋɡrɪlɪ] adv. 愤怒地

plead[pliːd] v. 请求，恳求
furious['fjuərɪəs] adj. 狂怒的
silly['sɪlɪ] adj. 愚蠢的，可笑的
nonsense['nɒnsəns] n. 没有意义的东西

march[mɑːtʃ] v. 快步走

selfish['selfiʃ] adj. 自私的

childish['tʃaɪldɪʃ] adj. 天真的，孩子气的

quietly['kwaɪətlɪ] adv. 安静地

calm down 平静下来，镇定下来

awake[ə'weɪk] adj. 醒的

aggravation[ægrə'veɪʃən] n. 烦恼，怒火

straight up 笔直，直线上升

pillow['pɪləʊ] n. 枕头

crumpled['krʌmpld] adj. 摺皱的

count out 点数，数出

grumble['grʌmbl] v. 抱怨，发牢骚

极品佳句背诵

1. A man came home from work late, tired and irritated to find his five-year-old son waiting for him at the door.
   男人带着一身的疲倦，恼火地回到家，这时天色已晚，他发现五岁的儿子在门口等他。

2. If the only reason you asked that is so you can borrow some money to buy a silly toy or some other nonsense, then you march yourself straight to your room and go to bed.
   如果你问这个问题，只是为了借钱买个愚蠢的玩具或一些废品，那你马上回到房间睡觉去。好好想想你这种自私的行为！

3. Daddy, I have $20 now. Can I buy an hour of your time? Please come home early tomorrow. I would like to have dinner with you.
   爸爸，我现在有20美元。我能买您一个小时的时间吗？明天请早点回家，我想和您一起吃晚饭。

Visit with a Tramp
一位流浪汉的到访

带着问题去阅读

1. 为什么妈妈要给流浪汉食物？
2. 文中的女孩家里富裕吗？
3. 流浪汉为什么来女孩家？

美文欣赏

译文

1 I was swinging on the front gate, trying to decide whether to walk down the street to play with Verna, my best friend in fifth grade. When I saw a tramp come up the road.

2 "Hello, little girl" he said, "Is your mother at home?"

3 I nodded and swung the gate open to him in the yard. He looked like all the tramps who came to our house from the hobo camp by the river during the Great Depression. His shaggy hair hung below a shapeless hat, and his threadbare shirt and trousers had been rained on and slept in.

1 我在院门口晃悠，想着要不要去下街找薇娜玩，她是我五年级最好的朋友。这时，我看见从街上走来一个流浪汉。

2 "你好，小姑娘，"他说，"你妈妈在家吗？"

3 我点点头，把门打开让他进了院子。经济大萧条时期，有许多流浪汉从河那边的游民营来过我家，他看起来跟他们一样，蓬乱的头发从那顶不成形的帽子下露了出来，破破烂烂的衬衣和裤子显然被雨水

He smelled like a bonfire.

4 He shuffled to the door . When my mother appeared, he asked "Lady, could you spare a bite to eat?"

5 "I think so. Please sit on the step."

6 He dropped onto the narrow wooden platform that served as the front porch of our two-room frame house. In minutes my mother opened the screen and handed him a sandwich made from thick slices of homemade bread and generous chunks of boiled meat. She gave him a tin cup of milk . "I thank you, lady."he said.

7 I swung on the gate ,watching the tramp wolf down the sandwich and drain the cup. Then he stood and walked back through the gate. "They said your mama would feed me." He told me on the way out.

8 Verna had said the hobos told one another who feed them. "They never come to my house." She had announced proudly.

9 So why does mother feed them? I wondered. A widow, she worked as a waitress in the mornings, and sewed at night to earn money.Why should she give anything to men who didn't work at all?

淋湿过，还穿着睡过觉。他浑身散发着一种篝火烧焦的味道。

4 他慢吞吞地走到门那儿，当妈妈出现时，他问道："夫人，能我给点吃的吗？"

5 "好的，请坐在台阶上等会儿。"

6 他坐在狭长的木板平台上，那是两间屋的走廊。不一会儿，妈妈打开帘子，递给他一个三明治，用家里自制的厚面包片夹着几大块熟肉。她还给了他一杯牛奶。"谢谢您，夫人。"他说。

7 我在门上一边摇晃着，一边看着这个流浪汉狼吞虎咽地吃下那个三明治，喝光牛奶，然后，他站起来，往外面走穿过了大门。"他们说你妈妈会给我东西吃。"他出门的时候对我说。

8 薇娜曾说过，谁给流浪汉们东西吃，他们就会互相转告。"他们从不去我家。"她骄傲地说道。

9 妈妈为什么要给他们东西吃呢？我很奇怪。妈妈是一个寡妇，上午在餐厅做服务员，晚上还要做缝纫来挣钱。她为什么要把东西给这些完全不工作的人吃呢？

10 I marched inside. "Verna's mother says those men are too lazy to work. Why do we feed them?"

11 My mother smiled. Her blue housedress matched her eyes and emphasized her auburn hair.

12 "Lovely, we don't know why those men don't work," she said, "but they were babies once. And their mothers loved them, as I love you." She put her hands on my shoulders and drew me close to her apron, which smelled of starch and freshly baked bread.

13 "I feed them for their mothers, because if you were ever hungry and had nothing to eat, I would want their mothers to feed you."

10 我大步走进屋子，"薇娜的妈妈说，这些人太懒了而不愿意工作。我们为什么要他们给吃的呢？"

11 妈妈笑了，她蓝色的围裙和眼睛很相称，也衬托着她赤褐色的头发。

12 "宝贝，我们不知道他们为什么不工作，"她说，"但他们也曾是孩子，他们的妈妈爱他们，就像我爱你一样。"她把双手放在我肩头，把我拉到她的围裙边，围裙散发出浆洗过的和新烤的面包的味道。

13 "我给他们东西吃，是为了他们的妈妈。如果你饿了，又什么吃的都没有，我很希望他们的妈妈也能给你东西吃。"

阅读无障碍

swing[swɪŋ] v. 摇摆，晃动

tramp[træmp] n. 流浪者

hobo['həʊbəʊ] n. 无业游民，流浪汉

Great Depression 经济大萧条

shaggy['ʃægɪ] adj. 头发蓬乱的，邋遢的

shapeless['ʃeɪplɪs] adj. 没有形状的，不成样子的

threadbare['θredbeə] adj. 毛绒已磨掉而露线的

bonfire['bɒnfaɪə] n.（为销毁垃圾而燃的）火堆

shuffle['ʃʌfl] v. 拖着脚步走，慢吞吞地走

narrow['nærəʊ] adj. 狭窄的

porch[pɔːtʃ] n. 门廊，走廊

frame[freɪm] n. 框架，结构

thick[θɪk] *adj.* 厚的

generous['dʒenərəs] *adj.* 大量的，
丰富的

chunk[tʃʌŋk] *n.* 大块

wolf down 狼吞虎咽地吃

drain[dreɪn] *v.* 喝干，喝光

widow['wɪdəʊ] *n.* 寡妇，孀妇

sew[səʊ] *v.* 缝纫，缝合，缝

auburn ['ɔːbən] *adj.* 赤褐色的

🐰 极品佳句背诵

1. His shaggy hair hung below a shapeless hat, and his threadbare shirt and trousers had been rained on and slept in.
   他蓬乱的头发从那顶不成形的帽子下露了出来，破破烂烂的衬衣和裤子显然被雨水淋湿过，还穿着睡过觉。

2. My mother smiled. Her blue housedress matched her eyes and emphasized her auburn hair .
   妈妈笑了，她蓝色的围裙和眼睛很相称，也衬托着她赤褐色的头发。

3. I feed them for their mothers, because if you were ever hungry and had nothing to eat, I would want their mothers to feed you.
   我给他们东西吃，是为了他们的妈妈。如果你饿了，又什么吃的都没有，我希望他们的妈妈也能给你东西吃。

Be My Valentine
我的情人节礼物

带着问题去阅读

1. 你在情人节通常会收到什么礼物？

2. 假如你是文中的女主角你会有什么感受？

3. 在你即将离开世界之前你会为你的另一半做一件什么事情？

美文欣赏

 译文

1　Red roses were her favorites, her name was also Rose. And every year her husband sent them to her, tied with pretty bows. The year he died, the roses were delivered to her door. The card said, "Be my Valentine," like all the years before.

2　Each year he sent her roses, and the note would always say, "I love you even more this year than last year on this day. My love for you will always grow, with

1　红玫瑰花是她的最爱，她的名字也叫露丝（英文中是玫瑰的意思）。每年她的丈夫都要送她用可爱蝴蝶结扎着的红玫瑰。他去世的那年，玫瑰花送到了她的门口，卡片上写着："我的情人节礼物"，跟往年一样。

2　每年他为她送红玫瑰，卡片上总这样说："我今年更爱你，比去年的今天更爱。随着逝去的岁月，我对你的爱一

every passing year". She knew this was the last time that the roses would appear. She thought, he ordered roses in advance before this day. Her loving husband did not know that he would pass away. He always liked to do things early. Then, if he got too busy, everything would work out fine. She trimmed the stems, and placed them in a very special vase. Then, set the vase beside the portrait of his smiling face. She would sit for hours, in her husband's favorite chair, staring at his picture and the roses sitting there.

3　A year went by, and it was hard to live without her mate. With loneliness and solitude, that had become her fate. Then, the very hour, as on Valentines before, the door-bell rang, and there were roses, sitting by her door. She brought the roses in, and then just looked at them in shock. Then, she went to get the telephone to call the florist shop. The owner answered, and she asked him, if he would explain, why would someone do this to her, causing her such pain?

4　"I know your husband passed away, more than a year ago," The owner said, "I knew you'd call, and you would want to know." "The flowers you received today were paid for in advance." "Your husband always planned ahead, he left nothing to chance."

直在增长。"她知道这将是最后一次收到玫瑰花。她想，他是提前订了玫瑰花。她亲爱的丈夫不知道，他将走了。他总喜欢把事情做在前头，这样，如果他很忙的话，每件事都照样做得妥妥当当。她整理好花茎，把它们插进一个特别的花瓶，然后，将花瓶放在他满脸笑容的相片旁，她会在她丈夫喜欢的椅子上坐上好几个小时，看着他的相片和放在那儿的玫瑰花。

3　一年过去了，没有他的日子很难过。孤独和寂寞，成了她的命运。然而，在情人节这天，跟以往送花的时间相同，门铃响了，在她的门口放着玫瑰花。她将玫瑰拿进屋，吃惊地看着它们。然后，拨通了花店的电话。她问店主能否向她解释一下，为什么有人要这么做，引起她的痛苦？

4　"我知道你的丈夫一年多前去世了，"店主说："我知道你会打电话来，你想知道是怎么回事。今天你收到的花，已经提前付了钱。你的丈夫总是提前计划，他做事从来不碰运气。"

5 "There is a standing order that I have on file down here. And he did pay, well in advance. You'll get them every year. There also is another thing that I think you should know. He wrote a special little card he did this year ago."

6 "I find out that he's no longer here. That's the card that should be sent to you the following year. "

7 She thanked him and hung up the phone, her tears now flowing hard. Her fingers were shaking, as she slowly reached to get the card. Inside the card, she saw that he had written her a note. Then, as she stared in total silence, this is what he wrote: "Hello my love, I know it's been a year since I've been gone, I hope it hasn't been too hard for you to overcome." "I know it must be lonely, and the pain is very real. For if it was the other way, I know how I would feel. The love we shared made everything so beautiful in life. I loved you more than words can say, you were the perfect wife."

8 "You were my friend and lover, you fulfilled my every need. I know it's only been a year, but please try not to grieve. I want you to be happy, even when you shed your tears. That is why the roses will be sent to you for years."

5 "我的存档里有一个固定的订单，他已经提前付了钱，你每年都会收到玫瑰花。还有另外一件事，我想你应该知道，他写了一张特别的小卡片，他去年就写好了的。"

6 "我知道他已不在人世了，这张卡片将在下一年送给你。"

7 她谢了他，挂了电话，眼泪夺眶而出，当她慢慢地伸手去拿卡片时，她的手指在颤抖。在卡片里，他看到了他写给她的短信。她默默地看着，他是这样写的："亲爱的，我知道我离开你已经一年了，我希望你所度过的这段日子不是太难。""我知道你肯定很孤独，而且这种痛苦是如此的真切。因为如果这样的事发生在我身上，我知道我会有怎样的感受。我们分享的爱让生命中的每件事都是那么的美好，我对你的爱无法用言语表达，你是最完美的妻子。"

8 "你是我的朋友和爱人，你总能满足我的每一个需求。我知道才过了一年，但是请你尽可能不要悲伤。我希望你快乐，即使流着泪。这就是为什么在今后的岁月里每年都会送玫瑰给你。"

9 "When you get these roses, think of all the happiness that we had together, and how both of us were blessed. I have always loved you and I know I always will. But, my love, you must go on, you have some living still."

10 "Please, try to find happiness, while living out your days. I know it is not easy, but I hope you find some ways. The roses will come every year, and they will only stop when your door's not answered, when the florist stops to knock."

11 "He will come five times that day, in case you have gone out. But after his last visit, he will know without a doubt. To take the roses to the place, where I've instructed him, and place the rose where we are together once again. Happy Valentine's Day."

9 "当你收到这些玫瑰花时，请想想我们一起度过的所有的幸福时光，我们是怎样受到祝福的。我一直爱着你，我知道我会永远爱着。但是，亲爱的，你必须继续生活下去，你还有好多日子要过。"

10 "哪怕我没有和你一起，也请你努力去寻找欢乐，我知道并不容易，但我希望你能找到一些方式。玫瑰每年都会送来，而且，只有当你不再应门时，只有当花店店主停止敲门时，它们才不会再来。"

11 "这一天，以防你出门不在，他会来 5 次。你是否还在，他最后一次拜访就会明了。他会将花送到我指定的地方，我们再次相聚的地方。情人节快乐。"

阅读无障碍

tie [taɪ] v. 系

bow [bəʊ] n. 蝴蝶结

deliver [dɪ'lɪvə(r)] v. 递送

in advance 提前

trim [trɪm] v. 修剪

stem [stem] n.（花草的）茎

portrait ['pɔːtreɪt] n. 肖像，人像

solitude ['sɒlɪtjuːd] n. 孤独

fate [feɪt] n. 命运

shock [ʃɒk] n. 震惊

florist ['flɒrɪst] n. 花匠

file [faɪl] v. 编档保存

flow [fləʊ] v. 流

overcome [,əʊvə'kʌm] v. 克服

fulfill [fʊlˈfɪl] *n.* 满足

grieve [griːv] *v.* 悲伤

shed [ʃed] *v.* 流出

bless [bles] *v.* 祝福

in case 以防万一

instruct [ɪnˈstrʌkt] *v.* 通知

🐰 极品佳句背诵

1. Each year he sent her roses, and the note would always say, "I love you even more this year than last year on this day. My love for you will always grow, with every passing year".

   每年他为她送红玫瑰，卡片上总这样说："我今年更爱你，比去年的今天更爱。随着逝去的岁月，我对你的爱一直在增长。"

2. When you get these roses, think of all the happiness that we had together, and how both of us were blessed.

   当你收到这些玫瑰花时，请想想我们一起度过的所有的幸福时光，我们是怎样受到祝福的。

3. Please, try to find happiness, while living out your days. I know it is not easy, but I hope you find some ways.

   哪怕我没有和你一起，也请你努力去寻找欢乐，我知道并不容易，但我希望你能找到一些方式。

Test of True Love
真爱的考验

带着问题去阅读

1. 你认为什么样的爱才是真爱？
2. 真爱需要考验吗？
3. 你会考验他/她对你的爱吗？

美文欣赏

 译文

1 My husband is an engineer.

2 Since the day we met, he has always been the rock in my life. I know he had his feet firmly planted on the ground, and it seemed that no matter what else went crazy, he would be the one constant.

3 Three years of romance and two years of marriage later, I was tired of him. He is the most unromantic man I know.

4 He never bought me flowers, he never surprised me, and nothing had changed in our marriage.

5 After some time, I finally found the courage to tell him that I wanted out. He

1 我丈夫是个工程师。

2 自从我们相遇，他一直是我生命中的磐石。我知道他很务实，好像不管其他一切变得多么疯狂，他都能始终如一。

3 三年的恋爱，两年的婚姻生活之后，我渐渐厌倦了他。他是我认识的最不浪漫的人。

4 他从不买花送我，也不给我惊喜。我们的婚姻生活永远一成不变。

5 一段时间过后，我终于鼓起勇气告诉他我想跟他离

just sat there, speechless. My heart froze: what kind of man was I married to who didn't even know what to say to make me stay? After a while, he spoke. "What can I do to change your mind?"

6　"I will stay if you can give me a good answer to this question." I replied coldly. "If I asked for a flower that grew on a cliff, and you knew that getting it for me meant certain death, would you still get it for me?"

7　His face grew troubled. "Can I give you the answer tomorrow morning?" with that, my heart sank. I knew that I could never be happy with a man who couldn't even give me an answer straight away.

8　The next morning, when I woke up, he was missing. In the living room, under a warm glass of milk, was a note. My eyes grew misty as I read it.

9　"Dear, I have my answer. I will never pick the flower for you if it meant certain death."

10　But before you leave, I hope you will give me a chance to give you my reasons.

11　You always sit in front of the computer and type the whole day. But you always end up in tears because your format goes all over the place. I need my fingers to do the formatting for you, so that your

婚。他只是坐在那里不说话。我的心凉了：跟我结婚的人怎么是这样的啊，他甚至不知道说些让我留下的话。过了一会儿，他说："我能做些什么才能让你改变主意呢？"

6　"如果你能对这个问题给我一个满意的答案，我就留下。"我冷冷地说："如果我要一朵开在悬崖上的鲜花，你也知道去那里采花意味着死亡，你还愿意为我采吗？"

7　他一脸不安的说："我能明早给你答案吗？"听到这话，我的心往下沉了。我明白和这样一个不能立马给我答案的人一起生活不会让我幸福的。

8　第二天早上，我醒来的时候没看见他。客厅里，一杯热牛奶的底下放了一张纸条。我读着读着眼睛模糊了。

9　"亲爱的，我有答案了。如果必死无疑的话，我是不会去采那朵花的。"

10　但在你离开之前，我希望你能给我一个机会让我告诉你理由。

11　你经常坐在电脑前整天打字，但是最后你总是被气哭了，因为你把格式弄得乱七八糟。我需要用我的手指为你调整格式，然后你会破涕为笑。

tears will become smiles.

12 You like to travel but always get lost. I need my eyes to take you to the nicest places on earth. Every time you leave the house, you forget your keys. I need my legs to run home and open the door for you.

13 You never know how to take care of yourself. I need my hands to help you get rid of the pesky, white hair that you hate so much when you grow old, to trim your nails and to feed you.

14 So you see, that's why I cannot pick the flower for you. Until I find someone who loves you more than I do, I will need my body to take care of you.

15 If you accept my reasons, open the door and I will be waiting with your favorite muffin.

16 With tears streaming from my eyes, I opened the door. And there he was with an extremely worried look on his face.

17 He still had nothing to say. He just stood there, waving the packet he had in his hand in front of me.

18 I knew then that I would never find another man who will love me as much as my husband does.

19 Just because someone does not love you the way you want him to, it doesn't mean that he does not love you with all he has.

12 你喜欢旅游，但经常迷路。我需要用我的眼睛带你到世界上最美丽的地方去。每一次你离开家总是忘记带钥匙，我需要用我的腿跑回来为你开门。

13 你从不知道照顾自己。当你年老的时候，我需要用我的手帮你拔掉你那么憎恨的烦人的白头发，帮你修剪指甲，喂饭给你吃。

14 所以你看，这就是我不能为你采花的原因。在找到一个比我更爱你的人之前，我需要用我的身体照顾你。

15 如果你接受了我的理由。请开门吧。我买了你最爱吃的松饼在等你。

16 我满脸泪水打开了门。他站在那儿，脸上显得很焦急。

17 他还是没说什么，只是站在那儿，在我眼前晃了晃他手上的一包松饼。

18 那时我知道我再也找不到比我丈夫更爱我的人了。

19 仅仅因为某人不是以你想要的方式来爱，这并不意味着他不是全身心地爱你。

阅读无障碍

engineer [endʒɪˈnɪə] *n.* 工程师

firmly [ˈfɜːmlɪ] *adv.* 坚固地，稳固地

crazy [ˈkreɪzɪ] *adj.* 疯狂的

constant [ˈkɒnst(ə)nt] *adj.* 不变的

romance [rəʊˈmæns] *n.* 浪漫故事（文章中指恋爱）

courage [ˈkʌrɪdʒ] *n.* 勇气

speechless [ˈspiːtʃlɪs] *adj.* 无言的，沉默的

freeze [friːz] *v.* 感到极冷

cliff [klɪf] *n.* 悬崖，绝壁

troubled [ˈtrʌb(ə)ld] *adj.* 不安的，困惑的

straight [streɪt] *adj.* 直接的

misty [ˈmɪstɪ] *adj.* 模糊的

format [ˈfɔːmæt] *n.* 格式，版式

get rid of 摆脱，除去

pesky [ˈpeskɪ] *adj.* 讨厌的，烦人的

trim [trɪm] *v.* 修剪

nail [neɪl] *n.* 指甲

muffin [ˈmʌfɪn] *n.* （涂牛奶趁热吃的）英格兰松饼

stream [striːm] *v.* 流，流眼泪

packet [ˈpækɪt] *n.* 小包

极品佳句背诵

1. I need my eyes to take you to the nicest places on earth.
   我需要用我的眼睛带你到世界上最美丽的地方去。

2. I need my hands to help you get rid of the pesky, white hair you hate so much when you grow old, to trim your nails and to feed you.
   当你年老的时候，我需要用我的手帮你拔掉你那么憎恨的烦人的白头发，帮你修剪指甲，喂饭给你吃。

3. Just because someone does not love you the way you want him to, it doesn't mean that he does not love you with all he has.
   仅仅因为某人不是以你想要的方式来爱，这并不意味着他不是全身心地爱你。

Love and Time
爱与时间

带着问题去阅读

1. 你认为爱人携手一生最重要的是什么?

2. 是否每一对夫妻都有其独特的相处之道?

3. 爱人之间是否需要彼此制造一些浪漫和温馨?

 美文欣赏

 译文

1 So often, when I'm alone with my thoughts,

2 I feel your presence enter me

3 like the morning sun's early light,

4 filling my memories and dreams of us

5 with a warm and clear radiance.

6 You have become my love, my life,

7 and together we have shaped our world

8 until it seems now as natural as breathing.

---

1 久久,当我独处,思索飞扬。

2 彼之浮影蹁跹,入我心肠。

3 譬如初阳,瑞彩千行。

4 若水清澈,暖我心房。

5 往昔追思,旧梦浮尘,洋溢满腔。

6 执手吾爱,漫漫人生路,与君话短长。

7 与君共书丹青,上下飞舞忙。

8 珠联璧合,相得益彰。

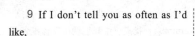

9 If I don't tell you as often as I'd like,

10 it's because I could never tell you enough

11 that I'm grateful for you

12 sharing your life with mine,

13 and that my love for you will live forever.

14 When my husband and I celebrated our 38th wedding anniversary at our favorite restaurant, Lenny, the piano player, asked, "How did you do it?"

15 I knew there was no simple answer, but as the weekend approached, I wondered if one reason might be our ritual of breakfast in bed every Saturday and Sunday.

16 It all started with the breakfast tray my mother gave us as a wedding gift. It had a glass top and slatted wooden side pockets for the morning paper kind you used to see in the movies. Mother loved her movies, and although she rarely had breakfast in bed, she held high hopes for her daughter. My adoring bridegroom took the message to heart.

9 无言与君对，不似旧时样。

10 滔滔东流水，怎及吾爱之浩荡。

11 诚此为幸，莫若君旁。

12 与卿携手，游戏人间，细品芬芳。

13 无尽爱恋，哪怕地老天荒。

14 当我和丈夫在我们最喜欢的饭馆庆祝结婚38周年纪念日时，那个弹钢琴的莱尼过来问道："你们是怎么走过来的？"

15 我知道，对于这个问题无法简简单单地来回答，但随着周末一天天的临近，我开始在想：或许其中的一个原因就是我们每逢星期六和星期天都在床上吃早餐。

16 一切都是从那个早餐托盘开始的，我妈把它作为结婚礼物送给我们。盘面是玻璃的，两边各有一个细长的木制侧袋用来放晨报——就像过去常常在电影中见到的那样。我妈很喜欢那些电影，尽管她自己很少在床上用餐，却非常希望女儿能这样。深爱着我的新郎把我母亲的话牢记在心里。

17 Feeling guilty, I suggested we take turns. Despite grumblings --"hate crumbs in my bed" ---Sunday morning found my spouse eagerly awaiting his tray. Soon these weekend breakfasts became such a part of our lives that I never even thought about them. I only knew we treasured this separate, blissful time read, relaxed, and forgot the things we should remember.

18 Sifting through the years, I recalled how our weekends changed, but that we still preserved the ritual. We started our family (as new parents, we slept after breakfast more than we read),but we always found our way back to where we started, just two for breakfast, one on Saturday and one on Sunday.

19 When we had more time, my tray became more festive. First it was fruit slices placed in geometric pattern; then came flowers from our garden just one blossom sprouting from a grapefruit half. This arranger of mine had developed a flair for decorating, using everything from amaryllis to the buds of a maple tree. My husband said my cooking inspired him.

17 出于心里有些愧疚，我提议由我们两个轮流准备早餐。星期天早上，虽然他嘴里嘟嘟囔囔地抱怨着——"我讨厌饭渣弄到床上。"——但我还是见到丈夫在急切地等候他的早餐。不久周末早餐就成为我们生活中的一部分，习以为常也就不去想它了。我只知道我俩都很珍视这段与其他时间有别的幸福时光——看看报、放松一下自己，忘记那些本该记在心里的事情。

18 细想逝去的岁月，我回忆起我们周末生活的诸多变化，但这个老习惯却依旧保留下来。我们建立起了这个家庭（初为父母时，早饭后的时间我们多半是睡一会儿，而不是阅读），但是我们总能够找到归路，返回起点——只是两个人的早餐，星期六一次，星期天一次。

19 当我们有了更多的时间，我的早餐托盘上就变得更加具有喜庆色彩。开始时是以几何图形排列的水果片，随后便是从自家花园里摘来的鲜花——有时候只是一朵，开在一半的葡萄柚当中。没想到这竟激发出我在装饰、点缀方面的天赋，各种各样的东西，从

Mother would have approved. Perhaps it was the Saturday when the big strawberry wore a daisy hat that I began to think, how can I top this? One dark winter night I woke with a vision of a snowman on a tray. That Sunday I scooped a handful of snow and in no time had my man made. With a flourish I put a miniature pinecone on his head.

20 As I delivered the tray, complete with a nicely frozen snowman, I waited for a reaction. There was none but as I headed down the stairs I heard a whoop of laughter and then, "You've won! Yes, sir, you've won the prize!"

孤挺花到枫树的叶芽，都成为我手下的装饰材料。丈夫说我做的早餐启发了他，妈妈也赞同他的说法。或许是在那个星期六，在一个大草莓上放一个雏菊做帽子之后，我开始在想：我怎么才能够比他做得更好？在一个漆黑的冬夜，我从梦中醒来，眼前仿佛看到有一个雪人站在托盘上。就在那个星期天，我铲来了一捧雪，很快就做好了一个雪人。我轻轻地把一个微型松果按在雪人的头上。

21 我端着早餐上楼，盘面上放着那个冻结实的小雪人，我期待着他的反应——什么也没有——但就在我下楼时，我听到他放声大笑起来，紧接着，他说道："你赢了！毫无疑问，你得奖了！"

阅读无障碍

radiance ['reɪdɪəns] n. 光辉
breathing ['briːðɪŋ] n. 呼吸
celebrate ['selɪbreɪt] v. 庆贺
anniversary [ˌænɪ'vɜːs(ə)rɪ] n. 周年纪念日
ritual ['rɪtʃʊəl] n. 惯例
bridegroom ['braɪdɡruːm] n. 新郎
guilty ['ɡɪltɪ] adj. 内疚的

crumb [krʌm] n. 碎屑
spouse [spaʊs] n. 配偶，夫或妻
blissful ['blɪsfl] adj. 极幸福的
geometric [ˌdʒiːə'metrɪk] adj. 几何图形的
sprout [spraʊt] v. 发芽，长芽
amaryllis [ˌæmə'rɪlɪs] n. 孤挺花，喇叭花

strawberry [ˈstrɔːb(ə)rɪ] *n.* 草莓

scoop [skuːp] *v.* 铲，掘取

flourish [ˈflʌrɪʃ] *n.* 装饰

miniature [ˈmɪnɪtʃə] *adj.* 微型的

pinecone [ˈpaɪnˌkɒn] *n.* 松果

frozen [ˈfrəʊzn] *adj.* 冻结的

whoop [wuːp] *n.* 呐喊，大叫

极品佳句背诵

1. You have become my love, my life, and together we have shaped our world until it seems now as natural as breathing.

   执手吾爱，漫漫人生路，与君话短长；与君共书丹青，上下飞舞忙；珠联璧合，相得益彰。

2. I knew there was no simple answer, but as the weekend approached, I wondered if one reason might be our ritual of breakfast in bed every Saturday and Sunday.

   我知道，对于这个问题无法简简单单地来回答，但随着周末一天天的临近，我开始在想：或许其中的一个原因就是我们每逢星期六和星期天都在床上吃早餐。

3. Sifting through the years, I recalled how our weekends changed, but that we still preserved the ritual.

   细想逝去的岁月，我回忆起我们周末生活的诸多变化，但这个老习惯却依旧保留下来。

Butterfly Kiss
蝶吻

带着问题去阅读

1. 你认为爱情应该是轰轰烈烈还是坚守一份平淡？
2. 幸福的婚姻就是一起慢慢变老吗？
3. 你认为真爱到底是什么？

美文欣赏

译文

1 My newlywed husband said the same thing every morning. "You're beautiful today."

2 One glance in the mirror revealed that it was far from the truth.

3 A skinny girl with mashed hair on one side of her head and no makeup smiled back at me. I could feel my sticky morning breath.

4 "Liar," I shot back with a grin.

5 It was my usual response. My mother's first husband was not a kind man

1 我的新婚丈夫每天早晨都对我说同样的话。"你今天真美。"

2 扫一眼镜子中的我就能证明他说的远非事实。

3 镜中的女孩瘦瘦的，乱乱的头发倒向头的一侧，素面朝天微笑地望着我。我还能感到早晨起来嘴里不大好闻的气味。

4 "骗子，"我咧着嘴笑，回敬了他一句。

5 我通常都是这样回答。我母亲的第一个丈夫可不是个

and his verbal and physical abuse forced her and her two children to find a safe place. He showed up on her doorstep one day with roses.

6 She let him in and he beat her with those roses and took advantage of her. Nine months later she gave birth to a 9 lb. 13 oz baby girl -- me.

7 The harsh words we heard growing up took root. I had trouble seeing myself as someone of value.

8 I had been married two years when I felt surprised. My husband wrapped his arms around me and told me I was beautiful.

9 "Thank you." I said.

10 The same thin girl with the mousy brown hair still stared back at me in the mirror, but somehow the words had finally blossomed in my heart.

11 A lot of years have passed.

12 My husband has grey in his hair. I'm no longer skinny. Last week I woke up and my husband's face was inches from mine.

13 "What are you doing?" I asked.

14 I covered my mouth, trying to hide my morning breath. He reached down and kissed my face.

15 "What I do every morning," he

善良之辈，他粗暴的语言攻击和身体虐待迫使我母亲带着两个孩子去寻找一个安全的地方。有一天他出现在母亲的门前，手里拿着玫瑰花。

6 她让他进了门，但他却用玫瑰花打她，并占了她便宜。9个月后她生了一个9磅13盎司重的女孩——就是我。

7 长大过程中我们听到的刺耳的话语在我心底生了根。我无法把自己看作一个值得珍视的人。

8 结婚两年后我感到惊讶了。我的丈夫双臂拥着我告诉我，我是美丽的。

9 "谢谢你。"我说。

10 同样是那个瘦弱，一头灰棕色头发的女孩在镜中盯着我，但是温柔的话语终于在我的心中开花了。

11 许多年过去了。

12 我的丈夫已经长出了白发。我也不再骨瘦如柴。上周的早晨我醒来时，我丈夫的脸离我只有几英寸。

13 "你在干什么？"我问。

14 我捂住嘴，不想让他闻到嘴里的气味。他俯身过来亲吻我的脸。

15 "做我每天早晨都做

said.

16　He leaves in the early hours of the morning while I sleep. I miss our morning conversations, but I had not realized that he continued to tell me that he loved me even while I slept. When he left, I rolled over and hugged my pillow. I envisioned the picture of me lightly snoring with my mouth open and giggled.

17　What a man! My husband understands my past.

18　He's been beside me as I've grown from an unsure young girl to a confident woman, mother, speaker and author.

19　But I'm not sure that he understands the part he played in that transition. The words I heard growing up pierced my soul, yet his words pierced even deeper.

20　This Anniversary Day I plan to wake early.

21　I want to tell Richard how much I love him. He may look in the mirror and see an extra pound or two, or wish for the day when his hair is dark and curly, but all that I'll see is the man who saw something in me when I couldn't see it myself, and who leaves butterfly kisses, even after twenty-three years of marriage.

的事。"他说。

16　他清晨就得离开家，而我常常还在熟睡。我错过了早上的谈话，但是我还未曾意识到他一直在告诉我他爱我，哪怕是在我还睡着时。他离开时，我翻过身去，抱着我的枕头。我想象着我睡觉时轻轻打鼾，嘴巴还微微张着的样子，不禁咯咯笑了。

17　这样一个男人！我丈夫知道我的过去。

18　他一直在我身边，看我从一个不自信的年轻女子变成一个成熟自信的女人、母亲、演讲者、作家。

19　但是我不确信他是否知道在这一过渡中他起着怎样的作用。伴我长大的话语曾刺入我的灵魂，而他的话语更是深深地打动了我的灵魂。

20　今年的结婚周年纪念日我打算早点醒来。

21　我要告诉查德我多么地爱他。他照镜子时也许会发现又增加了一两磅体重，或者期望有一天他的头发又是乌黑卷曲的，但是我所看到的是发现我身上具备什么东西，而我未能发现，即使是在结婚23年后也天天给我留下蝶吻的这样一个男人。

阅读无障碍

newlywed['nju:lɪwed] *adj.* 新婚的

reveal[rɪ'vi:l] *v.* 显示

skinny['skɪnɪ] *adj.* 皮包骨头的，极瘦的

response[rɪ'spɒns] *n.* 回答

verbal['vɜ:bl] *adj.* 口头的

harsh[hɑ:ʃ] *adj.* 刺耳的

wrap[ræp] *v.* 缠绕

mousy['maʊsɪ] *adj.* 灰褐色的

conversation[kɒnvə'seɪʃ(ə)n] *n.* 交谈

roll [rəʊl] *v.* 卷

pillow ['pɪləʊ] *n.* 枕头

envision [en'vɪʒ(ə)n] *v.* 想像

giggle ['gɪg(ə)l] *v.* 咯咯地笑，傻笑

unsure [ʌn'ʃʊə] *adj.* 不自信的

author['ɔ:θə] *n.* 作家

transition [træn''zɪʃn] *n.* 过渡，转变

pierce [pɪəs] *v.* 深深打动

curly['kɜ:lɪ] *adj.* 有卷发的

butterfly['bʌtəflaɪ] *n.* 蝴蝶

marriage['mærɪdʒ] *n.* 结婚

极品佳句背诵

1. I miss our morning conversations, but I had not realized that he continued to tell me that he loved me even while I slept.
   我错过了早上的谈话，但是我还未曾意识到他一直在告诉我他爱我，哪怕是在我还睡着时。

2. He's been beside me as I've grown from an unsure young girl to a confident woman, mother, speaker and author.
   他一直在我身边，看我从一个不自信的年轻女子变成一个成熟自信的女人、母亲、演讲者、作家。

3. The words I heard growing up pierced my soul, yet his words pierced even deeper.
   伴我长大的话语曾刺入我的灵魂，而他的话语更是深深地触动了我的灵魂。

Love Needs No Words
大爱无声

带着问题去阅读

1. 如果你是这位母亲会怎样做？
2. 你觉得什么是大爱？
3. 爱需要说出来吗？

1 "Can I see my baby?" the happy new mother asked. When the bundle was nestled in her arms and she moved the fold of cloth to look upon his tiny face, she gasped. The doctor turned quickly and looked out the tall hospital window.

2 The baby had been born without ears. Time proved that the baby's hearing was perfect. It was only his appearance that was marred.

3 When he rushed home from school one day and flung himself into his mother's arms. She sighed, knowing that his life

1 "我能看看我的孩子吗？"刚刚做了母亲的女人高兴地问。当襁褓被放到她怀里，她拿开挡着孩子小脸的布时，她倒吸了一口凉气。医生快速地转过身去，向外望去。

2 孩子天生没有耳朵。事实证明他的听力完全没有问题。只是容貌有缺陷。

3 一天，他从学校飞奔回家，投入妈妈的怀抱。她叹息着，知道他的一生将有一连

was to be a succession of heartbreaks. He blurted out the tragedy, "A boy, a big boy … called me a freak."

4 He grew up, handsome but for his misfortune. A favorite with his fellow students, he might have been class president, but for that. He developed a gift, a talent for literature and music.

5 The boy's father had a session with the family physician, "Could you nothing be done?"

6 "I believe I could graft on a pair of outer ears, if they could be gotten." The doctor declared. They searched for a person who could make such a great sacrifice for the young man.

7 Two years went by. One day, his father said to the son, "You're going to the hospital, son. Mother and I have someone who will donate the ears you need. But the identity of the donor is a secret."

8 The operation was a brilliant success, and a new person emerged. His talents blossomed into genius. School and college became a series of triumphs. He married and enter the diplomatic service.

9 He would ask his father: "Who gave me the ears? Who gave me so much? I could never do enough for him or her."

10 "I do not believe you could." Said

串的伤心。他说出了那件让人心碎的事情："一个男孩，大个子男孩，叫我怪物。"

4 他长大了，尽管有那个悲惨命运，他还是长得很英俊。他深受同学们喜欢，如果不是因为那个残疾，他本可以做班长的，他在文学和音乐方面很有天赋。

5 男孩的爸爸去问家庭医生："难道真的一点办法也没有吗？"

6 "办法是有的。如果能找到一双合适的外耳，我可以帮他植入。"医生说。他们开始寻找看有谁愿意为年轻人做出这样的牺牲。

7 两年过去了。一天，父亲告诉儿子："孩子，你终于可以做手术了。妈妈和我找到愿意为你捐耳朵的人了。但是，捐献者要求身份保密。"

8 手术非常成功，他脱胎换骨。他的才华宛如鲜花得到了释放。学业也取得了一连串的成功。后来，他结了婚，并做了外交官。

9 他问他的父亲：是谁给了我耳朵？谁给了我这么多？我从来都没有为他（她）做一点事。

10 "我不认为你有那个

the father, "but the agreement was that you are not to know… not yet."

11　The years kept their profound secret, but the day did come. He stood with his father over his mother's casket. Slowly, tenderly, the father stretched forth his hand and raised the thick, reddish-brown hair to reveal that the mother had no outer ears.

12　"Mother said she was glad she never got her hair cut," his father whispered gently, " and nobody ever thought mother less beautiful, did they?"

能力去报答，"爸爸说，"我们当初的协议中规定你不能知道是谁，至少现在还不能。"

11　父亲的守口如瓶使这个秘密保持了许多年，但是，这一天终于还是来了。他和爸爸站在妈妈的棺木前。慢慢地，轻柔地，爸爸伸出手撩起了妈妈那浓密的红色的头发，显露在孩子面前的竟是：妈妈没有耳朵！

12　"你妈说她很庆幸自己从来不用去理发，"爸爸低声说道，"但没人会认为你母亲因此减少了一丝一毫的美丽，不是吗？"

阅读无障碍

bundle['bʌndl] n. 包袱，襁褓
gasp[gæsp] v. 喘气，倒抽气
mar[mɑ:] v. 损毁，损伤，糟蹋
fling[flɪŋ] v. 投，使陷入
succession[sək'seʃən] n. 一系列，一连串
freak[fri:k] n. 畸形人，畸形物
misfortune[mɪs'fɔ:tʃən] n. 不幸，灾祸
literature['lɪtərɪtʃə] n. 文学
session['seʃən] n. 会谈
graft[grɑ:ft] v. 嫁接，移植

declare[dɪk'leə] v. 声明，宣称
sacrifice['sækrɪfaɪs] n. 牺牲
donate['dəʊneɪt] v. 捐赠
identity[aɪ'dentɪtɪ] n. 身份
brilliant['brɪljənt] adj. 卓越的，极棒的
emerge[ɪ'mə:dʒ] v. 浮现，形成
blossom['blɒsəm] v. 开花，兴旺发展
triumph['traɪəmf] n. 胜利，成功
casket['kæskɪt] n. 棺材
whisper['hwɪspə] v. 低声说

极品佳句背诵

1. The operation was a brilliant success, and a new person emerged. His talents blossomed into genius. School and college became a series of triumphs.

   手术非常成功，他脱胎换骨。他的才华宛如鲜花怒放般得到了释放。学业也取得了一连串的成功。

2. Slowly, tenderly, the father stretched forth his hand and raised the thick, reddish-brown hair to reveal that the mother had no outer ears.

   慢慢地，轻柔地，爸爸伸出手撩起了妈妈那浓密的红色的头发，显露在孩子面前的竟是：妈妈没有耳朵！

3. "Mother said she was glad she never got her hair cut," his father whispered gently, " and nobody ever thought mother less beautiful, did they?"

   "妈妈说她很庆幸自己从来不用去理发，"爸爸低声说道，"但没人会认为你母亲因此而减少了一丝一毫的美丽，不是吗？"

An Unforgettable Christmas
令人难忘的圣诞节

带着问题去阅读

1. 你最喜欢的圣诞礼物是什么？
2. 圣诞节会同家人一起做些什么？
3. 最令你难忘的一次圣诞节是什么时候？

 美文欣赏

 译文

1 I still can't believe what my husband has done for me.

2 He got me a CAR for Christmas; and I don't even know HOW to drive yet!

3 I woke up early Christmas morning, and after I got my bearings together and took my medications, I went to the living room, only to see the Christmas tree all lit up and all the presents underneath. I knew that "Santa Claus" had come, and I knew that the children would be all excited when they saw all the presents were underneath the tree; and that was when I heard some

---

1 我还是不能相信我丈夫为我做的一切。

2 圣诞节那天，他送给我一辆汽车，可是我还不会开车！

3 圣诞节的一大早我就起床了，吃完药后，刚走进起居室，便看到了圣诞树上的彩灯都点亮了，树下堆满了圣诞礼物。我知道"圣诞"老人已经来了，孩子们见到这些礼物一定会兴奋得大叫起来。这时，我听到从厨房传来响亮的笑声。厨房的灯亮着，我悄悄

loud laughter coming in from the kitchen. The kitchen light was on, and I slowly made my way to the kitchen, and much to my surprise, there was my husband, Roberto, chatting with my brothers, Keserian and Naiser! At the sight of my brothers, I screamed, and I started crying; I had NO idea they were coming! Keserian and Naiser both started crying when they saw me, and soon, we were hugging each other, and we were all crying from joy and excitement at seeing each other again!

4 I then heard the children from their rooms (Kibarake and Eshe were both crying sleepily, and Jubaki was yelling, "It's Christmas! It's Christmas! Did Santy come? Did Santy come??"), so I told Roberto to take care of the children while I visited with my brothers. I couldn't believe how well both Naiser and Keserian looked; and I was surprised at how well Keserian was getting around on forearm crutches and leg braces. The last time I saw Keserian back in Kenya last summer, he was still in the hospital, and at the time he couldn't walk, as he was recovering from his injuries.

5 After the kids were up, changed, washed up, and were dressed, Roberto then brought them in to the living room, and Jubaki was yelling, "He came! Oh, Santy came!! He brought presents for Jubaki!!"

的走向厨房，让我惊喜万分的是，我丈夫罗伯特，正在与我的两个哥哥凯撒瑞安和莱泽闲聊。看到两个哥哥，我激动的尖叫起来，喜极而泣。我没想到他们要来。两个哥哥见到我后，也激动得尖叫起来，互相拥抱后，我们又一次因见到彼此而掉下幸福、激动的泪水。

4 我听到了孩子们从房间传出来的声音（凯布莱克和艾施嚷嚷着喊困，朱百科叫嚷道："今天是圣诞节！今天是圣诞节！圣诞老人来了没有啊？"）。我让罗伯特去照看孩子，我留下和哥哥说话。我简直不敢相信自己的眼睛，凯撒瑞安和莱泽看起来气色很好。我很惊讶凯撒瑞安熟练地使用手中的拐杖和腿上的支架活动。最后一次见到他还是在去年夏天，那时他还在肯尼亚住院，根本不能走动，因为他当时正在恢复伤口。

5 孩子们起床、洗漱穿衣完毕后，罗伯特把他们带到起居室，朱百科叫道："他来了，圣诞老人来了！他给朱百科带礼物来了！"另外两个孪

and the twins were amazed at the sight of all the brightly wrapped presents under the lighted up Christmas tree. Roberto then started passing out presents after everyone was seated in the living room. The biggest cry came when Jubaki got his big gift, which, to my surprise, was a remote control Hummer. The Hummer was yellow, and it came with batteries and a remote control which could be operated by pushing a few buttons, and depending on which buttons you pressed, it could go forwards or backwards. I wasn't none too happy either when I found out that the toy remote-control Hummer cost $99.00 at WalMart!

6 After the presents had all been opened, Roberto then handed me an envelope that had my name on it. When I opened it, there were a set of car keys in it, and nothing else. I looked at him all confused; but then I heard the noise of a car horn beeping, and Roberto quickly got up, and when he looked out the front window, he grinned, and he said, "Honey, your present is here. Look out the front picture window, and you will see your Christmas present. It's from me." When I looked out, I nearly fainted. There, sitting in the driveway, was a beautiful orange Volkswagen Beetle that had a bright red Christmas bow wrapped around it and

生小兄弟惊异的看着闪闪发光的圣诞树下那些包装精美的礼物。他们坐好后，罗伯特开始分发礼物。接到礼物后，朱百科发出了兴奋的叫声。令我惊异的是，那是一个遥控的悍马玩具车，是一个配有电池和遥控器的黄颜色的悍马。只要按一下遥控器的按钮，就可以控制悍马。悍马会根据你按的不同按钮前后移动。但是，当我发现这个玩具在沃尔玛超市卖99美元时，我稍有些不悦。

6 所有的礼物都打开后，罗伯特递给我一个写有我名字的信封。打开后，里面只有一串车钥匙。我困惑的看着他，这时我听到了"嘟——嘟——嘟"的汽车喇叭声。罗伯特马上站起来，望着窗外，咧嘴笑道："亲爱的，你的礼物在这。从前窗望出去，你就会看到我送给你的圣诞礼物。"我望后，差点儿晕倒。那儿，一辆非常漂亮的桔色大众甲壳虫停在路上，车上系着一条红色的圣诞横幅，上面写道："圣诞快乐！爱你的罗伯特。"看到这辆车，我禁不住哭了，我对他

a sign on the front that said, "Merry Christmas, My beauty! With Love, your husband, Roberto". When I saw the car, I couldn't help BUT to start crying. I then said to him, "You got me a car?" and he said, "Yes! Merry Christmas, darling!"

7 Now it is two days after Christmas, and I still can't believe that my husband spent THAT kind of money on ME! He doesn't need to be doing that, you know...he's got kids and a wife to take care of; he doesn't need to be spending all that extra money on ME! Especially on stuff like remote-control Hummers, let alone, a real life car!! (Do you know that real Beetles cost at least$11,000? They aren't cheap!) And he expects me to learn to drive that thing? Oh—

说："你给我买车了？"他答道："是的，亲爱的，圣诞快乐！"

7 圣诞节已经过去两天了，我还是不能相信我丈夫把那么多钱用在我身上。其实，他无需这样做。要知道他有妻子和孩子要养活，他真的不用为我花多余的钱，尤其是像遥控悍马玩具车之类的，更别提那辆真车了（要知道甲壳虫要 1 万 1 千美元，可不便宜呢！）。他还在期望着我学开那辆车呢，噢——

阅读无障碍

medication[medɪˈkeɪʃən] n. 药物
light up 开灯，照亮，点燃
underneath[ʌndəˈniːθ] adv. 在下面
kitchen[ˈkɪtʃɪn] n. 厨房
chat[tʃæt] v. 聊天
scream[skriːm] v. 尖声叫
yell[jel] v. 大叫
forearm[ˈfɔːrɑːm] n. 前臂
brace[breɪs] n. 支架
remote[rɪˈməʊt] n. 遥控，遥控装置
Hummer 悍马

battery[ˈbætəri] n. 电池
operate[ˈɒpəreɪt] v. 操作，运转，开动
envelope[ˈenvɪləʊp] n. 信封；
confused[kənˈfjuːzd] adj. 困惑的
horn[hɔːn] n. 喇叭
grin[grɪn] v. 露齿而笑
faint[feɪnt] v. 昏晕
driveway[ˈdraɪvweɪ] n. 车道
extra[ˈekstrə] adj. 额外的，外加的

极品佳句背诵

1. I knew that "Santa Claus" had come, and I knew that the children would be all excited when they saw all the presents underneath the tree;

   我知道"圣诞"老人已经来了，孩子们见到这些礼物一定会兴奋得大叫起来。

2. Keserian and Naiser both started crying when they saw me, and soon, we were hugging each other, and we were all crying from joy and excitement at seeing each other again!

   两个哥哥见到我后，也激动得尖叫起来，互相拥抱后，我们又一次因见到彼此而掉下幸福、激动的泪水。

3. There, sitting in the driveway, was a beautiful orange Volkswagen Beetle that had a bright red Christmas bow wrapped around it and a sign on the front that said, "Merry Christmas. My beauty! With Love, your husband, Roberto".

   一辆非常漂亮的桔色大众甲壳虫停在路上，车上系着一条红色的圣诞横幅，上面写道："圣诞快乐！爱你的罗伯特。"

Lemonade and a Love Story
爱情故事

带着问题去阅读

1. 你还记得自己的初恋吗?

2. 你现在组建了自己的家庭、有自己的孩子吗?

3. 婚后的你是否会和自己的妻子相爱一生一世呢?

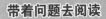

美文欣赏

译文

1 Driving down a deserted Indiana road, I saw a "fresh lemonade" sign and pulled over. I had expected a filling station or small store, but to my surprise, it was a house. An old man sat on the porch. I got out of my car, nobody else was around. He poured me some lemonade and offered me a seat. It was so peaceful.

2 We talked about the weather and my trip. He asked if I had family. I explained that I had just gotten married and hoped to have children someday. He seemed pleased

1 驱车经过印第安州一条废弃的马路,我看到了一个"新鲜柠檬汁"的招牌,便停下车。原本以为会有个加油站或者小商店什么的,但出乎我的意料,这里只有一间房子。一位老人坐在前廊。我走下车,发现四周空无一人。他给我倒了一杯柠檬汁,请我坐下歇息一会。一切是如此的宁静。

2 我们谈论天气和我的旅行。他问我是否成家。我说刚刚结婚,准备要个孩子。听到我这么在乎家庭他似乎很高

that family still mattered to some folks. Then he told me his story.

3 "There's something special about families. A wife, children, a home of your own. The peace of mind comes with doing the right thing. I remember being your age," he said. "I didn't think I'd have a chance at marriage. I didn't have the greatest family. But I persevered. Many nights I remember lying in bed, thinking, I'm not going to risk having divorce happen to me. A wife? A family? Why? I was convinced I would never risk exposing my kids to divorce. As a teenager, I experienced new emotions. I didn't believe in love, though. I thought it was only infatuation. I had this friend. In eighth grade she had a crush on me. But we just talked and she became my best friend all through high school." he grinned.

4 "She had problems in her family, too. I tried to help her out. I did my best to take care of her. She was smart and beautiful. Other young fellows wanted her to be theirs. But I wanted her to be mine, too. We tried going out once, but things blew up and we didn't talk for nine months. Then one day in class I got up the nerve to write her a note. She wrote back, and things slowly picked up again. Then

兴。然后给我讲他的故事。

3 "家庭对我们来说有种特殊的意义。妻子、孩子和你共同组建一个家庭。心灵的平静来自于我们从事正确的事情。还记得我和你差不多大时,"他说道。"我觉得自己这辈子都不会结婚,不会成家。但我仍然满怀期待。无数个夜晚,我躺在床上思索,我不会冒结婚又离婚的风险。娶妻? 成家? 为什么要这样做? 我说服自己决不能让自己的孩子经历父母离异的悲剧。当时还是个少年,正经历着情感的波动。但是我不相信爱情。我认为那仅仅是迷恋而已。我曾经有个朋友。八年级的时候她对我有好感。但我们只是聊聊天,整个高中都是我最好的朋友。"他笑了笑。

4 她的家庭也不太和谐。我努力帮她摆脱困境,所以尽力去照顾她。她很聪明,又漂亮。所以其他小伙子也想亲近她。但我也想拥有她。有一次我们准备出去约会,但后来事情告吹了,为此我们彼此九个月没说话。终于有一天在课堂上,我鼓起勇气给她写了一张纸条。她也给了我回复。我

she went to college in Minnesota, where her father lived," he reminisced. "I wanted to play baseball. I got rejection from school after school, and finally was accepted by a small school, also in Minnesota! It was so ironic. When I told her, she cried. So we began dating. I remember kissing her for the first time in my room. My heart beat so fast, I was afraid of rejection. But our relationship grew. After college, I did get to play baseball. Then, I married that sweet girl of mine. I never would have believed I'd be walking down the aisle."

5 "Did you have children?" I asked.

6 "Four of 'em!" he smiled. "Now they're all grown with kids of their own. When the kids left the house, my wife and I would go on trips together, holding hands like we were young again. That's the beauty of it, you see. I don't know how to explain the love I felt towards my wife," he said, "It never quit on us. It never died. It just got stronger. And nothing in this world is more powerful than love, not money, greed, hate or passion."

7 He looked at my empty glass. "I've kept you much longer than you had

们又和好如初了。后来她去明尼苏达州上大学了，她父亲也在那个州，"他回忆着。"而我喜欢打棒球。申请了一个又一个学校，辗转反复最终被一个不出名的学校录取了，正好也是在明尼苏达州！事情就是这么巧。当我告诉她这个消息时，她哭了。然后我们开始约会。我记得我们的初吻是在我的房间里。我的心跳得如此强烈，我害怕她拒绝。但是自那以后我们的关系大有进步。大学之后，我终于成了一名职业棒球运动员。之后，我就娶了心中的她。我从来没想过自己也会走上婚礼的红毯。"

5 "你有孩子吗？"我问道。

6 "四个。"他笑着回答。"现在他们已经长大成人有了自己的孩子。当孙子们离开我们后，我和老伴就会一起去旅游，牵着她的手，仿佛我们又回到了年轻的时候。你瞧，这就是爱情的魅力。我无法解释自己对老伴的爱，"他说，"但我们的爱情从未淡去，从未消失。反而越来越强烈。这个世界上最牢固的是爱情，而不是金钱、欲望、仇恨、激情。"

7 他发现我的杯子又空了。"很抱歉耽搁你这么长时

probably liked," he apologized. "I hope you enjoyed your lemonade. As you go, remember: love your wife and kids with everything you've got, every day of your life, because you never know when it may end."

8 Walking to my car, I felt the power of his words. It struck me that this man, who I assumed must have lost his wife years ago, still loved her with a passion. I was filled with sadness. As I set out on the road again, suddenly I realized I hadn't paid him for the lemonade, and so I turned the car around and drove back. When I walked over to the porch, the man was nowhere to be found. I bent to put the money on his chair and happened to glance in the window. And there was the old man, in the middle of the living room, slow dancing with his wife! I shook my head as I finally understood. He hadn't lost her after all. She had only been gone for the afternoon.

9 It's been years since that incident, yet I still think of that man and his wife. I hope to live the kind of life they lived and to pass our love on to my kids and grandchildren as they did. And, I hope to be a grandfather who can slow dance with his wife, knowing that indeed, there is no greater blessing than love.

间，"他不好意思的道歉。"希望你喜欢我的柠檬汁。在你走之前我还想说句话，记住：用你拥有的一切去爱你的妻子、孩子，天天如是。因为你不知道哪天一切就都变了。"

8 我朝着车走去，细细的品味着老人的话。突然意识到，这位老人的老伴儿也许已经过世好多年了，然而他依然深爱着她。心底涌起一阵悲伤。当我再次启程时，突然发现还没付老人饮料钱呢，于是我调转车头原路返回。当我返回时，发现老人已经不在前廊了。正准备把钱放在老人的椅子上时，我无意间朝窗户里瞟了一眼。原来老人正在客厅的中央，和他的老伴儿悠闲的跳着舞呢！我点点头终于明白了一切。他从来都没有失去过她。她只不过离开了一个下午而已。

9 这件事过去已经很多年了，然而我依然记得那位老人和他老伴儿的故事。我也希望自己能过上他那种生活，像他们一样把自己的爱传递给孩子们、孙子们。我也希望自己能当上外公，和自己的老伴儿悠闲的跳舞，并且深知：这世界上没有什么比爱情更伟大的祝福了。

阅读无障碍

lemonade [ˌleməˈneɪd] *n.* 柠檬水

pull over 停车

filling station 加油站

divorce [dɪˈvɔːs] *v.* 离婚

convince [kənˈvɪns] *v.* 说服

teenager [ˈtiːneɪdʒə] *n.* 青少年

infatuation [ɪnˌfætjuˈeɪʃən] *n.* 迷恋

have a crush on sb 对某人有好感

grin [grɪn] *v.* 咧嘴大笑

blow up（使）告吹

reminisce [ˌremɪˈnɪs] *v.* 追忆

date [ˈdeɪt] *n.* 约会

rejection [rɪˈdʒekʃən] *n.* 拒绝

aisle [aɪl] *n.* 过道

greed [griːd] *n.* 贪婪

passion [ˈpæʃən] *n.* 激情

apologize [əˈpɒlədʒaɪz] *v.* 道歉

assume [əˈsjuːm] *v.* 臆断

glance [glɑːns] *v.* 瞥一眼

incident [ˈɪnsɪdənt] *n.* 事件

极品佳句背诵

1. The peace of mind that comes with doing the right thing.
心灵的平静来自于我们从事正确的事情。

2. And nothing in this world is more powerful than love, not money, greed, hate or passion.
这个世界上最牢固的是爱情，而不是金钱、欲望、仇恨、激情。

3. As you go, remember: love your wife and kids with everything you've got, every day of your life, because you never know when it may end.
在你走之前我还想说句话，记住：用你拥有的一切去爱你的妻子、孩子，天天如是。因为你不知道哪天一切就都变了。

Chapter 2

谢谢你给我的温暖

The Differences a Teacher Can Make 老师改变了男孩的人生

带着问题去阅读

1. 你记忆中的学生时光是怎样的呢?
2. 学生时代的你也曾经是个"坏"学生吗?
3. 对你影响最大的是哪位老师?

美文欣赏

1 Steve, a twelve-year-old boy with alcoholic parents, was about to be lost forever, by the U.S. education system. Remarkably, he could read, yet, in spite of his reading skills, Steve was failing. He had been failing since first grade. Steve was a big boy, looking more like a teenager than a twelve-year-old, yet, Steve went unnoticed... until Miss White.

2 Miss White was a smiling, young, beautiful redhead, and Steve was in love! For the first time in his young life, he couldn't take his eyes off his teacher; yet, still he failed. He never did his homework,

译文

1 史蒂夫已经12岁了,他的父母都是酒鬼,他想彻底放弃学业了。然而很明显,他能够阅读,尽管考试总不及格。从一年级开始每回考试都不及格。史蒂夫长得很健壮,看上去比12岁的孩子要大。但他一直都被人忽略……直到有一天怀特小姐出现了。

2 怀特小姐总是笑容可掬,年轻,而且有一头迷人的红头发。史蒂夫非常喜欢她。这是他平生第一次,无法把眼睛从老师身上移开;然而,他

and he was always in trouble with Miss White. His heart would break under her sharp words, and when he was punished for failing to turn in his homework, he felt just miserable! Still, he did not study.

3 In the middle of the first semester of school, the entire seventh grade was tested for basic skills. Steve hurried through his tests, and continued to dream of other things, as the day wore on. His heart was not in school, but in the woods, where he often escaped alone, trying to shut out the sights, sounds and smells of his alcoholic home. But Steve never missed a day of school. One day, Miss White's impatient voice broke into his daydreams.

4 "Steve!!" Startled, he turned to look at her.

5 "Pay attention!"

6 Steve locked his gaze on Miss White with adolescent adoration, as she began to go over the test results for the seventh grade.

7 "You all did pretty well," she told the class, "except for one boy, and it breaks my heart to tell you this, but..." She hesitated, pinning Steve to his seat with a sharp stare, her eyes searching his face.

8 "...The smartest boy in the seventh grade is failing my class!" She just stared

还是不及格。他从不做作业，他总是找怀特小姐的碴。每次听到她尖刻的言辞，他感到自己的心都碎了。不交作业受到处罚时，他心里更是难受！但他依然不学习。

3 第一学期的期中考试来了，整个七年级要进行基础技能测验。史蒂夫匆匆写完了卷子，并继续幻想其他的事情，直到放学。他的心并不在学校，而在他经常独自躲藏的树林里，在那里，他试图摆脱酒鬼之家的声响和气味。但史蒂夫从没有旷过一次课。一天，怀特小姐急躁的声音打破了他的白日梦。

4 "史蒂夫！"他感到很吃惊，转过头去看着她。

5 "注意力要集中！"

6 当她宣布七年级测验结果的时候，史蒂夫用那种青春期特有的崇敬盯着怀特小姐。

7 "你们都考得很好，"她对全班说，"除了一个男生，他真让我感到伤心，但是……"她停顿了一下，眼光转向史蒂夫的座位，用犀利的目光在他的脸上搜寻着什么。

8 "我们七年级最聪明的孩子，我的科目考试竟然不及

at Steve, and Steve dropped his eyes and carefully examined his fingertips. After that, it was war! Steve still wouldn't do his homework. Even as the punishments became more severe, he remained stubborn.

9 "Just try it! ONE WEEK!" He was unmoved.

10 "You're smart enough! You'll see a change!" Nothing fazed him.

11 "Give yourself a chance! Don't give up on your life!" Nothing.

12 "Steve! Please! I care about you!"

13 Wow! Suddenly, Steve got it! Someone cared about him? Someone, totally unattainable and perfect, cared about him?

14 Steve went home from school, thoughtful, that afternoon. Walking into the house, he took one look around. Both parents were passed out, and the stench was overpowering! He, quickly, gathered up his camping gear, a jar of peanut butter, a loaf of bread, a bottle of water, and this time...his schoolbooks. Grim faced and determined, he headed for the woods.

15 The following Monday he arrived at school on time, and waited for Miss White to enter the classroom. Miss White,

格！"她盯着史蒂夫，而史蒂夫低下头，盯着自己的指尖。然而，在那之后，战争依然继续！史蒂夫依然不想做作业。即使惩罚更加严厉，他依然非常顽固。

9 "就试一下！一个星期也可以啊！"而他依然无动于衷。

10 "你非常聪明！你会有很大的变化！"任何话语都无法打动他。

11 "给自己一个机会！不要放弃自己的生活。"依然无动于衷。

12 "史蒂夫，求求你，我很关心你！"

13 天啊！突然间史蒂夫好像明白了什么！有人关心他？有人竟然不可思议地关心他？

14 那天下午，史蒂夫满怀思绪地回了家。进屋之后，他环顾了一下四周。发现父母已经睡了，屋子里的恶臭让人无法忍受！他迅速找齐自己的露营装备，一瓶花生酱，一块面包，一瓶水，而且这次他还带上了自己的课本。脸上带着严肃和决心，他又去了树林。

15 接下来的周一一早上，他准时到了学校，等着怀特小姐走进教室。怀特小姐立刻决

immediately, gave a quiz on the weekend homework. Steve hurried through the test, and was the first to hand in his paper. With a look of surprise, Miss White took his paper. Obviously puzzled, she began to look it over and was in total shock! She glanced up at Steve, then down, then up. Suddenly, her face broke into a radiant smile. The smartest boy in the seventh grade had just passed his first test! From that moment nothing was the same for Steve. Life at home remained the same, but life still changed. He discovered that not only could he learn, but he was good at it! Steve began to excel!

16 After high-school, Steve enlisted in the Navy, and had a successful military career. During his Naval career, he inspired many young people. Steve began a second career after the Navy, and he continues to inspire others, as an adjunct professor in a nearby college.

17 Miss White left a great legacy. She saved one boy who has changed many lives. You see, it's simple, really. A change took place within the heart of one boy, all because of one teacher, who cared.

定对周末的家庭作业进行测验。史蒂夫很快完成了测验，并且第一个交上了答卷。怀特小姐满脸惊奇地收下了他的卷子。很明显，她满怀疑惑的批阅着试卷。怀特小姐的脸上充满了惊奇。她瞟了一眼史蒂夫，然后又低下头去，但又再次抬起头来。突然，她的脸上绽放出了笑容。七年级最聪明的男孩终于第一次通过了测验。从那一刻起，史蒂夫如同换了一个人。虽然家里的生活依旧，但他的生活确实发生了变化。他发现自己不仅能够学习，而且能够学得很好！史蒂夫开始变得非常优秀。

16 高中毕业之后，史蒂夫应征加入了海军，并且在军队中也非常成功。在他的海军生涯中，他激励了很多年轻人。从海军退伍之后，史蒂夫开启了事业第二春，在附近的一所大学担任副教授，并继续启迪他人。

17 怀特小姐留下了宝贵的财产。她挽救了一个改变许多其他生命的男孩。看到了吗？其实就是这么简单。仅仅由于一个老师的关心，一个男孩的内心发生了巨大的变化。

阅读无障碍

alcoholic [ˌælkə'hɒlɪk] n. 酗酒者

in spite of 尽管

homework ['həʊmwɜːk] n. 作业

punish ['pʌnɪʃ] v. 惩罚

turn in 上交

miserable ['mɪz(ə)rəb(ə)l] adj. 悲惨的

semester [sɪ'mestə] n. 学期

impatient [ɪm'peɪʃ(ə)nt] adj. 急躁的

daydream ['deɪdriːm] n. 白日梦

adolescent [ˌædə'les(ə)nt] adj. 青春期的

hesitate ['hezɪteɪt] v. 犹豫

severe [sɪ'vɪə] adj. 严重的

stubborn ['stʌbən] adj. 固执的

stench [stentʃ] n. 恶臭

camping gear 露营设备

peanut butter 花生酱

quiz [kwɪz] n. 小测验

radiant ['reɪdɪənt] adj. 光芒四射的

adjunct professor 兼职教授

legacy ['legəsɪ] n. 遗产

极品佳句背诵

1. Steve, a twelve-year-old boy with alcoholic parents, was about to be lost forever, by the U.S. education system.

   史蒂夫已经12岁了，他的父母都是酒鬼，他想彻底放弃学业了。

2. His heart was not in school, but in the woods, where he often escaped alone, trying to shut out the sights, sounds and smells of his alcoholic home.

   他的心并不在学校，而在他经常独自躲藏的树林里，在那里，他试图摆脱酒鬼之家的声响和气味。

3. A change took place within the heart of one boy, all because of one teacher, who cared.

   仅仅由于一个老师的关心，一个男孩的内心发生了巨大的变化。

That's What Friends Do
朋友间就该这么做

带着问题去阅读

1. 你是否拥有一个刀子嘴豆腐心的朋友呢？
2. 你和朋友间的关系好吗？
3. 如果和朋友发生矛盾，你会主动认错吗？

美文欣赏

译文

1 Jack tossed the papers on my desk—his eyebrows knit into a straight line as he glared at me.

2 "What's wrong?" I asked.

3 He jabbed a finger at the proposal. "Next time you want to change anything, ask me first," he said. How dare he treat me like that? I thought angrily. I had changed one long sentence, and corrected grammar, something I thought I was paid to do. It's not that I hadn't been warned. One coworker already told me about him

1 杰克把文件扔在我桌上——当他气冲冲的盯着我时，他的眉毛拧成了一条直线。

2 "出什么问题了？"我问道。

3 他指着议案说，"下次做任何改动前要先通知我！"他怎么能这样对我，我生气的想着。我不过是改了一个长句子，修改了语法错误，做了自己应该做的事情而已。发生这样的事情并不是同事没有提醒我，自打我来的第一天同事就

the first day.

4 As the weeks went by, I grew to despise Jack. His actions made me question much that I believed in, such as turning the other cheek and loving your enemies. Jack quickly slapped a verbal insult on any cheek, then turned his way. One day another of his episodes left me in tears. I stormed into his office, prepared to lose my job if needed. I opened the door and Jack glanced up. "What?" he asked abruptly. Suddenly I knew what I had to do. After all, he deserved it.

5 I sat across from him and said calmly, "Jack, the way you've been treating me is wrong, and I can't allow it to continue. I want to make you a promise. I will be a friend," I said. "I will treat you as you deserve to be treated, with respect and kindness." I slipped out of the chair and closed the door behind me.

6 Jack avoided me the rest of the week. Proposals, specs, and letters appeared on my desk while I was at lunch. I brought cookies to the office one day and left a batch on his desk. Another day I left a note. "Hope your day is going great," it read. Over the next few weeks, Jack reappeared. He was reserved, but there were no other episodes.

已经提醒过我了。

4 又过了几周，我越来越讨厌杰克了。他的行为动摇了我要忍耐、爱自己的敌人的信念。只要你稍稍有些软弱，杰克立马会用刻薄的语言侮辱你。有一天又发生一件事情把我气哭了。我做好了被炒鱿鱼的准备，在他的办公室里大发雷霆。当我开门的瞬间，杰克抬头瞟了一眼。"又怎么了？"他粗鲁的吼着。突然间我意识到了此行的目的。反正是他活该。

5 我坐在他对面，平静地说，"杰克，你不该这么对我，我也不会让你这么对我了。我向你保证，以后我们会成为朋友。"我说，"我会用你应得的方式，友善地、尊敬地对待你。"说完我从椅子上起来，走出了办公室。

6 接下来的一周里杰克都躲着我。他总是在我吃饭的空档将议案、说明书、信件放在我的桌子上。有一天我带了一些曲奇饼去办公室，也往他的办公桌上放了一份。又有一天，我在他的桌上留了一张便条，上面写着"希望你的日子一切顺利。"接下来的几个星期，他终于又露面了，但多少

7 After that every time I saw Jack in the hall, I smiled at him. After all, that's what friends do.

8 One year after our "talk," I discovered I had breast cancer. I was thirty-two, the mother of three beautiful young children, and scared. The cancer had metastasized to my lymph nodes and the statistics were not great for long-term survival. After my surgery, friends and loved ones visited and tried to find the right words. No one knew what to say, and many said the wrong things. Others wept, and I tried to encourage them. I clung to encourage myself. One day, Jack stood awkwardly in the doorway of my small, darkened hospital room. I waved him in with a smile. He walked over to my bed without a word and placed a bundle beside me. Inside the package lay several bulbs.

9 "Tulips," he said.

10 I grinned, not understanding.

11 He shuffled his feet, and then cleared his throat. "If you plant them when you get home, they'll come up next spring. I just wanted you to know that I think you'll be there to see them when they come

7 从此以后每次我在大厅见到他，我都会微微一笑。毕竟，朋友间就该这么做。

8 我们这样"沟通"了一年之后，我发现自己患了乳腺癌。我那时才32岁，三个漂亮小孩的母亲，我害怕极了。癌细胞已经扩散到了淋巴结，各项检查也显示我剩下的日子不多了。手术之后，朋友、亲人们都来探望我，想给我打打气。但是没有一个人知道该说些什么，有些人说的话甚至适得其反。还有些人哭哭啼啼的，我反倒去安慰他们。我给自己加油鼓劲。有一天，杰克拘谨地站在我那间狭小黑暗的病房外的走廊里。我挥手，微笑着招呼他进来。他走到我的床边，默默的在我身旁放下一包东西。包裹里是一些郁金香球根。

9 "这是郁金香。"他说。

10 我咧嘴笑了笑，有些不明白。

11 他在地上磨蹭着鞋子，清了清嗓子，说"如果你病愈后回家把它们种起来，明年春天它们就会开花了。我只是想让你知道，我相信明年你

up."

12 Tears clouded my eyes and I reached out my hand. "Thank you." I whispered.

13 Jack grasped my hand and gruffly replied, "You're welcome. You can't see it now, but next spring you'll see the colors I picked out for you. I think you'll like them." He turned and left without another word.

14 For ten years, I have watched those red-and-white striped tulips push their way through the soil every spring. In a moment when I prayed for just the right word, a man with very few words said all the right things. After all, that's what friends do.

会看到它们的花朵。"

12 我眼睛里涌满了泪水，伸出手，啜泣着说道："谢谢你！"

13 他握住我的手，用粗哑的嗓音回答"不用谢。即使你现在看不到，但明年春天你一定会看到我给你选的花的颜色，你一定会喜欢的。"说完他转过身，默默的离开了。

14 10年来，我看着这些红白相间的郁金香开了一春又一春。回想当初我祈祷听到鼓励的话语时，一个寡言少语的男人居然说出了我想听的话。毕竟，朋友间就该这么做。

阅读无障碍

eyebrow ['aɪbraʊ] n. 眉毛

knit [nɪt] v. 皱眉

glare at 怒目而视

jab [dʒæb] v. 戳着

co-worker 同事

despise [dɪ'spaɪz] v. 看不起

enemy ['enɪmɪ] n. 敌人

insult [ɪn'sʌlt] v. 侮辱

episode ['epɪsəʊd] n. 小插曲

deserve [dɪ'zɜːv] v. 应得

respect [rɪ'spekt] n. 尊重

hall [hɔːl] n. 大厅

cancer ['kænsə] n. 癌症

metastasize [mə'tæstəsaɪz] v. 转移

lymph node 淋巴结

encourage [ɪn'kʌrɪdʒ] v. 鼓励

package ['pækɪdʒ] n. 包裹

tulip ['tjuːlɪp] n. 郁金香

whisper ['wɪspə] v. 耳语

soil [sɔɪl] n. 土地

极品佳句背诵

1. His actions made me question much that I believed in, such as turning the other cheek and loving your enemies.

   他的行为动摇了我要忍耐、爱自己的敌人的信念。

2. You can't see it now, but next spring you'll see the colors I picked out for you. I think you'll like them.

   即使你现在看不到，但明年春天你一定会看到我给你选的花的颜色，你一定会喜欢的。

3. For ten years, I have watched those red-and-white striped tulips push their way through the soil every spring.

   10年来，我看着这些红白相间的郁金香开了一春又一春。

The Price of a Miracle
奇迹的价格

带着问题去阅读

1. 当身处困境时，你相信奇迹吗？
2. 我们到底需要什么才能换到奇迹呢？
3. 你认为最美好的奇迹是什么？

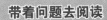 美文欣赏

1 Tess was eight-year-old when she heard her Mom and Dad talking about her little brother, Andrew. All she knew was that he was very sick and they were completely out of money. They were moving to an apartment complex next month because Daddy didn't have the money for both the doctor's bills and the house payment. "Only a very costly surgery could save him now and it was looking like there was no-one to loan them the money." She heard her Dad say to her mom, "Only a miracle can save him now."

2 Tess went to her bedroom and

 译文

1 听爸爸妈妈谈起小弟安德鲁的事情时，苔丝已是一个早熟的8岁小女孩。她只知道弟弟病得很厉害，父母却无钱给他医治。下个月他们要搬到一个公寓房，因为爸爸已经无力同时支付医药费和房款。"现在唯一可以救他的办法就是做手术，但手术费用非常昂贵，没有人肯借钱给我们了。"她听到爸爸对妈妈说，"现在只有奇迹可以救他了。"

2 苔丝回到房间，从壁

 90

pulled a glass jelly jar from its hiding place in the closet. She poured all the change out on the floor and counted it carefully. she counted it three times. The total had to be exactly perfect. No chance here for mistakes.

3 Carefully placing the coins back in the jar and twisting on the cap, she slipped out from the back door and made her way six blocks to Rexall's Drug Store with the big red Indian Chief sign above the door.

4 She waited patiently for the pharmacist to give her some attention but he was too intently talking to another man to be bothered by an eight-year-old at that moment. Tess twisted her feet to make a noise. Nothing. She cleared her throat with the most disgusting sound she could muster. No good. Finally she took a quarter from her jar and banged it on the glass counter. That did it!

5 "And what do you want?" the pharmacist asked in an annoyed tone of voice. "I'm talking to my brother from Chicago whom I haven't seen in ages." he said without waiting for a reply to his question. "Well, I want to talk to you about my brother." Tess answered back in the same annoyed tone. "He's really, really sick… and I want to buy a miracle."

6 "I beg your pardon?" said the

橱一个隐藏的地方拿出一个玻璃瓶子。她把里面所有的零钱倒在地上，仔细数了3次，直到确定无误。她一点错儿都不能犯。

3 她仔细地把硬币放回瓶子并把盖子拧好，悄悄地从后门溜出去，穿过六条街区，来到门上有红色印地安语大标志的雷克斯奥药店。

4 她耐心地等待着药剂师，可是药剂师忙着和另外一个人说话，并没有注意她。苔丝扭动着她的双脚，发出一种划伤似的噪音。没用！她就用喉咙发出她能够发出的、最令人厌恶的声音。药剂师还是没有注意到她。最后，她从瓶子里拿出个2角5分的硬币摔在玻璃柜台上，弄出清脆的响声。成功了！

5 "你到底想要什么？"药剂师不耐烦地问，"我在和我的弟弟说话，他从芝加哥来，我们很多年没见了。"他没等苔丝说话就接着说起来。"我想和你谈谈我弟弟，"苔丝用同样不耐烦的口气回答。"他真的，真的病得很严重……我想买一个奇迹。"

6 "你说什么？"药剂师

pharmacist. "His name is Andrew and he has something bad growing inside his head and my Daddy says only a miracle can save him now. So how much does a miracle cost?" "We don't sell miracles here, little girl. I'm sorry but I can't help you." the pharmacist said, softening a little.

7 "Listen, I have the money to pay for it. If it isn't enough, I will get the rest. Just tell me how much it costs." The pharmacist's brother stooped down and asked the little girl, "What kind of a miracle does your brother need?" "I don't know." Tess replied with her eyes welling up.

8 "I just know he's badly sick and Mommy says he needs an operation. But my Daddy can't pay for it, so I want to use my money."

9 "How much do you have?" asked the man from Chicago. "One dollar and eleven cents," Tess answered barely audibly. "And it's all the money I have, but I can get some more if I need to." "Well, what a coincidence." smiled the man. "A dollar and eleven cents — the exact price of a miracle for your little brother."

10 Then he said "Take me to where you live. I want to see your brother and meet your parents. Let's see if I have the kind of miracle you need." The pharmacist's brother was Dr. Carlton

问到。"他叫安德鲁，脑袋里长了一个非常糟糕的东西，爸爸说现在只有奇迹能救他。所以，请问奇迹多少钱？""我们这里不卖奇迹，小姑娘，很抱歉不能帮助你，"药剂师稍带温和地说。

7 "听着，我有钱。如果这些不够，我就回去取剩下的。就请告诉我奇迹多少钱吧。"药剂师的弟弟走下楼梯，问小女孩，"你弟弟需要什么样的奇迹呢？""我不知道。"苔丝的眼泪涌了上来。

8 "我只知道他病得非常厉害，妈妈说他需要做手术。但是爸爸支付不起手术费，所以我想用我自己的钱。"

9 "你有多少钱？"这个从芝加哥来的男人问。"一美元十一美分，"苔丝低声回答，声音勉强才能让人听得到。"这是我所有的钱，但是如果不够的话我会再想办法。""刚刚好。"男人笑着说，"一美元十一美分 —— 正好够为你弟弟买个奇迹。"

10 接着他说"带我去你住的地方，我想去看看你弟弟和你的父母。看看我是不是有你们需要的奇迹。"这药剂师的弟弟就是卡尔顿·阿姆斯壮，

Armstrong, a surgeon, specializing in neurosurgery.

11 The operation was completed without charge and it wasn't long until Andrew was home again and doing well. Mom and Dad were happily talking about the chain of events that had led them to this place. Her mom said, "That surgery was a real miracle. I wonder how much it would have cost?" Tess smiled. She knew exactly how much a miracle cost… one dollar and eleven cents … plus the faith of a little child.

著名的神经外科医生。

11 手术没有支付任何费用，安德鲁回家后不久就康复了。爸爸和妈妈高兴地谈论着这件事情。母亲低声自语，"这个手术真的是个奇迹，奇迹到底需要多少钱呢？"苔丝笑了。她知道奇迹的真正价值：一美元十一美分，加上一个小女孩的信念。

阅读无障碍

sick [sɪk] adj. 生病的
out of money 经济拮据
costly ['kɒs(t)lɪ] adj. 昂贵的
surgery ['sɜːdʒ(ə)rɪ] n. 手术
loan [ləʊn] v. 贷款
miracle ['mɪrək(ə)l] n. 奇迹
closet ['klɒzɪt] n. 衣橱
change [tʃeɪndʒ] n. 零钱
count [kaʊnt] v. 数数
mistake [mɪs'teɪk] n. 错误
coin [kɔɪn] n. 硬币

pharmacist ['fɑːməsɪst] n. 药剂师
bother ['bɒðə] v. 打扰
throat [θrəʊt] n. 喉咙
disgusting [dɪs'gʌstɪŋ] adj. 令人厌恶的
beg one's pardon 请某人重复一遍
pay for 为……付钱
audibly ['ɔːdəblɪ] adv. 听得见的
coincidence [kəʊ'ɪnsɪd(ə)ns] n. 巧合
neurosurgery [njʊərəʊ'sɜːdʒərɪ] n. 神经外科

1. They were moving to an apartment complex next month because Daddy didn't have the money for both the doctor's bills and the house payment.

   下个月他们要搬到一个公寓房，因为爸爸已经无力同时支付医药费和房款。

2. His name is Andrew and he has something bad growing inside his head and my Daddy says only a miracle can save him now.

   他叫安德鲁，脑袋里长了一个非常糟糕的东西，爸爸说现在只有奇迹能救他。

3. A dollar and eleven cents — the exact price of a miracle for your little brother.

   一美元十一美分 —— 正好够为你弟弟买个奇迹。

94

A Glass of Milk
一杯牛奶的温暖

带着问题去阅读

1. 什么是真正的善良？
2. 身陷困围的你还会估计自己的尊严吗？
3. 你依然相信这个社会上还有爱存在吗？

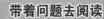 美文欣赏

 译文

1 One day, a poor boy who was trying to pay his way through school by selling goods door to door found that he only had one dime left. He was hungry so he decided to beg for a meal at the next house.

2 However, he lost his nerve when a lovely young woman opened the door. Instead of a meal he asked for a cup of water. She thought he looked hungry so she brought him a large glass of milk. He drank it slowly, and then asked, "How much do I owe you?"

1 一天，一个贫穷的小男孩为了攒够学费正挨家挨户地推销商品。当他摸遍全身，发现只有一角钱时，饥寒交迫的他决定向下一户人家讨口饭吃。

2 然而，当一位美丽的年轻女子打开房门的时候，这个小男孩却有点不知所措了。他没有要饭，只乞求给他一口水喝。这位女子看到他饥饿的样子，就倒了一大杯牛奶给他。男孩慢慢地喝完牛奶，问道："我应该付多少钱？"

3 "You don't owe me anything," she replied. "Mother has taught me never to accept pay for a kindness." He said, "Then I thank you from the bottom of my heart." As Howard Kelly left that house, he not only felt stronger physically, but it also increased his faith in God and the human race. He was about to quit before this point.

4 Years later the young woman became critically ill. The local doctors were baffled. They finally sent her to the big city, where specialists can be called in to study her rare disease. Dr. Howard Kelly, now famous was called in for the consultation. When he heard the name of the town she came from, a strange light filled his eyes. Immediately, he rose and went down through the hospital hall into her room.

5 Dressed in his doctor's gown, he went in to see her. He recognized her at once. He went back to the consultation room and determined to do his best to save her life. From that day on, he gave special attention to her case.

6 After a long struggle, the battle was won. Dr. Kelly requested the business office to pass the final bill to him for approval. He looked at it and then wrote something on the side. The bill was sent to her room. She was afraid to open it

3 "一分钱也不用付。"年轻女子微笑着回答。"我妈妈教导我，施以爱心，不图回报。"男孩说："那么，就请接受我由衷的感谢吧！"当霍华德·凯利道完谢离开了这户人家时，他不仅自己浑身是劲儿，而且更加相信上帝和整个人类。原本，他都打算放弃了。

4 数年之后，那位女子身患顽疾，当地医生对此束手无策。最后，她被转到大城市医治，由专家会诊治疗她罕见的病症。大名鼎鼎的霍华德·凯利医生也参加了医疗方案的制定。当他听到病人来自的那个城镇的名字时，一个奇怪的念头闪过他的脑际。他马上起身直奔她的病房。

5 身穿手术服的凯利医生来到病房。一眼就认出了恩人。回到会诊室后，他决心一定要竭尽所能来治好她的病。从那天起，他就特别关照这个对自己有恩的病人。

6 经过艰苦的努力，手术成功了。凯利医生要求财务处把医药费通知单送到他那里。他看了一下，便在通知单的旁边签了字。医药费通知单送到了她的病房。她不敢看，

because she was positive that it would take the rest of her life to pay it off. Finally she looked at it, and the note on the side of the bill caught her attention. She read these words...

7 "Paid in full of a glass of milk."

8 (Signed) Dr. Howard Kelly.

9 Tears of joy flooded her eyes as she prayed silently: "Thank You, God. Your love has spread through human hearts and hands."

因为她确信治病的费用将会花费她整个余生来偿还。最后，她还是鼓起勇气翻开了医药费通知单，旁边的那行小字引起了她的注意，她不禁轻声读了出来：

7 "医药费已付：一杯牛奶。"

8 (签名)霍华德·凯利医生。

9 喜悦的泪水溢出了她的眼睛，她默默地祈祷着："谢谢你，上帝，你的爱已通过人类的心灵和双手传播了。"

阅读无障碍

dime [daɪm] *n.* 10 美分
beg [beg] *v.* 乞讨
owe [əʊ] *v.* 欠……债
bottom ['bɒtəm] *n.* 底部
faith [feɪθ] *n.* 信心
quit [kwɪt] *v.* 放弃
baffle ['bæf(ə)l] *v.* 使困惑
specialist ['speʃ(ə)lɪst] *n.* 专家
consultation [kɒnsəl'teɪʃ(ə)n] *n.* 会诊
come from 来自
go down 下去

gown [gaʊn] *n.* 长袍
recognize ['rekəgnaɪz] *v.* 意识到
at once 马上
determine [dɪ'tɜːmɪn] *v.* 决定
do one's best 尽某人最大的能力
battle ['bætl] *n.* 战斗
bill [bɪl] *n.* 账单
pay off 偿还
catch one's attention 吸引某人注意力

极品佳句背诵

1. Mother has taught me never to accept pay for a kindness.
   我妈妈教导我，施以爱心，不图回报。

2. He went back to the consultation room and determined to do his best to save her life.
   回到会诊室后，他决心一定要竭尽所能来治好她的病。

3. She was afraid to open it because she was positive that it would take the rest of her life to pay it off.
   她不敢看，因为她确信治病的费用将会花费她整个余生来偿还。

My Life Was Saved by a Smile
一个微笑挽救了一条生命

带着问题去阅读

1. 一个微笑的力量究竟有多大?
2. 你是一个爱笑的人吗?
3. 你认为真情能笑容法律的冰川吗?

 美文欣赏

 译文

1 I was sure that I was to be killed. I became terribly nervous. I fumbled in my pockets to see if there were any cigarettes, which had escaped their search. I found one and because of my shaking hands, I could barely get it to my lips. But I had no matches, they had taken those. I looked through the bars at my jailer. He did not make eye contact with me.

2 I called out to him "Have you got a light?"

3 He looked at me, shrugged and came over to light my cigarette. As he came close and lit the match, his eyes

1 我肯定会被杀掉。意识到这一点让人不寒而栗。我又摸了摸衣兜,想找根烟抽。这次终于找到了一根。可是双手抖得厉害,烟几乎都递不到嘴边。但是却没有火柴,都给他们没收了。我望着牢房栅栏外的看守,他却并未与我对视。

2 我对他喊道:"有火吗?"

3 他看了我一眼,耸了耸肩,朝我走了过来。他过来给我点烟时,目光无意中跟我

inadvertently locked with mine. At that moment, I smiled. I don't know why I did that.

4 Perhaps it was nervousness, perhaps it was because, when you get very close, one to another, it is very hard not to smile. In any case, I smiled.

5 In that instant, it was as though a spark jumped across the gap between our two hearts, our two human souls. I know he didn't want to, but my smile leaped through the bars and generated a smile on his lips, too. He lit my cigarette but stayed near, looking at me directly in the eyes and continuing to smile.

6 I kept smiling at him, now aware of him as a person and not just a jailer. And his looking at me seemed to have a new dimension too.

7 "Do you have kids?" he asked.

8 "Yes, here, here." I took out my wallet and nervously fumbled for the pictures of my family.

9 He, too, took out the pictures of his family and began to talk about his plans and hopes for them.

10 My eyes were filled with tears. I said that I feared that I'd never see my family again, never have the chance to see them grow up. Tears came to his eyes, too.

接在了一起。那一刻，我对他微微一笑。我不晓得我为什么会对他微笑。

4 或许是由于紧张，也或许是因为彼此离得那么近，很难让人不微笑示意一下。在那种情况下，我都会笑一下。

5 那一刹那，两颗心灵，两个灵魂深处之间的鸿沟中似乎迸发出了一团火花。我知道他并不想对我微笑，然而，我的微笑却越过栅栏勾起了他唇边的笑意。给我点着了烟后，他就站在我的近旁，注视着我的双眼，微笑着。

6 我也对他微笑着，此刻，我感觉到他也是一个普通人，而不仅仅是个狱警。他望着我，目光里似乎有了与之前不同的东西。

7 "你有孩子吗？"他问道。

8 "有，有，在这儿，你看！"我掏出钱夹，手忙脚乱地翻出家人的相片。

9 他也拿出了家人的照片，开始跟我谈论对孩子的期望。

10 泪水涌满了我的眼眶，我对他说怕再也见不到家人，再也没有机会看着孩子们一天天的长大。他的眼睛也润

11 Suddenly, without another word, he unlocked my cell and silently led me out of the jail, quietly and by back routes, out of the town. There, at the edge of town, he released me. And without another word, he turned back toward the town.

12 My life was saved by a smile.

13 Yes, the smile—the unaffected, unplanned, natural connection between people.

14 I really believe that if that part of you and that part of me could recognize each other, we wouldn't be enemies; we couldn't have hate or envy or fear.

湿了。

11 忽然，没说一句话，他打开了牢门，放我出来。悄无声息地领着我出了牢房，沿着小路出了小镇。在小镇外，他放我逃走。一句话都没说，他转身向小镇走去。

12 一个微笑挽救了我的生命。

13 不错，是微笑——是那真挚、自然、不经意间显现的人与人之间的纽带，救了我一命。

14 我毫不怀疑：只要你我能彼此认同，我们就绝不会成为敌人；我们就不会有仇恨，妒忌或恐惧。

阅读无障碍

fumble ['fʌmb(ə)l] v. 摸索
pocket ['pɒkɪt] n. 口袋
cigarette [sɪɡə'ret] n. 香烟
escape [ɪ'skeɪp] v. 逃脱
lip [lɪp] n. 嘴唇
match [mætʃ] n. 火柴
jailer ['dʒeɪlə(r)] n. 狱警
look at 看着
smile [smaɪl] v. 微笑
spark [spɑːk] n. 火花

gap [ɡæp] n. 间隙
soul [səʊl] n. 灵魂
bar [bɑː] n. 栅栏
dimension [dɪ'menʃən] n. 方面
wallet ['wɑːlɪt] n. 钱包
fill with（使）充满
grow up 长大
suddenly ['sʌdnlɪ] adv. 突然的
cell [sel] n. 牢房
release [rɪ'liːs] v. 释放

阅读无障碍

1. As he came close and lit the match, his eyes inadvertently locked with mine.

   他过来给我点烟时，目光无意中跟我接在了一起。

2. In that instant, it was as though a spark jumped across the gap between our two hearts, our two human souls.

   那一刹那，两颗心灵，两个灵魂深处之间的鸿沟中似乎迸发出了一团火花。

3. I know he didn't want to, but my smile leaped through the bars and generated a smile on his lips, too.

   我知道他并不想对我微笑，然而，我的微笑却越过栅栏勾起了他唇边的笑意。

Tell Your Friend, I Love You
告诉你的朋友，我爱你

带着问题去阅读

1. 你通常是怎样度过情人节的？
2. 你和好友之间如何表达对彼此的情谊？
3. 你会在情人节送男女朋友之外的普通朋友礼物吗？

美文欣赏

1 Tomorrow is the one day of the year in which couples, in love, are required by Hallmark to say to another "Yes, it's true. I actually do love you. Here's a card, some flowers, let's go to eat a steak in the shape of a heart." This simple, restorative ritual suspends, for just one day, clearing up the fear that we've wound up with the completely wrong person.

2 But for far too long, boyfriends, girlfriends and married people have had a stranglehold on Valentine's Day. It's

译文

1 明天将是一年中的那个大日子，贺曼贺卡公司将要求共浴爱河的人们对彼此说："是的，没错，我确实爱你。这是送你的贺卡和鲜花，让我们一起去吃心形的牛排吧。"这个简单却有益的传统能消除你某天突然闪现的忧虑，让你意识到与自己共度一生的并不是一个完全错误的人。

2 但很长一段时间以来，男女朋友及夫妻们对情人节的看法都被束缚着：似乎贺曼公

as if Hallmark's High Holiday has been reserved for only the "in love". A day of consummation, not communion. Because you're not sharing a bed, you're not welcome. Isn't it time to allow everyone to participate in the Valentine tradition? To say "Hey, I love you, but not in that way." Because for many, best friends are spouses, family, our most cherished loved ones. And yet, for best friends there is no holiday celebrating their partnership and deeplycare for each other. Non-bed-sharers make tomorrow your day to tell someone you don't love in that way that you love them.

3 Here's how to say it without making them freak out. Guys, you can't give your best friend chocolates or flowers. Instead for Valentine's Day, get his car detailed-you know how he likes it. Or get him a card that says "Hey, I love your tie." But add somewhere "Hope my girlfriend gets me one just like it." Men can also get a buddy at the office a Valentine Greeting. He'll never hear from his girlfriend or wife "I love your work. Happy Valentine's Day." As a more daring gesture gentleman, a bit of the bard goes a long way: "Roses are red, violets are blue. Hey, I'm not gay, but dude, I love you." Ladies, there's always putting pen to paper with those three little

司这个火热的节日只为"爱河中的人"而存在；这是一个确定关系的日子，而不是促膝长谈的时机；如果还没有同床共枕，你们就不受欢迎。难道现在不是该让每一个人都加入情人节这个传统的时候吗？开始说"我爱你，但不是那种爱"吧。因为对许多人来说，最好的朋友是配偶、家人、那些我们最珍爱的人。然而，最好的朋友并没有一个节日来庆祝他们的友谊以及彼此之间深深的牵挂。并非同床共枕的人们，明天就向非性爱关系的朋友表达你的爱意吧！

3 下面让我们来看看如何将这种爱表达出来而不会让对方不知所措。小伙子们，你可不能在情人节送给你最好的朋友巧克力或鲜花，精心地布置他的车吧——你清楚他喜欢什么样儿。或者，也可以送他一张贺卡，写上："嘿，我喜欢你的领带。"再找个地方附上："真希望我女朋友也送我一条这样的。"男士们也可以向办公室里的好友们致以情人节的问候，而这将是他们在女朋友或配偶那里听不到的："我欣赏你的工作，情人节快乐！"如果你是一位举止优

words every woman loves to hear: "Your shoes rock." Or still, even more affectionate without any sexual overtones, "Oh my god, I love your hair." On Valentine's Day, tell her something she'll never hear from a guy, like "Hey, let's get a MAP" or "You were right." Send your boss a Valentine, send your letter carrier a Valentine, or a soldier, or heck, and send the president a Valentine that says: "I love you sir, for not eavesdropping on me."

雅的男士，摘写几句情人节诗句会更有意味："玫瑰是红的，紫罗兰是蓝的。嘿，我不是同志，但是哥儿们，我爱你。"女士们，一定要将每个女人都爱听的那些三字语句写下来："鞋真棒！"或者甚至更深情，但不带任何性暗示的话语："噢，天啊，我喜欢你的头发。"在情人节，告诉她一些她不可能从男人那里听到的话，如"让我们去做美白吧"或者"你是对的"。给你的上司送张情人节贺卡，邮递员、士兵或者你讨厌的家伙们都可以送。给总统寄张贺卡，写上："我爱你，先生，因为你不曾窃听我。"

4 A friend walk in

5 When the rest of the world walks out

6 Sometimes in life

7 You find a special friend

8 Someone who changes your life

9 Just by being part of it;

10 Someone who makes you laugh until you can't stop;

11 Someone who makes you believe that

12 There really is good in the world

4 当全世界都离你而去

5 一个朋友走近了你

6 有时在生命中

7 会有这样一个特别的朋友

8 他能改变你的生活

9 成为你生活的一部分

10 他能让你前仰后俯笑个不停

11 他会让你明白世间真的有真善美

12 他能让你相信真有一扇门

13 Someone who convinces you that

14 There really is an unlocked door just waiting for you to open it. This is Forever Friendship

15 This Valentine's Day, let your voice be heard. Even if you have no Valentine, no friends, let alone a spouse, aim Cupid's arrow at anyone. It might feel strange, but it'll hurt less than a chest full of birdshot.

16 We know that true friendship is rare and precious. In this world, no matter how the two souls seem irrelevant, they may be the most precious thing - a long-lasting friendship should be cherished!

17 Just remember the poem from Emily Brontë

18 Love is like the wild rose-briar; Friendship like the holly-tree.

19 The holly is dark when the rose-briar blooms, But which will bloom most constantly?

13 专为你而敞开

14 这就是永恒的友情

15 这个情人节，把你的心声传达出来吧！即使你没有情侣，没有朋友，更没有配偶，也要将你的丘比特之箭朝着每一个人瞄准！这可能会令别人感到怪异，可这种伤总比心伤到千疮百孔轻得多。

16 我们知道真正的友谊既难得又珍贵。在这个世界上，无论两个灵魂看起来是多么不相干，他们都可能获得最珍贵的东西——一份持久的，值得珍惜的友谊！

17 记住艾米利·勃朗特的诗中所说的吧

18 爱情像野玫瑰，友情像冬青。

19 当玫瑰开花的时候，冬青却墨绿着，但哪种能更持久盛开呢？

阅读无障碍

steak[steɪk] n. 牛排
restorative[rɪ'stɒrətɪv] adj. 恢复健康的
ritual['rɪtʃʊəl] n. 仪式
suspend[sə'spend] v. 停留，维持

stranglehold['stræŋɡlhəʊld] n. 束缚，压制
consummation [kɒnsə'meɪʃ(ə)n] n. 圆满，完成

communion[kəˈmjuːniən] n. 交 流，恳谈

cherish[ˈtʃerɪʃ] v. 珍惜，珍爱

freak out 吓坏，使不知所措

buddy[ˈbʌdɪ] n. 密友，好友

gesture[ˈdʒestʃə(r)] n. 行为，举止

dude[duːd] n.（俚）哥们，兄弟

affectionate[əˈfekʃənət] adj. 深情的

sexual[ˈsekʃuəl] adj. 性的

overtone[ˈəuvətəun] n. 暗示

eavesdrop[ˈiːvzdrɒp] v. 偷听（别人的谈话）

convince[kənˈvɪns] v. 说服，使相信

spouse[spaus] n. 配偶，夫妻

birdshot[bɜːdˈʃɒt] n.（射鸟用的）小号铅弹

bloom[bluːm] v. 开花

极品佳句背诵

1. We know that true friendship is rare and precious.
   我们知道真正的友谊既难得又珍贵。

2. In this world, no matter how the two souls seem irrelevant, they may be the most precious thing -- a long-lasting friendship should be cherished!
   在这个世界上，无论两个灵魂看起来是多么不相干，他们都可能获得最珍贵的东西——一份持久的，值得珍惜的友谊！

3. Love is like the wild rose-briar; Friendship like the holly-tree.
   爱情像野玫瑰，友情像冬青。

The Color of Friendship
友谊的色彩

带着问题去阅读

1. 在你心目中友谊是什么颜色的？
2. 你和朋友们之间通常会因为什么原因吵架？
3. 你们朋友之间吵架后会以怎样的方式言归于好？

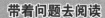 美文欣赏

 译文

1 Once upon a time the colors of the world started to quarrel.

2 All claimed that they were the best. The most important. The most useful. The favorite.

3 Green said: "Clearly I am the most important. I am the sign of life and of hope. I was chosen for grass, trees and leaves. Without me, all animals would die. Look over the countryside and you will see that I am in the majority."

4 Blue interrupted: "You only think about the earth, but consider the sky and

1 很久很久以前，世界上的各种颜色开始争吵起来。

2 各种颜色都宣称自己最棒、最重要、最有用、最漂亮、最惹人喜爱。

3 绿色说道："很明显，我最重要，因为我象征着生命和希望。小草、大树以及树叶都是绿色的。没有我，所有的动物都不能存活，看看我们的大地吧，绿色简直就是统治色。"

4 蓝色打断它说道："你只看到了大地，看看天空和海

the sea. It is the water that is the basis of life and drawn up by the clouds from the deep sea. The sky gives space and peace and serenity. Without my peace, you all would be nothing."

5 Yellow chuckled: "You are all so serious. I bring laughter, gaiety, and warmth into the world. The sun is yellow, the moon is yellow, the stars are yellow. Every time you look at a sunflower, the whole world starts to smile. Without me there would be no fun."

6 Orange started to blow her trumpet: "I am the color of health and strength. I may be scarce, but I am precious for I serve the needs of human life. I carry the most important vitamins. Think of carrots, pumpkins, oranges, mangoes, and papayas. I don't hang around all the time, but when I fill the sky at sunrise or sunset, my beauty is so striking that no one gives another thought to any of you."

7 Red could stand it no longer, so he shouted out: "I am the ruler of all of you. I am blood - life's blood! I am the color of danger and of bravery. I am willing to fight for a cause. I bring fire into the blood. Without me, the earth would be as empty as the moon. I am the color of passion and

洋吧。水是生命的基本组成部分，水由海水蒸发凝成云团降雨形成。天空是那么广阔、平和、安宁。没有象征着和平的蓝色，你们将什么都不是。"

5 黄色笑道："你们都太严肃了，只有我会给世界带来笑声、愉快和温暖。太阳是黄色的，月亮是黄色的，星星也是黄色的。每当你看太阳花时，全世界都在向你微笑。没有我，世界就没有欢乐。"

6 橙色开始自吹自擂："桔色代表着健康和力量。我也许令人感觉到恐惧，但是我能提供人类生命所需要的物质，因而显得异常珍贵。我的颜色携带者很多重要的维他命，想想胡萝卜、南瓜、桔子、芒果和木瓜吧，他们都是桔色。我并不是天天出现，但是日出或日落时，我给天空镶上一层无比漂亮的颜色，我的美丽是如此的突出，以至于没人会在意你们。"

7 红色再也忍受不了了，他大喊道："我是你们的统治者，我是血，生命的颜色！我象征着危险和勇敢，我愿为事业而奋战。我把火种带到我们的世界。没有我，地球将像月球一样荒凉一片。我代表着激

of love, the red rose, the poinsettia and the poppy."

8 Purple rose up to his full height: He was very tall and spoke with great pomp: "I am the color of royalty and power. Kings, chiefs, and bishops have always chosen me for I am the sign of authority and wisdom. People do not question me! They follow and obey."

9 Finally Indigo spoke, much more quietly than all the others, but with just as much determination: "Think of me. I am the color of silence. You hardly notice me, but without me you all become superficial. I represent thought and reflection, twilight and deep water. You need me for balance and contrast, for prayer and inner peace."

10 And so the colors went on boasting, each convinced of his or her own superiority. Their quarreling became louder and louder. Suddenly there was a startling flash of bright lightening thunder rolled and boomed. Rain started to pour down relentlessly. The colors crouched down in fear, drawing close to one another for comfort.

11 In the midst of the clamor, rain began to speak: "You foolish colors, fighting amongst yourselves, each trying to dominate the rest. Don't you know that

情和爱情，我也是红玫瑰、一品红和罂粟的颜色。"

8 紫色站起来，他非常高大，说起话来气势磅礴："我象征着皇室和权力，国王、领袖、主教选我为他们的代表色，因为我象征着权力和智慧。人们不会怀疑我，他们听从、服从我。"

9 最终靛蓝色说话了，语气较之其他几种颜色平和许多，但是同样的富有决心："想想我吧，我是安静的象征。你们很少注意到我，但是没有我，你们都将沦为肤浅。我象征着思考和深思，象征着曙光和一池深水。我使你们保持协调、形成对比，你们需要我来祈祷和保持内心的平和。"

10 颜色之间一直在互相吹嘘，夸捧着自己比其他颜色好，他们的争吵声越来越大。突然，一道闪光从天空划过，雷声慢慢袭来，雨猛烈的下了起来。各种颜色恐惧的蹲下身来，紧凑在一起寻求安慰。

11 喧闹声中，雨开始说道："你们真愚蠢，竟然互相攻击，试图去统治别人。难道你们不知道你们每种颜色都有

you were each made for a special purpose, unique and different? Join hands with one another and come to me."

12 Doing as they were told, the colors united and joined hands.

13 The rain continued: "From now on, when it rains, each of you will stretch across the sky in a great bow of color as a reminder that you can all live in peace. The rainbow is a sign of hope for tomorrow." And so, whenever a good rain washes the world, and a rainbow appears in the sky, let us remember to appreciate one another.

自己特定的用处，你们各自都独特、与众不同吗？现在，你们手拉手一块跟我来。"

12 按照雨的指示，颜色们手拉手团结起来向雨走过去。

13 雨继续说道："从现在开始，只要一下雨，你们每种颜色都要加入到天空中去，彩虹代表着你们颜色间的和平相处。彩虹是明天希望的象征。"因此，每当一场及时雨清洗了我们的世界后，天空便会横挂一条彩虹，让我们记住去欣赏每一种颜色吧。

阅读无障碍

quarrel ['kwɒr(ə)l] v. 吵架

majority [mə'dʒɒrɪtɪ] n. 多数

interrupt [ɪntə'rʌpt] v. 打断

chuckle ['tʃʌk(ə)l] v. 咯咯的笑

gaiety ['geɪətɪ] n. 欢乐

sunflower ['sʌnflaʊə] n. 向日葵

trumpet ['trʌmpɪt] n. 吹嘘

precious ['preʃəs] adj. 宝贵的，珍贵的

pumpkin ['pʌm(p)kɪn] n. 南瓜

striking ['straɪkɪŋ] adj. 突出的，显著的

bravery ['breɪv(ə)rɪ] n. 勇敢，勇气

poinsettia [ˌpɔɪn'setɪə] n. 一品红

poppy ['pɒpɪ] n. 罂粟

royalty ['rɔɪəltɪ] n. 皇室，王权

bishop ['bɪʃəp] n. 主教

indigo ['ɪndɪgəʊ] n. 靛蓝色

twilight ['twaɪlaɪt] n. 黎明

boast [bəʊst] v. 自吹自擂

clamor ['klæmə] v. 喧闹，叫嚷

rainbow ['reɪnbəʊ] n. 彩虹

🐰**极品佳句背诵**

1. I am the color of passion and of love, the red rose, the poinsettia and the poppy."

   我代表着激情和爱情，我也是红玫瑰、一品红和罂粟的颜色。

2. Don't you know that you were each made for a special purpose, unique and different?

   难道你们不知道你们每种颜色都有自己特定的用处，你们各自都独特、与众不同吗？

3. And so, whenever a good rain washes the world, and a rainbow appears in the sky, let us remember to appreciate one another.

   因此，每当一场及时雨清洗了我们的世界后，天空便会横挂一条彩虹，让我们记住去欣赏每一种颜色吧。

Best Friends
最好的朋友

带着问题去阅读

1. 在你最脆弱的时刻是谁帮助你渡过难关？
2. 你和最好的朋友是怎么相识的？
3. 你对你的好朋友表达过谢意吗？

 美文欣赏　　 译文

1 One day, when I was a freshman in high school, I saw a kid from my class walking home from school. His name was Kyle. It looked like he was carrying all of his books. I thought to myself, "Why would anyone bring home all his books on a Friday? He must really be a nerd."

2 I had quite a weekend planned (parties and a football game with my friends tomorrow afternoon), so I shrugged my shoulders and went on. As I was walking, I saw a bunch of kids running toward him. They ran at him, knocking all his books out of his arms and tripping him

1 那年我还是高中新生。一天，看见我们班的同学凯尔，正搬着他所有的书回家，我暗自想道："为什么在星期五搬这么多书啊？真是个书呆子。"

2 我的周末计划得满满的（聚会，明天下午和朋友去足球比赛），因此，我不屑的耸耸肩，继续往前走。这时一群孩子向凯尔跑过来，他们把他撞倒了，书从他的手臂上掉了下来，他摔倒在地。他的眼

113

so he landed in the dirt. His glasses went flying, and I saw them land in the grass about ten feet from him. He looked up and I saw this terrible sadness in his eyes. My heart went out to him. So, I jogged over to him and as he crawled around looking for his glasses, and I saw a tear in his eye. As I handed him his glasses, I said, Those guys are jerks. They really should get lives. He looked at me and said, "Hey thanks!" There was a big smile on his face. It was one of those smiles that showed real gratitude.

3 I helped him pick up his books, and asked him where he lived. As it turned out, he lived near me, so I asked him why I had never seen him before. He said he had gone to private school before now. I would have never hung out with a private school kid before. We talked all the way home, and I carried some of his books.

4 He turned out to be a pretty cool kid. I asked him if he wanted to play football with my friends. He said yes. We hung out all weekend and the more I got to know Kyle, the more I liked him, and my friends thought the same of him.

5 Monday morning came, and there was Kyle with the huge stack of books again. I stopped him and said, "Boy, you are gonna really build some serious muscles with this pile of books everyday!"

镜飞到了离他 10 英尺远的草地上，他抬起了头，我看到他眼中那无限的悲哀。我的同情心油然而生。我小跑过去，他在地上慢慢挪动着身体去找他的眼镜，我看到了他眼里的泪水。我把眼镜捡回来，递给他说："这些蠢人，他们不得好死。"他看着我，脸上绽放着笑容，那是一种充满感激之情的微笑，然后对我说："谢谢。"

3 我帮他把书捡好，问他家住哪儿。原来，我们住的是那么近，问他为什么之前从没见过，他回答说他一直上的是私立学校。我此前从未跟私立学校的小孩玩过。我帮他拿着书，就这样我们聊了一路。

4 其实，他是一个很酷的孩子。我问他愿不愿意和我还有我的朋友们一起去踢足球，他说愿意。我们整个周末都玩在一起，我发现，越了解凯尔，就会越喜欢他，我的朋友们也有这种感觉。

5 星期一的早上，我又看到凯尔搬了一大摞书。我截住他，说道，"嗨，你每天都搬这么一大摞书，锻炼肌肉呀！"他只是笑笑，然后把一

He just laughed and handed me half the books. Over the next four years, Kyle and I became best friends. When we were seniors, we began to think about college. Kyle decided on Georgetown and I was going to Duke. I knew that we would always be friends, that the miles would never be a problem. He was going to be a doctor, and I was going for business on a football scholarship.

6 Kyle was valedictorian of our class. I teased him all the time about being a nerd. He had to prepare a speech for graduation. I was so glad it wasn't me having to get up there and speak. Graduation day, I saw Kyle. He looked great. He was one of those guys that really found himself during high school. He actually looked good in glasses. He had more dates than I had and all the girls loved him. Boy, sometimes I was jealous. Today was one of those days. I could see that he was nervous about his speech. So, I smacked him on the back and said, "Hey, big guy, you'll be great!" He looked at me with one of those looks (the really grateful one) and smiled. "Thanks."he said.

7 As he started his speech, he cleared his throat, and began with "Graduation is a time to thank those who helped you make it through those tough years. Your parents, your teachers, your siblings,

半书给了我。四年里，我和凯尔成了最要好的朋友。四年级的时候，我们开始考虑考大学了。凯尔决定去乔治敦大学，而我决定去杜克大学，但我知道，距离不是问题，我们将是永远的朋友。他立志做一名医生，而我则决定用足球奖金开始创业。

6 凯尔是我们班致告别辞的代表。我经常讥笑他是个书虫，他必须准备他的毕业讲话稿了。我很庆幸不是我站在那儿致毕业词。毕业那天，我看见了凯尔，他状态不错，他的高中过的很精彩。他戴着眼镜显得那么英俊。他比我的约会多，所有的女孩子都喜欢他。唉，有时，我还真的嫉妒他，今天也是。我可以看出他有点儿紧张，所以我拍了拍他的后背，说道："嗨，伙计，你一定能成的！"他还是以那种表情看着我（充满感激之情的表情），笑道："谢谢。"

7 他清了清喉咙开始了演讲。"毕业的时刻，要感谢那些所有帮助过你度过困境的人，包括你的父母、老师、兄弟、姐妹、教练……但是，最

maybe a coach...but mostly your friends...
I am here to tell all of you that being a
friend to someone is the best gift you can
give them. I am going to tell you a story."
I just looked at my friend with disbelief as
he told the story of the first day we met.
He had planned to kill himself over the
weekend. He talked of how he had cleaned
out his locker so his Mom wouldn't have to
do it later and was carrying his stuff home.
He looked hard at me and gave me a little
smile. "Thankfully, I was saved. My friend
saved me from doing the unspeakable." I
heard the gasp go through the crowd as this
handsome, popular boy told us all about
his weakest moment. I saw his Mom and
dad looking at me and smiling that same
grateful smile. Only then did I understand
the meaning and depth of smile.

重要的要感谢你的朋友。这里
我想说，友情是你可以给别人
的最好礼物。接下来，我要给
你们讲一个故事。"我简直不
敢相信，他讲起了我们初次相
遇的那一天。他讲道，那天，
他计划好在周末自杀，他把他
的橱柜彻底的清理干净，这样
他妈妈就不用替他再清理了，
那天他正在把所有的东西往家
运。他盯着我，露出了浅浅的
微笑。"幸运的是，我被解救
了，我的朋友把我从那难以启
齿的罪恶中救出来了。"人群
中发出惊诧的叹息声，大家听
着眼前这个英俊的，那么受欢
迎的男生讲述着他生命中最脆
弱的那一刻。我看到他的父母
微笑地看着我，那一模一样的
充满感激的微笑，直到那时我
才明白那微笑的含义和深度。

阅读无障碍

freshman['freʃmən] *n.* 一年级新生

nerd [nɜːd] *n.* 呆子，傻瓜

shrug [ʃrʌg] *v.* 耸肩（以表冷淡，怀
    疑等）

shoulder ['ʃəuldə(r)] *n.* 肩膀

dirt [dɜːt] *n.* 污泥，泥土

jog [dʒɒg] *v.* 慢跑

crawl [krɔːl] *v.* 缓慢行进，爬行

gratitude ['grætɪtjuːd] *n.* 感谢，感激

private ['praɪvət] *adj.* 私人的，私有
    的

hang out 闲逛

stack [stæk] *n.* 堆，垛

muscle ['mʌsl] *n.* 肌肉

scholarship ['skɒləʃɪp] *n.* 奖学金

valedictorian [ˌvælɪdɪk'tɔːrɪən] *n.* 致
告别辞者

tease [tiːz] *v.* 取笑，戏弄

jealous ['dʒeləs] *adj.* 妒忌的，羡慕的

smack [smæk] *v.* 拍打

sibling ['sɪblɪŋ] *n.* 兄弟姐妹

disbelief [ˌdɪsbɪ'liːf] *n.* 怀疑，不相信

gasp [gɑːsp] *n.*（尤指惊讶、震惊时
的）喘息，倒抽气

极品佳句背诵

1. Graduation is a time to thank those who helped you make it through those tough years.

   毕业的时刻，要感谢那些所有帮助过你度过困境的人.

2. I am here to tell all of you that being a friend to someone is the best gift you can give them.

   这里我想说，友情是你可以给别人的最好礼物。

3. I heard the gasp go through the crowd as this handsome, popular boy told us all about his weakest moment.

   人群中发出惊诧的叹息声，大家听着眼前这个英俊的，那么受欢迎的男生讲述着他生命中最脆弱的那一刻。

The Love
爱

带着问题去阅读

1. 爱的力量有多大？
2. 是爱带来的奇迹吗？
3. 文中主人公是幸运还是不幸？

1　It was well after mid night, wrapped in my warm fleecy robe I stood silently staring out the ninth floor window of the daunting New York Hospital. I was staring at the 59th Street Bridge. It was as sparkling and beautiful as a Christmas tree. New York City has always been special to me; the Broadway theatre, the music, the restaurants from the deli's to the Tavern-On-the-Green. "This is what the city is supposed to be about." I thought, dreading the morning to come and all the uncertainty it held. But the morning did come and at nine a.m. on that March 17th,

1　时间早就过了午夜了，我裹着暖暖的柔软睡袍静静地站在这座令人生畏的纽约医院的九楼病房，凝视窗外。我望着眼前的第59街大桥，它像圣诞树般闪闪发光，美丽动人。纽约对于我来说一直很特别，纽约的百老汇的戏院，音乐，和形形色色、档次各异的餐馆都很特别。"这个城市本来就应该是这样的。"我想着，担心着即将到来的一天和它将带来的未知之数。但那天还是来了，就在那天，3月

I was wheeled into an operating room. Eleven hours and forty-five minutes later I was wheeled into a recovery room and a very few hours after being returned to my own hospital room I found myself actually on my feet, half walking, half propelled by medical equipment and members of my family.

2　It was then that I first saw him. I saw him through a haze of, drugs, pain and the dreamy unreality that this could be happening to me. He was standing in the doorway of a hospital room. In my twilight, unfocused state I saw him almost as a spirit shape rather than a full blown person.

3　This became my daily routine for the next three weeks. As I gained a little more strength the man would be standing in the doorway, smiling and nodding as I would pass with one or more members of my family. On the fourth week I was allowed to solo up the corridor. As I passed his room, there was my faithful friend in the doorway. He was a slender dark complexioned man. I stopped a minute to chat. He introduced me to his wife and his son who was lying listlessly in a hospital bed. The next day as I made my scheduled walk, he came out and walked with me

17 日的早上 9 点，我被推进了手术室。11 个小时 45 分钟后，我又被推进了恢复室，在被送回自己的病房后，仅仅几个小时，我就已经能下地行走了——在我自己的努力，器械的辅助和家人的搀扶下走着。

2　就在那时，我第一次看到他。在药物和疼痛的作用下，我透过朦胧的双眼看到了他，那景象感觉很不真实，我也不肯定自己究竟看到了什么。他当时正站在一间病房的门口。我当时正处于那种迷糊无神的状态中，他对我来说，就像个幽灵，而不是一个完整的人影。

3　在以后的三个星期里，在医院的长廊里行走成了我的日常行动。在我的力气稍微恢复之后，我在家人的陪同下走过他站立的门口，我会看到他站在那里向我微笑、点头。到了第四个星期，我可以自己在长廊上走了，每当我经过他的房间，我这位忠实的朋友都会站在门口。这是一个肤色稍黑，身体瘦小的男人。我停下来与他谈了一会儿。他把我介绍给他的妻子和儿子。他的儿子躺在病床上，看上去没精打

119

to my room. He explained that he and his wife had brought their teenage son to this hospital of hope from Iran. They were still hoping but things were not going well. He told me of how I had encouraged him on that first dreadful night's walking tour and how he was rooting for me. For three more weeks we continued our conversations, each giving the other the gift of caring and friendship. He told me of how he enjoyed seeing my family as they rallied around me and I was saddened by the loneliness of that small family so far from home.

4 Miraculously, there did come a day when the doctor told me I would be discharged the following morning. That night I told my friend. The next morning he came to my room. I had been up and dressed since dawn. My bright yellow dress gave me hope, and I almost looked human. We talked a bit. I told him I would pray for his son. He thanked me but shrugged his shoulders indicating the hopelessness. We knew we would never see each other again, in this world. This man in his sorrow was so happy for me. I felt his love. He took my hand and said, "You are my sister." I answered back and said, "You are my brother." He turned and left the room.

采的样子。第二天，我又按时地在走廊里走动，他从房间里走出来，陪我走回我的病房。他告诉我，他和他的妻子满怀希望地把他十几岁的儿子从伊朗带到这家医院。尽管现在他们还是抱有希望，但情况确实不容乐观。他告诉我，我手术后第一个难熬的晚上艰辛的行走使他倍受鼓舞，他也在暗暗为我加油。在接下来的三个多星期里，我们在一起交谈，互相关心，彼此关爱。他很高兴看到我的家人很关心和支持我，而我也为这个三口之家远离故土的孤独而感到伤感。

4 奇迹出现了，终于有一天医生告诉我说，第二天早上我就可以出院了。那晚，我把这个消息告诉了我的朋友。第二天一早，他来到我的房间。那天，我早早地就起床了，并换好了衣服。我那鲜黄色的衣服给了我希望。我总算康复了。我们俩谈了一会儿。我对他说，我会为他的儿子祈祷的。他在感谢我的同时，耸了耸肩，表示他也不抱很大希望。我们都知道我们再也不会见面了。这个忧伤的人很为我感到高兴，我能感受到他对我的关爱。他握着我的手

5 My family came to retrieve me. Doctors and nurses, to say their goodbyes and give orders. All business had been taken care of. After seven and a half weeks I was leaving the hospital room I had walked into with so much trepidation.

6 As I turned to walk down the corridor to the elevator, my brother stood in the doorway, smiling, nodding and giving his blessing.

7 It was 14 years ago today on March 17th 1990 that I entered that operating room and much has happened to the world since my brother and I said our last farewell. Yet I think of him often and he is always in my heart as I feel I am in his. I remember his intense, dark brown eyes as we pledged ourselves as brother and sister. At that moment, I knew without a doubt that the Spirit of God hovered over us smiling, nodding and blessing us with the knowledge that we are all one.

说："你就是我的妹妹。"我回答道："你就是我的哥哥。"说完，他转过身，走出了房间。

5 我的家人来接我了。医生和护士向我道别，嘱咐我出院后该怎么做。所有事情都安排好了。在我怀着忐忑不安的心情走进医院的七个半星期后，我终于要离开这间病房了。

6 就在我沿着走廊向电梯走去时，我哥哥站在他的病房门口，冲我微笑点头，传递着他的祝福。

7 我进手术室的那天，也就是14年前的今天，1990年3月17日。自从我与我哥哥告别后，这个世界发生了很大的变化。但我还会经常会想起他，他一直都在我的心里，而我相信我也一直在他心中。我记得我们互称兄妹时，他那双真诚的深褐色的眼睛。在那一刻，我毫不怀疑上帝正在天堂微笑地看看我们，向我们点头，为我们祝福。因为他知道，我们都与彼此同在。

阅读无障碍

wrap [ræp] v. 包，裹

fleecy ['fliːsɪ] adj. 柔软的

daunting ['dɔːntɪŋ] adj. 使人畏缩的

sparkling ['spɑːklɪŋ] adj. 闪耀的

dread [dred] v. 害怕

uncertainty [ʌn'sɜ:tənti] n. 不确定

recovery [rɪ'kʌv(ə)rɪ] n. 恢复

propel [prə'pel] v. 推进

equipment [ɪ'kwɪpm(ə)nt] n. 设备

unreality [ˌʌnrɪ'ælətɪ] n. 非现实

twilight ['twaɪlaɪt] adj. 朦胧的

unfocused ['ʌn'fəukəst] adj. 未聚焦的

routine [ru:'ti:n] n. 日常工作

corridor ['kɒrɪdɔ:] n. 走廊

faithful ['feɪθful] adj. 忠实的

complexioned [kəm'plekʃənd] adj. 肤色…的

scheduled ['ʃedju:əld] adj. 预先安排的，定期的

dreadful ['dredful] adj. 可怕的

miraculously [mɪ'rækjuləslɪ] adv. 神奇地

nod [nɒd] v. 点头

 极品佳句背诵

1. For three more weeks we continued our conversations, each giving the other the gift of caring and friendship.
   在接下来的三个多星期里，我们在一起交谈，互相关心，彼此关爱。

2. I was staring at the 59th Street Bridge. It was as sparkling and beautiful as a Christmas tree.
   我望着眼前的第 59 街大桥，它像圣诞树般闪闪发光，美丽动人。

3. At that moment, I knew without a doubt that the Spirit of God hovered over us smiling, nodding and blessing us with the knowledge that we are all one.
   在那一刻，我毫不怀疑上帝正在天堂微笑地看着我们，向我们点头，为我们祝福。因为他知道，我们都与彼此同在。

Gifts of Love
爱的礼物

带着问题去阅读

1. 在过节的时候你最想收到什么礼物？

2. 在节日里你通常会给亲人朋友赠送什么礼物？

3. 曾经是否有一件事改变了你的生活态度？

美文欣赏

译文

1 On the last day of Christmas, I hurried to the supermarket to buy the remaining gifts I hadn't managed to get earlier. When I saw all the people there, I started to mutter to myself: "It's going to take forever here and I still have so many other places to go…Christmas really is getting more and more annoying every year. How I wish I could just lie down, go to sleep and only wake up after it's over…"

2 Nonetheless, I made my way to the toy section, and there, I started to curse the prices as I wondered if kids really played with such expensive toys. While looking

1 圣诞节前一天，我匆匆到超市去买早些时候没买上的礼物。当我看见很多人在那时，我咕哝着："在这还要呆很长时间，而我还有很多地方要去……圣诞节真是越过越烦人，我多么希望我能躺下来，睡一觉，等到它结束了我再醒来……"

2 尽管如此，我还是挤着走到玩具部，在那儿，我又开始抱怨价格，我怀疑小孩根本就不会玩这些昂贵的玩具。

around the shelves, I noticed a boy of about five, pressing a doll against his chest.

3　He kept touching the hair of the doll and looked quite sad, I wondered who the doll was for. Then the boy turned to an old woman beside him:

4　"Granny, are you sure I don't have enough money?"She replied, "You know that you don't have enough to buy his doll, my dear."

5　Then she asked him to stay there for five minutes while she looked around. She left quickly and the boy continued to hold the doll in his hand. I walked towards him and asked who he wished to give the doll to.

6　"It is the doll my sister loved most and wanted so much for Christmas. She was so sure that Santa Claus would bring it to her."

7　I told him that maybe Santa Claus would bring it after all, and not to worry. But he said sadly, "No, Santa Claus cannot take it where she is now. My sister has gone to be with God. Daddy says mummy will go to see God very soon, so I thought that she could take the doll with her to give my sister."

8　My heart nearly *stopped*. The boy looked up at me and added, "I told daddy to tell mummy not to go yet. I asked him to

我顺着货架到处看的时候，发现一个五岁的小男孩把洋娃娃紧紧抱在胸前。

3　他不停地摸洋娃娃的头发，看起来很伤心。我很好奇他会把洋娃娃送给谁。男孩转过身对旁边的老妇人说：

4　"奶奶，你确定我没有足够的钱吗？"奶奶说："亲爱的，你知道你没有足够的钱买这个洋娃娃的。"

5　于是她叫他在这儿呆五分钟，她再去四处看看。她很快离开了，男孩还是把那个洋娃娃握在手中。我向他走去，问他想把洋娃娃送给谁。

6　"这是我妹妹最喜欢的洋娃娃，是她想要的圣诞礼物。她相信圣诞老人会送给她的。"

7　我告诉他圣诞老人最终会带给他妹妹的，不用担心，但是他伤心地说："不，圣诞老人不能送到她现在所在的地方。我妹妹随上帝走了。爸爸说妈妈也将很快去见上帝，我想妈妈可以把这个洋娃娃带给妹妹。"

8　我的心几乎停止跳动了。小男孩看着我接着说："我叫爸爸告诉妈妈先不要

wait until I'm back from the supermarket."
"Then he showed me a nice photo in which he was laughing.

9 "I also want mummy to take this photo with her so that she will not forget me. I love my mummy and I wish she didn't have to leave me. But daddy says she has to go to be with my little sister. "

10 Then he looked again at the doll, silently. I quickly reached for my wallet, took out a few notes and said to him, "What if we checked again just in case you have enough money?"

11 "Okay," he replied. I added some of my money to him without his noticing, and we started counting. There was enough for the doll, and some change.

12 The boy looked at me and said, "Last night, before going to bed, I asked God to make sure I have enough money to buy this doll so mummy can give it to my sister. He heard me."

13 "I also wanted some money to buy a white rose for my mummy, but I didn't dare ask God for too much. You know, my mummy loves white roses."

14 A few minutes later, the old lady came again and I left with my trolley. I finished my shopping in a totally different state from when I started. I couldn't get the boy out of my mind.

走，等我从超市回来。"接着他给我看了一张漂亮的照片，照片上他笑得很灿烂。

9 "我还想让妈妈把照片带着，希望她不要忘记我。我爱妈妈，不希望她离开我，但是爸爸说她要去陪妹妹。"

10 他又看了一眼洋娃娃，陷入了沉默。我马上伸手去拿我的钱包，拿出几张钱后对他说："我们再来数数，万一你的钱够了呢？"

11 "好的，"他说。我趁他不注意把几张钱塞进了他的钱里面，然后我们开始数，这下买洋娃娃的钱够了，还有一些剩余。

12 男孩看着我说："昨晚睡觉前我祈求上帝让我有足够的钱买这个洋娃娃，然后妈妈就可以带去给我妹妹。上帝听到了。"

13 "我还想给我妈妈买一支白玫瑰，但是我没有向上帝要更多的钱。我妈妈喜欢白玫瑰。"

14 几分钟后，老奶奶回来了。我推着购物车走了，带着和刚开始完全不同的心情结束了购物。那个小男孩的影子始终在我脑海里，挥之不去。

15 Then I remembered a newspaper report from two days back, about a drunk who had hit a car driven by a young woman, who was with her little girl. The girl died instantly and the mother is now in a coma. Is this the family of the little boy?

16 Two days after our encounter in the supermarket, I read that the young mother had died.

17 I couldn't stop myself. I bought a bunch of white roses and went to the mortuary, where her body lay for visitors to pay their last respects. She was in her coffin, with a beautiful white rose in her hand and the photo of the boy and the doll over her chest. I left crying. I felt as if my life had been changed forever.

15 然后我回想起了前两天在报纸上看过的一则报道，一个卡车司机酒后驾车，撞到了一辆小汽车，车上是一位年轻的妈妈和她的小女儿。小女孩当场就死亡，妈妈现处于昏迷状态。她们会不会就是这个小男孩的家人呢？

16 在超市遇到小男孩的两天后，我在报纸上看到年轻妈妈去世的消息。

17 我不能自已，买了一束白玫瑰来到她的灵堂，在那里来访者向死者做最后的道别。她躺在棺材里，手上拿着漂亮的白玫瑰花，胸脯上放着小男孩的照片和那个洋娃娃。我哭着离开，感觉我的生命像是从此永远被改变了。

阅读无障碍

Christmas['krɪsməs] n. 圣诞节

remaining [rɪ'meɪnɪŋ] adj. 剩下的，余下的

mutter ['mʌtə] v. 咕哝，喃喃自语

nonetheless [nʌnðə'les] adv. 尽管如此，但是

expensive [ɪk'spensɪv] adj. 昂贵的

stop [stɒp] v. 停止，中断

supermarket ['su:pəma:kɪt] n. 超市

wallet ['wɒlɪt] n. 钱包

rose [rəʊz] n. 玫瑰花

totally ['təʊtəlɪ] adv. 完全地

remember [rɪ'membə] v. 记得

newspaper ['nju:zpeɪpə] n. 报纸

instantly ['ɪnst(ə)ntlɪ] adv. 立即地，马上地

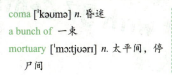

coma ['kəʊmə] *n.* 昏迷

a bunch of 一束

mortuary ['mɔːtjʊərɪ] *n.* 太平间，停
尸间

visitor ['vɪzɪtə] *n.* 来访者

coffin ['kɒfɪn] *n.* 棺材

chest [tʃest] *n.* 胸部

forever [fə'revə] *adv.* 永远地，永久地

极品佳句背诵

1. Daddy says mummy will go to see God very soon, so I thought that she could take the doll with her to give my sister.
   爸爸说妈妈也将很快去见上帝，我想妈妈可以把这个洋娃娃带给妹妹。

2. I also wanted some money to buy a white rose for my mummy, but I didn't dare ask God for too much.
   我还想要一些钱给我妈妈买一支白玫瑰，但是我没有向上帝要更多。

3. She was in her coffin, with a beautiful white rose in her hand and the photo of the boy and the doll over her chest.
   她躺在棺材里，手上拿着漂亮的白玫瑰花，胸脯上放着小男孩的照片和那个洋娃娃。

A Church Built with 57 Cents
57美分建成的教堂

带着问题去阅读

1. 教堂是用什么建成的？
2. 小女孩的心愿是什么？
3. 57美分能够做些什么？

1 A sobbing little girl stood near a small church from which she had been turned away because it "was too crowded." "I can't go to Sunday school." she sobbed to the pastor as he walked by.

2 Seeing her shabby, unkempt appearance, the pastor guessed the reason and, taking her by the hand, took her inside and found a place for her in the Sunday school class. The child was so happy, that she went to bed that night thinking of the children who have no place to worship Jesus.

1 一个衣服破旧的小女孩站在一个小教堂的外面，她哭着向从她身边走过的牧师说："我不能去参加主日学校（星期天学习圣经的班）了，因为里面太挤了。"

2 见她衣衫褴褛的样子，牧师便猜出她为何被拒之门外了。牧师拉着她的手，走进那座小教堂，在儿童主日学习班里，为她找到了一个座位，为此她感到很开心！那天晚上她睡觉的时候，还在想那些无法参加敬拜上帝的孩子们该怎么办。

3 Some two years later, this child lay dead in one of the poor tenement buildings and the parents called for the kindhearted pastor, who had befriended their daughter, to handle the final arrangements. As her poor little body was being moved, a worn and crumpled purse was found which seemed to have been rummaged from some trash dump. Inside was found 57 cents and a note scribbled in childish handwriting which read, "This is to help build the little church bigger so more children can go to Sunday school."

4 For two years she had saved for this offering of love. When the pastor tearfully read that note, he knew instantly what he would do. Carrying this note and the cracked, red pocketbook to the pulpit, he told the story of her unselfish love and devotion. He challenged his deacons to get busy and raise enough money for the larger building.

5 But the story does not end there! A newspaper learned of the story and published it. It was read by a Realtor who offered them a parcel of land worth many thousands. When told that the church could not pay so much, he offered it for 57 cents payment.

6 Church members made large

3 两年后，小女孩去世了。她的父母请那位和他们女儿作朋友的慈祥的牧师帮助他们处理小女孩的后事。当大家挪动小女孩瘦小的躯体时，从她身上突然滑落了一个皱巴巴、破烂不堪的、像是从垃圾堆里翻出来的红色小钱包，里面有57美分和一张小纸条。上面的字迹歪歪扭扭，写着："这些钱将用来帮助扩大教堂，让更多的孩子参加主日学习。"

4 这57美分是她经过两年时间积攒下来的。当那位牧师泪流满面的读完这张字条，他立刻意识到他该做些什么。他带着这张纸条和那个破旧的红色钱包走上讲道台，向他人讲述小女孩的故事，她无私的爱和奉献。牧师还向教堂的执事提议，通过募集资金来扩建这座小教堂。

5 事情至此并未结束！当地的一家报纸转载了小女孩的故事，一位房地产开发商倍受感动，愿意将一块价值上千的土地给教会建教堂。当被告知教会付不起时，他说，他愿意把那块地以57美分的价格卖给教会。

6 教区的人们捐助了一

donations. Checks came from far and wide. Within five years the little girl's gift had increased to $250,000.00—a huge sum for that time (near the turn of the century). Her unselfish love had paid large dividend.

7　When you are in the city of Philadelphia, look up Temple Baptist Church, with a seating capacity of 3,300 and Temple University, where hundreds of students are trained. Have a look, too, at the Good Samaritan Hospital and at a Sunday school building which houses hundreds of Sunday schoolers, so that no child in the area will ever need to be left outside during Sunday school time.

8　In one of the rooms of this building may be seen the picture of the sweet face of the little girl whose 57 cents, so sacrificially saved, made such remarkable history. Alongside of it is portrait of her kind pastor, Dr. Russel H. Conwell, author of the book, "Acres of Diamonds" A true story, which goes to show WHAT GOD, CAN DO WITH 57 cents?

大笔钱，馈赠的支票也从四面八方汇集而来。短短五年的时间，捐款的数字已从当初小女孩的 57 美分增加到 25 万美元——这在 20 世纪初，可是一笔相当可观的财富！她无私的爱收获巨大的回馈。

7　现在，如果您到费城，请参观一下拥有 3300 个座位的坦普尔大教堂和坦普尔大学，成千上万的学生在那儿接受教育。也不要忘了去看一看，撒马利亚慈善医院以及扩建后的星期日学校，如今，教区的数百名活泼可爱的儿童都可以进入星期日学校，没人会被拒之门外。

8　这座建筑内有一个房间专门用来陈列这个小女孩的画像，画面上的小女孩是那么可爱，这个贫穷的小女孩用节俭下来的 57 美分创造了一段非同寻常的历史。画像旁边陈列着那位好心牧师的肖像，《万亩钻石》的作者——鲁塞 ·H· 康威尔 (Russell H. Conwell) 博士。这是一个真实的故事，它告诉我们上帝用 57 美分能做什么。

阅读无障碍

sob [sɒb] v. 哭诉，啜泣

pastor ['pɑːstə] n. 牧师

shabby ['ʃæbɪ] adj. 破旧的

unkempt [ʌn'kem(p)t] adj. 蓬乱的，不整洁的

worship ['wɜːʃɪp] v. 拜神，做礼拜

tenement ['tenəm(ə)nt] n. 租住的房屋

kindhearted ['kaɪnd'hɑːtɪd] adj. 仁慈的，好心肠的

worn [wɔːn] adj. 用旧的

rummage ['rʌmɪdʒ] v. 仔细搜查，翻找出

trash [træʃ] n. 垃圾，废物

scribble ['skrɪb(ə)l] v. 乱写，滥写，潦草地书写

tearfully ['tɪəfəlɪ] adv. 含泪地，泪汪汪地

instantly ['ɪnst(ə)ntlɪ] adv. 立即地，马上地

cracked [krækt] adj. 破裂的

pocketbook ['pɒkɪtbʊk] n. 钱包

devotion [dɪ'vəʊʃ(ə)n] n. 献身，奉献

donation [də(ʊ)'neɪʃ(ə)n] n. 捐款

dividend ['dɪvɪdend] n. 红利，股息

remarkable [rɪ'mɑːkəb(ə)l] adj. 卓越的，非凡的

portrait ['pɔːtrɪt] n. 肖像，半身雕塑像

极品佳句背诵

1. The child was so happy, that she went to bed that night thinking of the children who have no place to worship Jesus.
为此她感到很开心！那天晚上她睡觉的时候还在想那些因教堂太小无法敬拜上帝的孩子们该怎么办。

2. Carrying this note and the cracked, red pocketbook to the pulpit, he told the story of her unselfish love and devotion.
他带着这张纸条和破旧的红色钱包走上讲道台，向他人讲述小女孩的故事，她无私的爱和奉献。

3. In one of the rooms of this building may be seen the picture of the sweet face of the little girl whose 57 cents, so sacrificially saved, made such remarkable history.
这座建筑内有一个房间专门用来陈列这个小女孩的画像，画面上的小女孩是那么可爱，这个贫穷的小女孩用节俭下来的 57 美分创造了一段非同寻常的历史。

The Power of Love
爱的力量

带着问题去阅读

1. 在生活中你是否感到过抑郁和缺少爱？
2. 你想拥有一份怎样的爱情？
3. 你知道如何去爱别人吗？

美文欣赏

1 Love is as critical for your mind and body as oxygen. It's not negotiable. The more connected you are, the healthier you will be both physically and emotionally. The less connected you are, the more you are at risk.

2 It is also true that the less love you have, the more depression you are likely to experience in your life. Love is probably the best antidepressant, because one of the most common sources of depression is feeling unloved. Most depressed people don't love themselves and they do not feel

译文

1 爱对你的情绪和身体来说，跟氧气一样重要。这点无需置疑。你和别人关系越紧密，就会越健康，不仅在身体上，情绪方面也是如此。如果与别人越疏离，来自健康的威胁就会越大。

2 同样，你拥有的爱越少，你一生中就可能经历更多的抑郁。爱，可能是最好的抗抑郁药，因为陷入抑郁最重要的原因之一就是感觉失去了他人的关爱。大多数抑郁的人不爱自己，也感觉不到有人爱他

loved by others. They also are very self-focused, making them less attractive to others and depriving them of opportunities to learn the skills of love.

3　There is a mythology in our culture that love just happens. As a result, the depressed often sit around passively waiting for someone to love them. But love doesn't work that way. To get love and keep love you have to go out and be active and learn a variety of specific skills.

4　Most of us get our ideas of love from popular culture. We come to believe that love is something that sweeps us off our feet. But the pop-culture ideal of love consists of unrealistic images created for entertainment, which is one reason so many of us are set up to be depressed. It's part of our national vulnerability, like eating junk food, constantly stimulated by images of instant gratification. We think it is love when it's simply distraction and infatuation.

5　Knowing that love is a learned skill, not something that comes from hormones or emotion particularly, Erich Fromm called it "an act of will." If you don't learn the skills of love you virtually guarantee that you will be depressed, not only

们。他们总是把注意力集中在自己身上，这大大降低了他们的吸引力，也使他们丧失了学会去爱的机会。

3　在我们的文化里，人们相信爱情是可遇不可求的。正因如此，那些郁闷的人总是守株待兔，被动地等着别人来爱他们。不过，爱情并不是这样。得到爱、维持爱，必须走出去、主动地学习一系列专门的方法。

4　我们中的大多数人通过流行文化来了解爱情。我们开始相信爱情是突然到来、让我们猝不及防、无力招架的东西。不过流行文化中的理想爱情包括了很多为了娱乐效果而特地制造出来的、不现实的情景，这也是我们陷入抑郁的一个陷阱。我们天生就有脆弱的一面，比如大嚼垃圾食品、总被那些立即让人满足的画面所打动。我们认为那就是爱情了，而实际上那不过是分心或是迷恋罢了。

5　爱是一种后天习得的能力，而不是从荷尔蒙或者情绪直接演变出来的产物，埃里克·弗洛姆把它称作"意志行为"。如果你学不会爱的技巧，很容易会沮丧，这不单是因为

because you will not be connected enough but because you will have many failure experiences. Learn good communication skills. They are a means by which you develop trust and intensify connection. The more you can communicate the less depressed you will be because you will feel known and understood.

6 There are always core differences between two people, no matter how good or close you are, and if the relationship is going right those differences surface. The issue then is to identify the differences and negotiate them so that they don't distance you or kill the relationship. You do that by understanding where the other person is coming from, who that person is, and by being able to represent yourself. When the differences are known you must be able to negotiate and compromise on them until you find a common ground that works for both.

7 Focus on the other person. Rather than focus on what you are getting and how you are being treated, read your partner's need. What does this person really need for his/her own well-being? This is a very tough skill for people to learn in our narcissistic culture. Of course, you don't lose yourself in the process; you make sure you're also doing enough self-care. Help someone else. Depression keeps

你不能和对方心灵相通，还因为你会经历很多次的失败。学习良好的交流技巧。这是产生信任、加深默契的方法。越会交流，也就越少抑郁，因为你会感到自己被了解、被理解。

6 两个人之间总会有些根本的差异，不论他们多要好、多亲密。如果你们的关系发展正常，这些差异就会浮现出来。接下来要解决的问题就是明确这些差异，并协调差异，这样两个人之间才不会有距离、关系才能维持下去。你要了解另一半从何处而来、是怎样的人，还要表达你自己。发现差异之后，你们还要对这种差异进行协商和折衷，直到找到一个对两人都可行的方法。

7 把注意力放在另一半身上。与其注意自己得到什么、关注对方如何对待自己，不如去了解对方的需要。从他／她的幸福出发，对方到底需要什么？在我们这个自恋的文化中，学习这种能力并不容易。当然，也不要在这个过程中迷失自我，你还要确保有足够的自我保护。帮助别人。抑

people so focused on themselves they don't get outside themselves enough to be able to learn to love. The more you can focus on others and learn to respond and meet their needs, the better you are going to do in love. Develop the ability to accommodate simultaneous reality. The loved one's reality is as important as your own, and you need to be as aware of it as of your own. What are they really saying, what are they really needing?

8 Recognize that the internal voice is strong but it's not real. Talk back to it. "I'm not really being rejected, this isn't really evidence of inadequacy. I made a mistake." Or "this isn't about me, this is something I just didn't know how to do and now I'll learn." When you reframe the situation to something more adequate, you can act again in an effective way and you can find and keep the love that you need.

郁让人们过分关注自己，他们不能走出自我去学习如何去爱。如果能够更关注他人、学习如何去应对、满足别人的需求，你也会在爱情中做的更好。培养适应与现实同步的能力。爱人的现实和你自己的现实同样重要，你需要和了解自己一样去了解对方的实际情况。他们到底说的是什么？到底需要什么？

8 要认识到内心的声音虽然强烈但并不是现实。跟它针锋相对。"我并不是真的被拒绝，这不能证明我没用。我只是犯了个错。"或者这样，"这不是针对我，我只是不知道该怎么做，现在我会去学习。"当你重新调节情形至更为合适的时候，你将能再次进行有效的行动，找到并拥有一份自己需要的爱情。

阅读无障碍

critical [ˈkrɪtɪk(ə)l] adj. 决定性的
negotiable [nɪˈɡəʊʃəb(ə)l] adj. 可磋商的
antidepressant [ˌæntɪdɪˈpres(ə)nt] n. 抗抑郁药
deprive [dɪˈpraɪv] v. 剥夺，使丧失

passively [ˈpæsɪvlɪ] adv. 被动地
pop-culture n. 流行文化
unrealistic [ˌʌnrɪəˈlɪstɪk] adj. 不切实际的
entertainment [entəˈteɪnm(ə)nt] n. 娱乐，消遣

135

vulnerability [ˌvʌlnərəˈbɪləti] *n.* 弱点

gratification [ˌɡrætɪfɪˈkeɪʃn] *n.* 喜悦，满足

distraction [dɪˈstrækʃ(ə)n] *n.* 注意力分散

infatuation [ɪnˌfætʃʊˈeɪʃ(ə)n] *n.* 迷恋，醉心

virtually [ˈvɜːtjʊəli] *adv.* 实际上

intensify [ɪnˈtensɪfaɪ] *v.* 加强

compromise [ˈkɒmprəmaɪz] *v.* 妥协，折中

narcissistic [ˌnɑːsɪˈsɪstɪk] *adj.* 自我陶醉的，自恋的

simultaneous [ˌsɪm(ə)lˈteɪnɪəs] *adj.* 同时的

inadequacy [ɪnˈædɪkwəsɪ] *n.* 不适当，不充分

reframe [rɪˈfrem] *v.* 重新构筑

adequate [ˈædɪkwət] *adj.* 适当的

🐰 极品佳句背诵

1. Love is probably the best antidepressant, because one of the most common sources of depression is feeling unloved.
   爱，可能是最好的抗抑郁药，因为陷入抑郁最重要的原因之一就是感觉没人爱。

2. If you don't learn the skills of love you virtually guarantee that you will be depressed, not only because you will not be connected enough but because you will have many failure experiences.
   如果你学不会爱的技巧，很容易会沮丧，这不单是因为你不能和对方心灵相通，还因为你会经历很多次的失败。

3. When you reframe the situation to something more adequate, you can act again in an effective way and you can find and keep the love that you need.
   当你重新调节情形至更为合适的时候，你将能再次进行有效的行动，找到并拥有一份自己需要的爱情。

An Unknown Friend
陌生朋友

带着问题去阅读

1. 你怎么看待人与人之间的关系？
2. 我们应该相信陌生人吗？
3. 你相信陌生人的好意和缘分吗？

美文欣赏

1 The roads were wet from the rains that lashed the city the whole of the previous night. It was still drizzling early morning when Priya, with an umbrella to protect her from getting wet, walked onto the morning roads to get a rickshaw to take her to the station from where her train leaves at 6:55 a.m.

2 She had a 45 minute travel to her office in the other part of the city. As the climate was cool and damp due to the continuous downpour there was hardly anyone on the roads at that early hour.

3 Just as she saw a cycle rickshaw

译文

1 经过昨晚倾盆大雨的洗礼，城市感觉湿漉漉的。普瑞雅手持一把雨伞出门时，天空中仍飘着毛毛细雨。她走向洒满晨光的小路准备搭乘人力车去车站乘坐早晨 6 点 55 分出发的火车。

2 她需要花 45 分钟的车程才能到达位于城市另一端的办公室。持续的大雨使空气阴凉而潮湿，此时几乎无人行走在小路上。

3 她看见一辆人力车恰

coming that way and waved her hand to stop it. It stopped and she got in.

4 The ricksha wallah was young, nearly about her age as she observed, and she reached the station ten minutes before the train's departure, earlier than usual. At the station entrance, while she was searching for change to give the ricksha wallah, he engaged himself in buying some flowers to keep on the cycle.

5 From the flowers he bought, he offered Priya rose. She smiled, took it, said thanks, gave him the fare and hurried to catch the train.

6 She reached her office ten minutes before eight and hit the computers. She was just 22 and was working as an assistant editor for a monthly magazine in the city. Her passion for writing and reporting things had led her to do her bachelor in journalism and immediately after completion of her degree she had been offered this job, which she accepted. Along with the job she was also pursuing her masters. A diligent and hardworking girl with a pretty face and short stature, she was liked by everyone in the office and had gained praises for her work.

7 She caught her evening train at 4:30 and reached her evening class at 5:30. After the two hour class she either walked home or took a rickshaw.

好顺路而来就挥手叫车停下。车一停，她便上了车。

4 据她观察，这人力车夫很年轻，与她年纪相仿。普瑞雅在火车开车前十分钟到了车站，比平常略早一些。在车站入口，当她找得零钱给车夫时，他正在买一些鲜花，准备把花插在车上。

5 车夫从鲜花中拿出一支玫瑰送给普瑞雅。普瑞雅接过玫瑰，微笑着道谢，付了车费，匆匆去赶火车

6 普瑞雅在7点50到达办公室，打开电脑。她仅22岁，是本市一家月刊的编辑助理。她对写作和新闻报道的热爱之情使她取得新闻专业学士。在她结束学业时，这家杂志社向她伸出橄榄枝，她就接受了这份工作。在工作期间，她还在攻读硕士学位。普瑞雅是一个刻苦勤奋、兢兢业业的女孩，有着漂亮的面孔和娇小的身材。她在公司里招人喜欢且工作也获得认可。

7 她赶上下午4点半的火车，在5点半赶到了夜大教室。在两小时的课程结束后，她会步行或乘人力车回家。

8 And today as it happened she got the same cycle rickshaw that she had traveled in the morning.

9 The rickshaw wallah chatted lightly as he pedaled on, "Where do you work in the city?"

10 "For Times Magazine. Office is in the eastern part of the city." "Oh! So you are a press worker!" She smiled a little smile. After sometime he asked, "You didn't like the flower I gave you, did you? I can't see it on your hair."

11 Priya mumbled some excuses saying she left it in the flower vase in the office and that she liked roses while she had actually lost it somewhere on her train journey. He dropped her at her house. "Goodbye." "Goodnight."

12 The next morning it happened so that Priya got the same rickshaw. Then he came to pick her up every morning and also brought her back in the evening. During their trips they got to know each other better. Afterwards they became friends.

13 In fact, the relationships among people is very subtle, especially the warmth of strangers.

8 今天很凑巧，她遇见了早晨搭乘的那辆人力车。

9 当人力车夫踩起脚踏板出发时她轻轻地聊起来"你在哪里上班啊？"

10 "时代周刊，办公室在城市东部。""哦！那你是新闻工作者了！"她微微地笑了笑。少顷，他问道："你不喜欢我送你的花吗？我看你没带在头上。"

11 普瑞雅含糊地说，她喜欢玫瑰并且把花插在了办公室的花瓶里；事实上她早在乘火车途中把花弄丢了。他把她送到家门口，道声"再见"。"晚安"。

12 很巧的是，第二天早上普瑞雅又遇见了那个车夫，所以她又搭乘他的车。于是，以后的每一天早上他都来接她，晚上再把她送回家。在他们每天的旅程中，他们对彼此更加了解，后来便成为了朋友。

13 其实，人与人之间的关系很微妙，尤其是素不相识的人带给你的温暖。

阅读无障碍

lash[læʃ] v. 猛击，冲击

drizzle['drɪz(ə)l] v. 下毛毛雨

rickshaw['rɪkʃɔː] n. 人力车

damp[dæmp] adj. 潮湿的

continuous[kən'tɪnjʊəs] adj. 继续的，持续的

downpour['daʊnpɔː] n. 倾盆大雨

ricksha wallahn. 人力车夫

observe[əb'zɜːv] v. 观察，注意到

departure[dɪ'pɑːtʃə] n. 启程，离开

change[tʃeɪn(d)ʒ] n. 零钱

engage in 参加，从事于

bachelor['bætʃələ] n. 学士

pursue[pə'sjuː] v. 追求，追逐

stature['stætʃə] n. 身材

pedal['ped(ə)l] v. 踩踏板，骑车

press[pres] n. 新闻

mumble['mʌmb(ə)l] v. 含糊地说

excuse[ɪk'skjuːz] n. 借口

somewhere['sʌmweə] n. 某个地方

subtle['sʌt(ə)l] adj. 微妙的

极品佳句背诵

1. As the climate was cool and damp due to the continuous downpour there was hardly anyone on the roads at that early hour.
持续的大雨使空气阴凉而潮湿，此时几乎无人行走在小路上。

2. Priya mumbled some excuses saying she left it in the flower vase in the office and that she liked roses while she had actually lost it somewhere on her train journey.
普瑞雅含糊地说，她喜欢玫瑰并且把花插在了办公室的花瓶里；事实上她早在乘火车途中把花弄丢了。

3. In fact, the relationships among people is very subtle, especially the warmth of strangers.
其实，人与人之间的关系很微妙，尤其是素不相识的人带给你的温暖。

The Right Thing to Do
应做之事

带着问题去阅读

1. 达利斯为什么没投中罚球?
2. 约翰为什么要上场比赛?
3. 球员们的行为说明了什么?

美文欣赏

1　Darius and John have a lot in common. They are both talented high school seniors. They both love basketball. They are both captains of their respective high school basketball teams. But on one Saturday night in February, they were forever linked in the minds of all who were present for mutual act of courage, sportsmanship, and respect.

2　The remarkable moment came during a game between Darius's small-town Illinois team and John's big-city team in Wisconsin—a game that almost wasn't played. Just hours before the tip-off John's mother lost her five-year battle with

译文

1　达利斯和约翰有许多共同点。他俩都是优秀的高三在读生,都热爱篮球,是各自所在高中的篮球队队长。二月里一个周六的晚上,两人所共同表现出的勇气、体育精神以及对彼此的尊重,让他俩的形象永远紧紧相连,铭刻在了现场每一位观众的心中。

2　这次比赛是达利斯率领的来自伊利诺斯小镇的篮球队对抗约翰率领的来自威斯康星这个大城市的篮球队——这是一场差点儿就没打成的比赛。那非凡的一刻就发生在这

cervical cancer. Her death was sudden and devastating to all who knew her, and John's coach wanted to cancel the game. But John insisted that the game should be played, and so with heavy hearts his teammates prepared to honor their captain's wishes and to play—and hopefully win—without him. What they weren't prepared for was John's appearance in the gym mid-way through the first half.

3 As soon as he saw him, John's coach called a time out, and players and fans surrounded the grieving young man to offer love and support. The coach asked him if he wanted to sit on the bench with the team.

4 "No," John said. "I want to play."

5 Of course his team was thrilled to have him. But because John wasn't on the pre-game roster, putting him in the game at that point would result in a technical foul and two free throws for the opposing team. John's coach was OK with that. He could see that this was the teenager's way of coping with his loss—the points didn't matter.

6 The opposing team understood the

场比赛中。开赛前的几个小时，约翰的妈妈在与子宫癌的5年抗争中败下阵来。她的突然辞世对一个认识她的人来说，都是一个沉重的打击。约翰的教练打算取消这场比赛，但约翰坚持要按原计划比赛。出于对队长意愿的尊重，队友们怀着沉重的心情准备上场——希望在队长缺席的情况下还能拿下这场比赛。出乎他们的意料，上半场进行到一半的时候，约翰就出现在了体育馆里。

3 一见到约翰，教练马上就要求暂停。队友和球迷们纷纷包围住这位经受丧亲之痛的年轻人，给予其安慰和支持。教练问约翰是否想和队友们一起坐在长凳上。

4 "不，"约翰说道，"我要上场比赛。"

5 他要上场比赛，这当然令他的队友们都兴奋不已。但因为约翰的名字不在赛前登记的运动员名册上，若他此时上场，就会造成该队技术犯规，对方球队会获得两个罚球机会。约翰的教练对此并没有意见。他看得出，约翰这个青年是想借此缓解其丧亲之痛——比分并不重要。

6 对方球队也理解此时

142

situation and told the referees to let John play and to forget the technical foul. The referees argued that a rule is a rule, and the free throws would have to be taken before the game could proceed.

7　For possibly the first time in basketball history, officials had to force a team to accept and take the technical free throws. As team captain, Darius volunteered to take the shots. One would have expected he was looking for an opportunity to keep his team close in a hard-fought game against a big city school. Or one could even assume he wanted a chance to add a couple of points to his personal statistics.

8　In either case, one would be wrong.

9　Darius took the ball from the official, looked at the basket, and calmly shot the ball.

10　Now, basketball purists know that the free throw line is 15 feet from the basket. Darius's first shot only traveled about four feet. His second shot only traveled two.

11　Immediately John and his teammates understood what Darius was doing. They stood and applauded the gesture of sportsmanship as Darius made

的状况。他们对裁判表示，让约翰上场，不用判对方球队技术犯规。但裁判回答，必须严格执行比赛规则，得先罚球再继续进行比赛。

7　或许在篮球史上，由裁判强制一个球队接受因对方技术犯规而获得的罚球，这还是头一次。作为队长，达利斯主动出来投射罚球。有人可能会以为，与来自大城市一所高中的篮球队苦战到了这刻，达利斯想借此凝聚全队士气，又或者想借此在个人得分上添上两分。

8　无论哪一种想法，都错了。

9　达利斯从裁判手中接过球，看着篮球筐，平静地射球。

10　在场所有熟知篮球比赛规则的人都知道，罚球线距离篮板 15 英尺（约 4.57 米），可达利斯的第一个罚球却只投出了 4 英尺（约 1.22 米），而第二个罚球也只投出 2 英尺（约 0.61 米）。

11　约翰特尔和他的队友们立刻明白了达利斯的用意。当达利斯走回场外长凳时，约翰特尔和他的球友们都站了起

his way back to his bench. So did all of the big city fans.

12 "I did it for the guy who lost his Mom," Darius told the Milwaukee Journal Sentinel after the game. "It was the right thing to do."

13 For those who are concerned about such things, John's team rode the emotion of the night to a 15-point victory. But as the two teams met after the game for pizza and sodas, nobody on either side was too concerned with wins or losses or personal stats.

14 "This is something our kids will hold for a lifetime," Darius's coach said. "They may not remember our record 20 years from now, but they will remember what happened in that gym that night."

来，为达利斯展现的运动精神鼓掌喝彩。而大城市篮球队的球迷亦掌声不断。

12 赛后，达利斯对《密尔沃基哨兵报》表示："我之所以这么做，是为了那个刚失去母亲的球员，就该这样做。"

13 那晚，约翰特尔所率领的篮球队没有辜负关注他们球队的人的期望，他们以领先15分的优势取得了胜利。但赛后，两队的队员碰头一起去吃比萨饼喝汽水的时候，双方都没太在意比赛输赢或是个人得分情况。

14 "我们的孩子将会终生铭记那一刻，"达利斯的教练说道，"20年后，他们或许不会记得这场比赛的结果，但却一定会记得那一晚在体育馆里发生的一切。"

阅读无障碍

respective[rɪ'spektɪv] adj. 分别的，各自的

mutual['mju:tʃuəl] adj. 共同的；相互的，彼此

sportsmanship['spɔːtsmənʃɪp] n. 运动员精神，运动道德

cervical['sɜːvɪk(ə)l] adj. 子宫颈的

devastating['devəsteitiŋ] adj. 毁灭性的

gym[dʒɪm] n. 体育馆

grieve[gri:v] v. 悲痛，哀悼

thrilled[θrɪld] adj. 非常兴奋的；极为激动的

roster['rɒstə] n. 球员名单，花名册

foul[faʊl] *n.* 犯规

opposing[əˈpəʊzɪŋ] *adj.* 反对的；相
　对的；

cope[kəʊp] *v.* 处理；对付

referee[refəˈriː] *n.* 裁判员

free throw 罚球

proceed[prəˈsiːd] *v.* 开始；继续进行

hard-fought[hɑːdˈfɔːt] *adj.* 激烈的；
　努力争取来的

assume[əˈsjuːm] *v.* 假设

statistics[stəˈtɪstɪks] *n.* 统计

applaud[əˈplɔːd] *v.* 喝彩；鼓掌欢迎

victory[ˈvɪkt(ə)rɪ] *n.* 胜利；成功

极品佳句背诵

1. But on one Saturday night in February, they were forever linked in the minds of all who were present for mutual act of courage, sportsmanship, and respect.

   二月里一个周六的晚上，两人所共同表现出的勇气、体育精神以及对彼此的尊重，让他俩的形象永远紧紧相连，铭刻在了现场每一位观众的心中。

2. As soon as he saw him, John's coach called a time out, and players and fans surrounded the grieving young man to offer love and support.

   一见到约翰，教练马上就要求暂停。队友和球迷们纷纷包围着这位承受着丧亲之痛的年轻人，给予其安慰和支持。

3. They may not remember our record 20 years from now, but they will remember what happened in that gym that night.

   20年后，他们或许不会记得这场比赛的结果，但却一定会记得那一晚在体育馆里发生的一切。

The Value of Friendship
友谊的价值

带着问题去阅读

1. 该怎样选择朋友？
2. 人们该如何经营一份友谊？
3. 知心好友会因分开而陌生吗？

美文欣赏

译文

1 Friendship is both a source of pleasure and a component of good health. People who have close friends naturally enjoy their company. Of equal importance are the concrete emotional benefits they derive. When something sensational happens to us, sharing the happiness of the occasion with friends intensifies our joy. Conversely, in times of trouble and tension, when our spirits are low, unburdening our worries and fear to compassionate friends alleviates the stress. Moreover, we may even get some practical suggestions for solving a particular problem.

1 友谊既是快乐的源泉，又是保持健康的重要因素。有挚友的人自然可以享受朋友的陪伴，同样重要的是他们在精神上可以得到快乐。遇到高兴的事情时，与朋友分享会更加开心。反之，在不如意时，情绪低落，向富有同情心的朋友倾诉衷肠，会减轻痛苦。此外，我们甚至还可以得到一些实际的建议去解决一个特殊的问题。

2 From time to time, we are insensitive and behave in a way that hurt someone's feelings. Afterward, when we feel guilty and down in the dumps, friends can reassure us. This positive interaction is therapeutic, and much less expensive than visits to a psychologist.

3 Throughout life, we rely on small groups of people for love, admiration, respect, moral support, and help. Almost everyone has a "network" of friends; co-workers, neighbors, and schoolmates. While both men and women have such friends, evidence is accumulating that indicates men rarely make close friends. Men are sociable and frequently have numerous business acquaintances, golf buddies, and so on. However, friendship does not merely involve a sharing of activities; it is a sharing of self on a very personal level. Customarily, men have shied away from close relationships in which they confide in others. By bottling up their emotions, men deprive themselves of a healthy outlet for their negative feelings.

4 Because friendships enhance our lives, it is important to cultivate them. Unfortunately, it is somewhat difficult to make long-lasting close friends. People are mobile and mobility puts a strain on friendships. Long distances between

2 有时我们感觉迟钝，甚至行为中不知不觉伤害了他人的感情。事后我们感到愧疚和沮丧，这时朋友会安慰我们。这种积极的双向行为犹如一剂良药，远远比求助于心理学家合算。

3 我们在一生中都有赖于一些小团体来获得友爱，赏识，尊重，道义上的支持和帮助。几乎人人都有一个"友谊网"：同事，邻居和同学。尽管男人和女人都有这样一些朋友，但越来越多的迹象表明，男人不容易交上挚友。男人喜欢社交，结识很多生意上的朋友，高尔夫球友等。然而，友谊不仅包括参与活动，也包括在纯粹私人的范围内分享对方的一切。在一般情况下，男人总是避开那种可以向对方交心的亲密关系。男人因为掩盖自己的情感而丧失了抒发消极情绪的健康途径。

4 正因为友谊可以提高我们的生活质量，所以我们应该用心经营它。遗憾的是，要结交经得起时间考验的挚友尤其困难。人免不了走南闯北，这种变化，时刻考验着友情。

friends discourage intimacy, long distance telephone conversations are costly, and letter writing is not a deeply ingrained habit. Divorce is also destructive to friendship. In many cases, when divorce occurs, friendships disintegrate because couples usually prefer to associate with other couples.

5 People choose some friends because they are fun to be with, they "make things happen". Likewise, common interests appear to be a significant factor in selecting friends. Families with children, for instance, tend to gravitate toward families with Children. It is normal to befriend people who have similar lifestyles, and organizations such as Parents without Partners have appeared on the scene as a natural outgrowth of this tendency. These groups provide an opportunity to socialize, make new acquaintances and friends, obtain helpful advice in adapting smoothly to a new lifestyle. Other groups focus on specific interest such as camping or politics. It is perfectly acceptable to select friends for special qualities as long as there is a balanced giving and taking that is mutually satisfying.

6 Very close and trusted friends share confidences candidly. They feel secure that they will not be ridiculed or derided, and their confidences will be honored.

相隔两地不利于保持亲密的友谊。长途电话花费太大，至于写信，很难长期坚持下去。离婚也会毁灭友情，因为大多数情况下，夫妻一旦分手，友谊便随之土崩瓦解，因为已婚夫妇通常更愿意与其他夫妻交往。

5 人们选择一些朋友，是因为和他们在一起很开心。朋友使你的生活生机勃勃。同样，共同的兴趣是择友的一个重要因素。例如，有孩子的家庭之间容易相互吸引。生活方式相似的人互相交友也是正常的。像"离异父母协会"这样的组织的出现，也正是这种趋势的必然结果。这类组织给人提供参加社交的机会，结识新的朋友，给予有助于顺利适应新生活的好建议。还有类团体关注特定的爱好，比方说野营和政治。选择与有特性的人交友，这是无可厚非的，只要给予与索取保持平衡，双方都会感到满足。

6 亲密而相互信任的朋友，他们彼此坦诚相待。他们不会互相攻击和嘲笑，因而心里踏实自在。他们之间的这种

Betraying a trust is a very quick and painful way to terminate a friendship.

7　As friendships solidify, ties strengthen. Intimate relationships enrich people's lives. Some components of a thriving friendship are honesty, naturalness, and some common interests.

8　Circumstances and people are constantly changing. Some friendships last "forever"; others do not. Nevertheless, friendship is an essential ingredient in the making of a healthful, rewarding life.

信任也会受到尊重。背信弃义则会迅速而痛苦地断送友谊。

7　随着友谊日益巩固，友谊的纽带也会更加坚固。亲密的友谊会使人的生活丰富多彩。确保友谊之花兴盛不败的诸要素是：诚实，质朴，体谅和某些共同兴趣。

8　环境和人都处于不断变化和发展中。有的友谊天长地久，有的昙花一现。然而，友谊的确是使人健康且过得有意义所不可缺少的组成部分。

阅读无障碍

source [sɔːs] *n.* 来源

naturally [ˈnætʃ(ə)rəlɪ] *adv.* 自然地

company [ˈkʌmp(ə)nɪ] *n.* 陪伴

concrete [ˈkɒnkriːt] *adj.* 具体的

derive [dɪˈraɪv] *v.* 得到

conversely [ˈkɒnvɜːslɪ] *adv.* 相反地

tension [ˈtenʃən] *n.* 紧张（状态）

compassionate [kəmˈpæʃ(ə)nət] *adj.* 富于同情心的

therapeutic [ˌθerəˈpjuːtɪk] *adj.* 有益身心的

psychologist [saɪˈkɒlədʒɪst] *n.* 心理学者

evidence [ˈevɪd(ə)ns] *n.* 迹象

buddy [ˈbʌdɪ] *n.* 伙伴

customarily [ˈkʌstəm(ə)rɪlɪ] *adv.* 通常

outlet [ˈaʊtlet] *n.* 出口

destructive [dɪˈstrʌktɪv] *adj.* 破坏的

likewise [ˈlaɪkwaɪz] *adv.* 同样地

obtain [əbˈteɪn] *v.* 获得

mutually [ˈmjuːtʃʊəlɪ] *adv.* 互相地

solidify [səˈlɪdɪfaɪ] *v.* 巩固

rewarding [rɪˈwɔːdɪŋ] *adj.* 有益的，有所得的

极品佳句背诵

1. Friendship is both a source of pleasure and a component of good health.

   友谊既是快乐的源泉，又是保持健康的重要因素。

2. Because friendships enhance our lives, it is important to cultivate them. Unfortunately, it is somewhat difficult to make long-lasting close friends.

   正因为友谊可以提高我们的生活质量，所以我们应该用心经营它。遗憾的是，要结交经得起时间考验的挚友尤其困难。

3. As friendships solidify, ties strengthen. Intimate relationships enrich people's lives. Some components of a thriving friendship are honesty, naturalness, and some common interests.

   亲密而相互信任的朋友，他们彼此坦诚相待。他们不会互相攻击和嘲笑，因而心里踏实自在。他们之间的这种信任也会受到旁人的尊重。背信弃义则会迅速而痛苦地断送友谊。

Support
支持

带着问题去阅读

1. 当朋友需要帮助时，你会伸出援手吗？
2. 你如何看待乐于助人？
3. 当你悲伤时，谁在陪伴你？

美文欣赏

译文

1 "There are two ways of spreading light: to be the candle or the mirror that reflect it."

2 —Wharton

3 You support someone when you willingly step forward to help him through a challenging time. Yet the great irony is that when you support others, you are also, in fact, supporting yourself. When you withhold support from others, it is usually an indicator that you are also withholding support from yourself.

4 We are most often called upon to support others in friendship. One of my

1 "传播光明的方法有两种：要么做一根蜡烛，要么做一面镜子去反射蜡烛的光明。"

2 ——沃顿

3 如果你能自愿上前帮助他人渡过难关，你这就是在支持他。但是奇异之处在于，当你在支持他人时，你其实就是在支持自己。相反，如果你拒绝给予他人支持，这通常表明你也在拒绝帮助自己。

4 我们常常被召唤去支持朋友。最近，我的一位熟人

acquaintances, Donna, told me a story recently that clearly illustrates the magic of support and its potential as an emotional mirror.

5 Several years ago, Donna had been feeling very depressed. She had just broken up with her boyfriend of two years, and she was having a very difficult time accepting the loss. She had been laid up with a knee injury for several days, and the time alone at home certainly was not helping. Her misery was only compounded by her frustration at herself for not being able to pull it together and stop crying all the time.

6 Early one morning, Donna received a phone call with some terrible news: her best friend's brother had been killed in a car accident. Donna had known this friend, Mary, and her brother nearly her entire life, and the news was devastating. However, Donna quickly pulled herself together, got in the car, and drove to her friend's house to be there with her.

7 Over the course of the next few days, amid the haze of the funeral and hundreds of visitors, Donna was 100 percent present for Mary. She held her close while she cried endless tears, sat by her side as the waves of grief washed over her friend, and slept on the floor next to Mary's bed to make sure she did not wake up alone in the middle of the night. During

唐娜向我讲述了一个故事，这正好清楚地阐述了支持的神奇魔力以及它作为情感之镜的潜在作用。

5 几年前，唐娜曾一度萎靡不振，因为她与交往了两年的男友刚刚分手，非常难以接受这种失去的现实。接着她又因为膝盖受伤卧床数天。这样独自在家的日子，肯定是难捱的。她为自己未能自控、成天哭个不停而沮丧、懊恼，这加剧了她的痛苦。

6 一天清晨，唐娜接到一个电话，得知了一个噩耗：她最要好的朋友的弟弟在车祸中丧生。唐娜和这位朋友玛丽和她的弟弟有着多年的交情，可以算是一辈子的朋友，这一消息令唐娜悲痛万分。但是她很快控制住自己，立刻开车赶到了玛丽家里陪伴她。

7 在以后的几天里，在忙着张罗葬礼、接待众多吊唁者的同时，唐娜一刻不离的陪在玛丽身边。当玛丽失声痛哭不能自已时，唐娜紧紧的搂着她；当玛丽悲伤过度，痛不欲生时，唐娜紧伴其左右；夜晚，为了让玛丽不会在黑夜里独自惊醒，唐娜就睡在玛丽

that time she hardly felt any pain in her knee at all and none of the depression she had been experiencing.

8 Several weeks later, when life began to return to normal, Donna realized that the level of support she had given Mary far exceeded any support she had offered herself during her dark time. She was able to use the support she had given her friend as a mirror for the support she had been withholding from herself. She realized that her own tears required as much attention and nurturing from her as anyone else's, and that if she could give it to another, she must be able to also give it to herself.

9 So, when you find yourself unable to support someone else, look within and see if perhaps there is something within yourself that you are not supporting. Conversely, when you give complete support to others, it will mirror those places within you that require the same level of attention.

的床边的地板上。在那段时间里，唐娜几乎忘记了她膝盖的伤痛以及自己曾经经历的消沉。

8 几星期后，生活恢复了正常。这时唐娜意识到自己给予了玛丽极大的支持，远远超出自己失意的时候给予自己的支持。给朋友的支持犹如一面镜子，使唐娜认识到自己吝于支持自我。她认识到自己的眼泪与别人的一样，也需要得到她的关心和爱护；而且如果她可以关心、爱护别人，她也必定能够关心、爱护自己。

9 所以，当你发现自己无法给予他人支持、安慰时，你应该扪心自问，看看自己是否在某些地方，未自我支持。反过来，如果你能够不遗余力地去支持他人，你也会因此发现自己也有某些值得同样关心、爱护的脆弱之处。

阅读无障碍

spread[spred] v. 传播
candle['kændl] n. 蜡烛
reflect[rɪ'flekt] v. 反射，反映，
irony['aɪrəni] n. 反话，讽刺，

withhold[wɪð'həʊld] v. 拒给
indicator['ɪndɪkeɪtə] n. 指示，信号
acquaintance[ə'kweɪnt(ə)ns] n. 相识的人，熟人

illustrate['ɪləstreɪt] v. 举例说明

potential [pə'tenʃəl] n. 潜能，潜力

injury['ɪn(d)ʒ(ə)rɪ] n. 伤害

misery['mɪz(ə)rɪ] n. 悲惨，不幸，穷困

compound[kəm'paʊnd] v. 使复杂化，加重

frustration[frʌ'streɪʃn] n. 挫败，挫折，受挫

devastating['devəsteɪtɪŋ] adj. 令人震惊的，毁灭性的

haze[heɪz] n. 混乱，迷糊

funeral['fjuːn(ə)r(ə)l] n. 丧葬，葬礼

grief[griːf] n. 悲痛，伤心事，不幸，忧伤

exceed[ɪk'siːd] v. 超越，胜过

nurture['nɜːtʃə] v. 养育，给与营养物，教养

conversely['kɒnvɜːslɪ] adv. 相反地

极品佳句背诵

1. There are two ways of spreading light: to be the candle or the mirror that reflect it.
   传播光明的方法有两种：要么做一根蜡烛，要么做一面镜子去反射蜡烛的光明。

2. You support someone when you willingly step forward to help him through a challenging time.
   如果你能自愿上前帮助他人渡过难关，你这就是在支持他。

3. Conversely, when you give complete support to others, it will mirror those places within you that require the same level of attention.
   反过来，如果你能够不遗余力地去支持他人，你也会因此发现自己也有某些需要同等关心、爱护的脆弱之处。

To Be a Better Friend
做个更好的朋友

带着问题去阅读

1. 你有多久没给好朋友打电话了？
2. 你有一份历经岁月的友谊吗？
3. 你是如何同朋友相处的？

美文欣赏

1　Back when we were kids, the hours spent with friends were too numerous to count. There were marathon telephone conversations, all-night studying and giggling sessions. Even after boyfriends entered the picture, our best friends remained irreplaceable. And time was the means by which we nurtured those friendships. Now as adult women we never seem to have enough time for anything. Husbands, kids, careers and avocations--all require attention; too often, making time for our friends comes last on the list of priorities. And yet, ironically, we need

译文

1　在孩提时代，我们和朋友呆在一起的时间不计其数：马拉松式的电话交谈，整夜在一起学习和玩耍。即使在交了男朋友之后，我们最好的朋友的位置依然不可取代。正是相互在一起的时间培养了我们之间的友谊。女孩长成为女人后，时间似乎总不够用。丈夫、孩子、事业和业余爱好都要投入精力，因而很多时候朋友反而是最不重要的了。然而有讽刺意义的是，我们在成年时和儿童时代一样需要友谊。

our friends as much as ever in **adulthood**. A friendship network is absolutely crucial for our well-being as adults. We have to do the hard work of building and sustaining the network. Here are some important ways for accomplishing this.

2　Let go of your less central friendships. Many of our friendships were never meant to last a lifetime. It's natural that some friendships have time limits. Furthermore, now everyone has a busy social **calendar**, so pull back from some people that you don't really want to draw close to and give the most promising friendship a fair chance to grow.

3　Be willing to "drop everything" when you're truly needed. You may get a call from a friend who is really depressed over a certain problem when you are just sitting down to enjoy a **romantic** dinner with your husband. This is just one of those instances when a friend's needs mattered more. Sometimes, because of our unbreakable commitments or other **circumstances**, we simply can't give a needy friend the time we'd like. If you can't be there at that given moment, say something like, "I wish I could be with you—I can hear that you're in pain. May I call you tomorrow?" Be sure your friend knows she's cared about.

4　Take advantage of the mails . Nearly

一个由友谊编织成的网络对我们成年人的幸福至关重要。我们必须努力去建立和保持这个网络。以下便是达到这个目的的几个重要方法。

2　放弃无足轻重的友情，许多友情本来就不能终生维持。有的友情随时光的流逝而消失是情理之中的事。此外，现在每个人都那么忙碌，所以，放弃那些你并不想真正接近的人，以更多的时间去培养那些最重要的友情。

3　必要的时候愿意"放下手头的一切事情"。当你刚刚坐下想和丈夫享受一顿浪漫的晚餐时，你的朋友却突然打来电话，她正为某一问题沮丧不已。在一些情况下，朋友之需显得更为重要，这只是其中的一个例子。有时候，因为我们有事无法分身或别的原因，我们虽然想助朋友一臂之力，但苦于没有时间。如果你不能及时给朋友以帮助，那么不妨对她说，"我真希望能陪陪你——我能听出来你很痛苦。我明天给你打电话行吗？"一定要让你的朋友知道你对她的关心。

4　利用鸿雁传书。几乎

all of us have pals living far away--friends we miss very much. Given the limited time available for visits and the high price of phone calls, writing is a fine way to keep in touch—and makes both sender and receiver feel good. Besides, letters, cards and postcards have the virtue of being tangible--friends can keep them and reread them for years to come.

5　Risk expressing negative feelings when time together is tough to come by, it's natural to want the mood during that time to be upbeat. And many people fear that others will think less of you if you express the negative feelings like anger and hurt. Remember honesty is the key to keeping a friendship real. Sharing your pain will actually deepen a friendship.

6　Don't make your friends' problems your own. Sharing your friend's grief is the way you show deep friendship. But taking on your friend's pain doesn't make that pain go away. There's a big difference between empathy or recognizing a friend's pain, and overidentification, which makes the sufferer feel even weaker "I must be in worse pain than I even thought, because the person I'm confiding in is suffering so much!" Remember troubled people just need their friends to stay grounded in their own feelings.

7　Never underestimate the value of

我们所有人都有远在异地让我们非常想念的朋友。考虑到抽不出时间去走访，电话费又那么贵，那么写信是保持联系的好方法。这种方式让写信人和收信人都感到很高兴。另外，信件、卡片和明信片都是看得见摸得着的，朋友可以将其保存，以后还可以再读。

5　敢于袒露心中的抑郁，大家聚在一起不容易时，自然希望彼此都有个好心情。好多人都担心，把自己的心事——愤怒和受伤害等吐露出来会让人家瞧不起。记住以诚相待是保持友谊真实的关键。让朋友分担你的痛苦反倒会加深你们的友谊。

6　不要把朋友的问题变成自己的问题。分担朋友的痛苦是表露友情的一种方式。但是承受朋友的痛苦并不能消除其痛苦。心灵相通（即理解朋友的痛苦）与过分卷入朋友的痛苦有很大区别。过分卷入使对方感到自己更脆弱—"我的痛苦肯定比我感受到的更可怕，因为听我倾诉的朋友都如此难过。"记住，处于逆境中的人需要的只是朋友的理解和支持。

7　切勿低估忠诚的价值。

loyalty. Loyalty has always been rated as one of the most desired qualities in friends. True loyalty can be a fairly subtle thing. Some people feel it means that, no matter what, your friend will always take your side. But real loyalty is being accepting the person, not necessarily of certain actions your friend might take.

8 Give the gift of time as often as time allows. Time is what we don't have nearly enough of—and yet, armed with a little ingenuity, we can make it to give it to our friends. The trick is remembering that a little is better than none and that you can do two things at once. For instance, if you both go for a weekly aerobics, go on the same day. If you both want to go on vacation, schedule the same destination.

忠诚一直被列为朋友间最需要的品质之一。真正的忠诚是件相当微妙的事情。有人认为忠诚意味着不管你做什么，你的朋友总是站在你这一边。但真正的忠诚指的是接受其人，而不一定赞同其所有的行为。

8 巧妙利用时间，增进友谊。时间似乎总是不够用，但稍微变通一下便可以为朋友挤出时间来。重要的是要记住时间即使少一点也总比没有好，而且有时你可以一箭双雕。比如说，如果你和某位朋友每个星期都要去做一次健美操，那么就安排同一天去。如果双方都要去度假，那么不妨选择同一个去处。

阅读无障碍

numerous[ˈnjuːmərəs] *adj.* 众多的，许多的，无数的

marathon[ˈmærəθən] *n.* 马拉松赛跑，耐力的考验

giggle[ˈɡɪɡl] *v.* 哈哈地笑

irreplaceable[ˌɪrɪˈpleɪsəb(ə)l] *adj.* 不能调换的，不能代替的

avocation[ˌævəˈkeɪʃ(ə)n] *n.* 副业，业余爱好

priority[praɪˈɒrɪtɪ] *n.* 先，前，优先，优先权

ironically[aɪˈrɒnɪklɪ] *adv.* 说反话地，讽刺地

adulthood[əˈdʌlthud] *n.* 成人期

calendar[ˈkælɪndə] *n.* 日历，历法

romantic[rə(ʊ)ˈmæntɪk] *adj.* 浪漫的

circumstance[ˈsɜːkəmst(ə)ns] *n.* 环境，详情，境况

tangible['tæn(d)ʒɪb(ə)l] *adj.* 实体的，
　有形的

negative['neɡətɪv] *adj.* 否定的，消
　极的

upbeat['ʌpbiːt] *adj.* 快乐的，乐观的

empathy['empəθɪ] *n.* 同感，感情移
　入

confide[kən'faɪd] *v.* 倾诉

underestimate[ʌndə'estɪmeɪt] *v.* 低
　估，看轻

loyalty['lɔɪəltɪ] *n.* 忠诚，忠实

ingenuity[ɪndʒɪ'njuːɪtɪ] *n.* 机灵，独
　创性

aerobics [eə'rəʊbɪks] *n.* 健美操

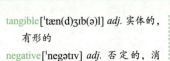 极品佳句背诵

1. Let go of your less central friendships. Many of our friendships were never meant to last a lifetime. It's natural that some friendships have time limits.
   舍得放弃无足轻重的友情，许多友情本来就不能终生维持。有的友情随时光的流逝而消失是情理之中的事。

2. Given the limited time available for visits and the high price of phone calls, writing is a fine way to keep in touch--and makes both sender and receiver feel good.
   考虑到抽不出时间去走访，电话费又那么贵，那么写信是保持联系的好方法。这种方式让写信人和收信人都感到很高兴。

3. Never underestimate the value of loyalty. Loyalty has always been rated as one of the most desired qualities in friends.
   切勿低估忠诚的价值。忠诚一直被列为朋友间最需要的品质之一。真正的忠诚是件相当微妙的事情。

Chapter 3

爱是永恒的主题

A Walk in the Woods
林中漫步

带着问题去阅读

1. 真正的爱情是什么？
2. 时间真的是爱情的敌人吗？
3. 最能打动人心的真情到底是什么呢？

1 I was puzzled! Why was this old woman making such a fuss about an old copse which was of no use to anybody? She had written letters to the local paper, even to a national, protesting about a projected by-pass to her village, and, looking at a map, the route was nowhere near where she lived and it wasn't as if the area was attractive. I was more than puzzled, I was intrigued.

2 The enquiry into the route of the new by-pass to the village was due to take place shortly, and I wanted to know what

1 我实在不明白！为什么这个年老妇人会对一片毫无用处的老灌木林如此紧张呢？她给当地报纸写了信，甚至给全国性的报纸也写了信，对拟将在她们村子里修建小路的方案表示抗议。但从地图上看，这条拟建的小路离她家并不近，那一带也谈不上风景优美。这不仅使我感到更加不解，还激起了我的好奇心。

2 很快就要对新修小路进行预先调查了，我想了解一下她反对的原因。于是我敲响

162

it was that motivated her. So it was that I found myself knocking on a cottage door, being received by Mary Smith and then being taken for a walk to the woods.

3 "I've always loved this place," she said, "it has a lot of memories for me, and for others. We all used it. They called it 'Lovers lane'. It's not much of a lane, and it doesn't go anywhere important, but that's why we all came here. To be away from people, to be by ourselves," she added.

4 It was indeed pleasant that day and the songs of many birds could be heard. Squirrels gazed from the branches, quite bold in their movements, obviously few people passed this way and they had nothing to fear. I could imagine the noise of vehicles passing through these peaceful woods when the by-pass was built, so I felt that she probably had something there but as I hold strong opinions about the needs of the community over-riding the opinions of private individuals, I said nothing. The village was quite a dangerous place because of the traffic especially for old people and children, their safety was more important to me than an old woman's whims.

5 "Take this tree," she said pausing after a short while. "To you it is just that,

了小屋的门，一位叫玛丽·史密斯的老妇接待了我，然后她带我到林中散步。

3 "我一直深爱这个地方，"她说，"这里珍藏了我和其他许多人的回忆。我们都曾在这个地方呆过。人们称它为'情人路'。实际上它算不上一条路，也不通往什么重要的地方，但这正是我们来这里的原因。远离他人，只有我们自己。"她补充说道。

4 那天林间实在迷人，小鸟唱着歌，松鼠在树枝间张望，自由自在的活动着，显然这里人迹罕至，它们一点都不害怕。我能想象得出，在小路修好后，汽车通过这片宁静的树林将会是怎样的喧闹，因此我猜这对她来说可能意味着些什么。但我坚持认为社区的需要高于个人的意见，所以我没说什么。村里目前的交通，特别是对于老人和小孩来说，尤其危险，所以对我来说他们的安全比这个老妇的怪念头更重要。

5 "拿这棵树来说吧，"她停了一会儿说，"对你来说

a tree. Not unlike many others here." She gently touched the bark. "Look here, under this branch, what can you see?"

6 "It looks as if someone has done a bit of carving with a knife," I said after a cursory inspection.

7 "Yes, that's what it is!" she said softly. "There are letters and a lover's heart."

8 I looked again, this time more carefully. The heart was still there and there was a suggestion of an arrow through it. The letters on one side were indistinct, but on the other an 'R' was clearly visible with what looked like an 'I' after it. "Some budding romance?" I asked, "did you know who they were?"

9 "Oh yes, I knew them", said Mary Smith, "it says RH loves MS."

10 I realized that I could be getting out of my depth, and longed to be in my office, away from here and this old lady, snug, and with a mug of tea in my hand.

11 She went on, "He had a penknife with a spike for getting stones from a horse's hoof, and I helped him to carve my initials. We were very much in love, but

它只是一棵普通的树，与这里其它的树没什么区别。"她轻轻地摸着这棵树的树干说："看这，在这个树枝下面，你看见了什么？"

6 "好像有人用小刀在这里刻过什么东西。"我略略看了一眼后说。

7 "是的，是有刻过！"她轻轻地说，"是一些字母和一颗爱人的心。"

8 我又看了一下，这回格外认真了些。刻的那颗心还在那，此外还依稀可以看见支箭穿心而过。心一边的字母已无法辨认了，但在另一边，字母"R"清晰可见，后面还有个像"I"的字母。"初恋罗曼史？"我问道，"你知道他们是谁吗？"

9 "嗯，我知道。"玛丽·史密斯说，"写的是'RH爱MS'。"

10 我意识到我可能涉入太深了，真希望自己身在办公室，远离这个地方和这位老妇，手里还端着杯茶，舒舒服服地享受着一切。

11 她继续讲着，"他拿着一把袖珍折刀，折刀上嵌有长钉，那种长钉可以用来挖出夹在马蹄上的碎石块，我们一

he was going away, and could not tell me what he was involved in the army. I had guessed of course. It was the last evening we ever spent together, because he went away the next day, back to his Unit."

12 Mary Smith was quiet for a while, then she sobbed. "His mother showed me the telegram. Sergeant R Holmes ... Killed in action in the invasion of France."

13 'I had hoped that you and Robin would one day get married,' she said, 'He was my only child, and I would have loved to be a Granny, they would have been such lovely babies' - she was like that!

14 "Two years later she too was dead. Pneumonia, following 'a chill on the chest' was what the doctor said, but I think it was an old fashioned broken heart. A child would have helped both of us."

15 There was a further pause. Mary Smith gently caressed the wounded tree, just as she would have caressed him. "And now they want to take our tree away from me." Another quiet sob, then she turned to me. "I was young and pretty then, I could have had anybody, I wasn't always the old woman you see here now. I had everything I wanted in life, a lovely man, health and a future to look forwards to."

起刻了我名字的第一个字母。我们深爱着彼此，但他却要离开了，而且不知道他将在军队里干什么。当然我也曾猜想过。那是我们在一起度过的最后一个夜晚，因为他第二天就回部队去了。

12 玛丽·史密斯停了一会儿，接着抽泣起来。"他母亲给我看了那封电报。'R·荷尔姆斯军士…在解放法国的战役中牺牲。"

13 "我本来希望将来你会和罗宾结婚。"她母亲说，"我只有他一个孩子，我本希望能做祖母，有非常可爱的小宝宝。"——她真是那么说的！

14 "两年后她也去世了。医生说是'肺炎，胸部伤寒引起的'，但我认为这是典型的伤心过度。如果有个孩子那我们俩就都不会这样了。"

15 玛丽·史密斯又停了会儿没说话。她轻柔地抚摸着那棵被刻过的树，就仿佛她曾经抚摸他一样。"现在他们却想把我们的树夺走。"她又轻轻地抽噎了一下，然后她转过身来对着我。"当时我年轻漂亮，我嫁给谁都可以，我当时可不是你看到的这副衰老的样子。我拥有生命里所想要的一

16 She paused again and looked around. The breeze gently moved through the leaves with a sighing sound. "There were others, of course, but not a patch on my Robin!" she said strongly. "And now I have nothing - except the memories this tree holds. If only I could get my hands on that awful man who writes in the paper about the value of the road they are going to build where we are standing now, I would tell him. Has he never loved, has he never lived, does he not know anything about memories? We were not the only ones, you know, I still meet some who came here as Robin and I did. Yes, I would tell him!"

17 I turned away, sick at heart.

16 她顿了顿，朝四周看了一眼。微风轻轻吹拂着树叶，发出叹息般的沙沙声。"当然，那时还有其他人，但他们连罗宾的一丝一毫都比不上！"她肯定地说。"现在我一无所有——只剩下残留在这棵树上的记忆。那个可恶的家伙竟建议把路修在我们所站的这个地方，我真希望掐死他，我会质问他。难道他从没爱过吗，他活过吗，他从不知道什么叫记忆吗？你知道，不仅仅是我们，现在我仍能看见些男男女女像当年的我和罗宾那样到这儿来。是的，我一定要对他说！"

17 我转过身去，心里感到很难过。

🐱 **阅读无障碍**

puzzle ['pʌzl] v. 困惑
make a fuss about 大惊小怪
copse [kɒps] n. 杂树林
knock on 敲门
squirrel ['skwɪrəl] n. 松鼠
gaze [geɪz] v. 凝视
bold [bəʊld] adj. 大胆的
vehicle ['viːɪkəl] n. 汽车

cursory ['kɜːs(ə)rɪ] adj. 仓促的
suggestion [sə'dʒestʃən] n. 建议
arrow ['ærəʊ] n. 箭
snug [snʌɡ] adj. 温暖舒适的
penknife ['pennaɪf] n. 折叠式小刀
initial [ɪ'nɪʃəl] n. 首字母
unit ['juːnɪt] n. 部队
sob [sɒb] v. 呜咽

telegram ['telɪgræm] *n.* 电报

pneumonia [nju: 'məʊnɪə] *n.* 急性肺炎

sergeant ['sɑ:dʒənt] *n.* 中士

breeze [bri:z] *n.* 微风

极品佳句背诵

1. I was more than puzzled, I was intrigued.
   这不仅使我感到迷惑，还激起了我的好奇心。
2. The enquiry into the route of the new by-pass to the village was due to take place shortly, and I wanted to know what it was that motivated her.
   很快就要对新修小路进行预先调查了，我想了解一下她反对的原因。
3. The village was quite a dangerous place because of the traffic especially for old people and children, their safety was more important to me than an old woman's whims.
   村里目前的交通，特别是对于老人和小孩来说，尤其危险，所以对我来说他们的安全比这个老妇的怪念头更重要。

A Good Heart to Lean On
善心可依

带着问题去阅读

1. 你心中的父爱是什么？
2. 何所谓"善良的心"？
3. 仔细思量一下，你自己履行了为人子的责任了吗？

美文欣赏

译文

1 When I was growing up, I was embarrassed to be seen with my father. He was severely crippled and very short, and when we would walk together, his hand on my arm for balance, people would stare. I would inwardly squirm at the unwanted attention. If he ever noticed or was bothered, he never let on.

2 It was difficult to coordinate our steps — his halting, mine impatient — and because of that, we didn't say much as we went along. But as we started out, he

1 在我成长的过程中，我一直羞于让别人看见我和父亲在一起。我的父亲身材矮小，腿上有严重的残疾。当我们一起走路时，他总是挽着我以保持身体平衡，这时总招来一些异样的目光，令我无地自容。可是如果他注意到了这些，不管他内心多么痛苦，也从不表现出来。

2 走路时，我们的步伐很难协调一致——他的步子慢慢腾腾，我的步子焦燥不安——所以一路上我们都很少交谈。

always said, "You set the pace. I will try to adjust to you."

3　Our usual walk was to or from the subway, which was how he got to work. He went to work sick, and despite nasty weather. He almost never missed a day, and would make it to the office even if others could not. A matter of pride.

4　When snow or ice was on the ground, it was impossible for him to walk, even with help. At such times my sisters or I would pull him through the streets of Brooklyn, NY, on a child's sleigh to the subway entrance. Once there, he would cling to the handrail until he reached the lower steps that the warmer tunnel air kept ice-free. In Manhattan the subway station was the basement of his office building, and he would not have to go outside again until we met him in Brooklyn on his way home.

5　When I think of it now, I marvel at how much courage it must have taken for a grown man to subject himself to such indignity and stress. And at how he did it — without bitterness or complaint.

6　He never talked about himself as an object of pity, nor did he show any envy of the more fortunate or able. What he looked for in others was a "good heart", and if he

但是每次出行前，他总是说，"你走你的，我会跟上你的"。

3　我们常常往返于从家到他上班乘坐地铁的那段路。即使生病他也要上班，更不管天气如何恶劣。他几乎从未误过一天工，即使别人都旷班，他也要设法去上班。这的确是件骄傲的事！

4　每当冰封大地，雪花飘飘的时候，即使有人帮助，他也是举步维艰。每当这时，我或我的姐妹们就用儿童雪橇托着他经过纽约布鲁克林区的街道，一直送到地铁站的入口处。一到那儿，他便握着扶手一直走到底下的台阶，因为地下通道的空气更暖和，使得地面上没有结冰。到了曼哈顿，地铁站就在他办公楼的地下一层，所以我们在布鲁克林接他回家之前他无须再走出楼来。

5　如今每当我想起这些，我惊叹一个成年男人要经受住这种侮辱和压力得需要多么大的勇气啊！叹服他竟然能够做到这一点——没有任何痛苦，没有丝毫抱怨。

6　他从不说自己可怜，也从不嫉妒别人的幸运和能力。他所期望的是人家"善良的心"，当他得到时，人家真

found one, the owner was good enough for him.

7　Now that I am older, I believe that is a proper standard by which to judge people, even though I still don't know precisely what a "good heart" is. But I know the times I don't have one myself.

8　Unable to engage in many activities, my father still tried to participate in some way. When a local sandlot baseball team found itself without a manager, he kept it going. He was a knowledgeable baseball fan and often took me to Ebbets Field to see the Brooklyn Dodgers play. He liked to go to dances and parties, where he could have a good time just sitting and watching.

9　On one memorable occasion a fight broke out at a beach party, with everyone punching and shoving. He wasn't content to sit and watch, but he couldn't stand unaided on the soft sand. In frustration he began to shout, "I'll fight anyone who will tit down with me!"

10　Nobody did. But the next day people kidded him by saying it was the first time any fighter was urged to take a dive even before the bout began.

11　I now know he participated in some things vicariously through me, his only son. When I played ball (poorly), he

7　如今我已经长大成人，我明白了"善良的心"是评价人最合适的标准，尽管我仍不很清楚它确切的涵义，但是我却知道我有缺乏善心的时候。

8　虽然父亲不能参加许多活动，但他仍然想方设法以某种方式参与其中。当一个地方棒球队发现缺少一个领队时，他便作了领队。因为他是个棒球迷，有丰富的棒球知识，他过去常带我去埃比茨棒球场观看布鲁克林的道奇队的比赛。他喜欢参加舞会和晚会，乐意默默地坐在一旁，欣赏着别人的快乐。

9　在一次记忆深刻的海滩晚会上，有人打架，动了拳头，大家相互推推搡搡。他不甘于置身事外，但又无法在松软的沙滩上自己站起来。于是，失望之下，他吼了起来："有哪个人想要和我打一架？"

10　没有人响应。但是第二天，人们都取笑他说比赛还没开始，拳击手就被劝认输，这还是头一次看见。

11　现在我知道一些事情他是通过我—他唯一的儿子来做的。当我打球时（尽管我打

"played" too. When I joined the Navy he "joined" too. And when I came home on leave, he saw to it that I visited his office. Introducing me, he was really saying, "This is my son, but it is also me, and I could have done this, too, if things had been different." Those words were never said aloud.

12 He has been gone many years now, but I think of him often. I wonder if he sensed my reluctance to be seen with him during our walks. If he did, I am sorry I never told him how sorry I was, how unworthy I was, how I regretted it. I think of him when I complain about trifles, when I am *envious* of another's good fortune, when I don't have a "good heart".

13 At such times I put my hand on his arm to regain my balance, and say, "You set the pace, I will try to adjust to you."

得很差)，他也在"打球"。当我参加海军时，他也"参加"。当时我放假回家时，他一定要让我去他的办公室，在介绍我时，他坦坦荡荡地说，"这是我儿子，他完成了我的梦想。假如事情不是这样的话，我也会去参军的。"但他从未大声说过这些话。

12 父亲离开我们已经很多年了，但是我时常想起他。我不知道他是否意识到我曾多么不情愿让人看到和他走在一起。假如他知道这一切，我现在感到很遗憾，因为我从没告诉过他我是多么愧疚、多么不孝、多么悔恨。每当我抱怨一些琐事，妒忌别人的好运时，自己缺乏"善心"时，我就会想起我的父亲。

13 此时，我会挽着他的胳膊保持身体平衡，然后说一句，"你走你的，我会跟上你的。"

阅读无障碍

cripple ['krɪpəl] v. 使残疾
inwardly ['ɪnwədlɪ] adv. 在内心
squirm [skwɜːm] v. 蠕动
let on 泄密

coordinate [kəʊˈɔːdɪneɪt] v.（使）配合
adjust to 调整，使适合于
nasty ['nɑːstɪ] adj. 肮脏的，不愉快的

sleigh [sleɪ] *n.* 雪橇

cling to 抓紧

handrail ['hændreɪl] *n.*（楼梯）扶手

basement ['beɪsmənt] *n.* 地下室

marvel at 诧异

subject...to 使……经历

indignity [ɪn'dɪɡnɪtɪ] *n.* 轻蔑，侮辱

punch [pʌntʃ] *v.*（用拳头）猛砸

shove [ʃʌv] *v.* 推，乱推

frustration [frʌs'treɪʃən] *n.* 失望

take a dive 认输

bout [baʊt] *n.* 拳击比赛

envious ['envɪəs] *adj.* 妒忌的

极品佳句背诵

1. When I think of it now, I marvel at how much courage it must have taken for a grown man to subject himself to such indignity and stress.

   如今每当我想起这些，我惊叹一个成年男人要经受住这种侮辱和压力得需要多么大的勇气啊！

2. He never talked about himself as an object of pity, nor did he show any envy of the more fortunate or able.

   他从不说自己可怜，也从不嫉妒别人的幸运和能力。

3. I think of him when I complain about trifles, when I am envious of another's good fortune, when I don't have a "good heart".

   每当我抱怨一些琐事时，妒忌别人的好运时，自己缺乏"善心"时，我就会想起我的父亲。

The Best Kind of Love
天底下最真挚的爱情

带着问题去阅读

1. 你相信平平凡凡的真爱吗?
2. 在你眼中爱情保鲜的秘诀又是什么呢?
3. 我们应该保持怎样一种恋爱观呢?

美文欣赏

1 I have a friend who is falling in love. She honestly claims the sky is bluer. Mozart moves her to tears. She has lost 15 pounds and looks like a cover girl.

2 "I'm young again!" she shouts exuberantly.

3 As my friend raves on about her new love, I've taken a good look at my old one. My husband of almost 20 years, Scott, has gained 15 pounds. Once a marathon runner, he now runs only down hospital halls. His hairline is receding and his body

译文

1 我有一个朋友正谈着恋爱。在她看来,天空更蓝了,莫扎特也能将人感动落泪;她减肥成功,掉了15磅秤,看上去有点像杂志上的封面女孩。

2 她兴高采烈地大喊:"我更年轻了!"

3 在我的朋友因为她的恋爱而喋喋不休的时候,我开始审视我的那一位,我的丈夫斯科特,我们结婚已经快20年了。他长胖了15磅。他曾经是一名马拉松队员,现在却

shows the signs of long working hours and too many candy bars. Yet he can still give me a certain look across a restaurant table and I want to ask for the check and head home.

4 When my friend asked me "What will make this love last?" I ran through all the obvious reasons: commitment, shared interests, unselfishness, physical attraction, communication. Yet there's more. We still have fun. Spontaneous good times. Yesterday, after slipping the rubber band off the rolled up newspaper, Scott flipped it playfully at me: this led to an all-out war. Last Saturday at the grocery, we split the list and raced each other to see who could make it to the checkout first. Even washing dishes can be a blast. We enjoy simply being together.

5 And there are surprises. One time I came home to find a note on the front door that led me to another note, then another, until I reached the walk-in closet. I opened the door to find Scott holding a "pot of gold" (my cooking kettle) and the "treasure" of a gift package. Sometimes I leave him notes on the mirror and little presents under his pillow.

6 There is sharing. Not only do we

只在医院里跑来跑去。他的发际线已经开始后移，身体也因长时期的工作和太多的甜食而衰退。然而，他依然能从我眼中读出饭桌对面的我的心思，知道我想要付账回家了。

4 当我的朋友问我"什么能使爱情长久？"时，我的脑海中浮现出所有明显的理由：忠诚、共同的爱好、无私、好身材、沟通。当然还有更多的。我们仍然拥有发自内心的快乐时光。昨天，在把捆报纸堆的橡皮圈弄掉后，斯科特嬉戏着把它扔到了我的身上，而这引起了我们之间的"战争"。上周六在杂货店里，我们撕碎了购物单，还比赛着看谁能先跑到收银台。甚至连洗碗都会大斗一番。只要在一起，我们就很开心。

5 我们之间充满惊喜。有一次，我回家时发现前门贴着一张便条，于是顺着它我找到了第二张、第三张……直到我走进了步入式衣橱。我打开门发现斯科特正拿着一个金罐子（我的做饭用的锅）和"财富"礼包。有的时候我也会在镜子上给他留便条，还在他的枕头下藏小礼物。

6 我们乐于分享。我们

share household worries and parental burdens - we also share ideas. Scott came home from a convention last month and presented me with a thick historical novel. But he already read it on the plan, and just wanted to share with me when I finished it.

7　There is forgiveness. When I'm embarrasssingly loud and crazy at parties, Scott forgives me. When he confessed losing some of our savings in the stock market, I gave him a hug and said, "It's okay. It's only money."

8　There is faith. Last Tuesday a friend came over and confessed her fear that her husband is losing his courageous battle with cancer. On Thursday a neighbor called to talk about the frightening effects of Alzheimer's disease on her father-in-law's personality. On Friday a childhood friend called long-distance to tell me her father had died. I hung up the phone and thought, this is too much heartache for one week. Through my tears, as I went out to run some errands, I noticed the boisterous orange blossoms of the gladiolus outside my window. I caught sight of a wedding party emerging from a neighbor's house. The bride, dressed in satin and lace, tossed her bouquet to her cheering friends. That

不仅共同承担家庭的烦恼和抚养孩子的重任，我们也一起交流思想。上个月，斯科特开完会回来，送给我一本厚厚的历史小说。但他已经在飞机上读完了这本小说，因为他想和我分享我的读后感。

7　我们相互原谅。当我在聚会上大声、疯狂的吵闹，令人难堪时，斯科特原谅了我。当他坦白承认用我们的积蓄炒股亏了钱时，我给了他一个拥抱，告诉他，"没关系。我们还可以再赚。"

8　我们都有信念。上周二一个朋友来访时告诉我，她担心丈夫渐渐失去了和癌症对抗的勇气；周四一个邻居打电话时谈到了老年痴呆症对她公公人格上造成的可怕影响；周五发小打长途电话告诉我她父亲去世了。我挂掉电话，想着这一周发生了太多让人心痛的事情。泪眼模糊中，我出了门，准备去干点什么。这时我注意到了窗外的剑兰正茂盛地开着橘黄色的花；我看到了一个邻居家正在举办婚宴，美丽的新娘身着绸缎和蕾丝的婚纱，正把她的捧花抛向高兴的朋友们。那天晚上，我把这些

night, I told my husband about these events. We helped each other acknowledge the cycles of life and that the joys counter the sorrows. It was enough to keep us going.

9 Finally, there is knowing. I know Scott will throw his laundry just shy of the hamper every night; he'll be late to most appointments and eat the last chocolate in the box. He knows that I sleep with a pillow over my head; I'll lock us out of the house at a regular basis, and I will also eat the last chocolate.

10 I guess our love lasts because it is comfortable. No, the sky is not bluer: it's just a familiar hue. We don't feel particularly young: we've experienced too much that has contributed to our growth and wisdom, taking its toll on our bodies, and created our memories. I hope we've got what it takes to make our love last. As a bride, I had Scott's wedding band engraved with Robert Browning's line "Grow old along with me!" We're following those instructions.

11 "If anything is real, the heart will make it plain."

事情告诉了丈夫。我们相互安慰，明白了生命的轮回，悲喜的交替。这就足够了，让我们生活下去。

9 最后，我们彼此相知。我知道斯科特会每晚害羞得把他的衣服扔向洗衣房；会在大多数约会的时候迟到；会吃掉盒子里的最后一块巧克力。而他知道，我喜欢蒙着枕头睡觉；我经常会把我们全家锁在门外；我也会吃掉最后一块巧克力。

10 我猜想我们的爱情能够长久是因为双方都很感到很惬意。天空没有变蓝，它对于我们来说还是熟悉的色彩。我们也不觉得特别年轻。我们一起经历了太多。这些经历使我们成长，使我们更加睿智；虽然我们的身体在其中衰老，但这些经历也构成了我们的回忆。我希望我们已经理解了爱情长久的秘诀。结婚时，斯科特给我的戒指上刻着罗伯特布朗宁的诗句"陪我一起到老吧！"我们一直都守候着这份誓言。

11 若世上的一切都是真的，那么一颗真诚的心会把它变得平淡。

阅读无障碍

fall in love 坠入爱河

exuberantly [ɪgˈzjuːbərəntɪ] *adv.* 兴高采烈的

rave on 喋喋不休

hairline [ˈheəlaɪn] *n.* 发髻线

head [hed] *v.* 朝……地方走

obvious [ˈɒbvɪəs] *adj.* 明显的

commitment [kəˈmɪtmənt] *n.* 誓言

grocery [ˈgrəʊsərɪ] *n.* 杂货店

closet [ˈklɒzɪt] *n.* 衣橱

treasure [ˈtreʒə] *n.* 宝藏

pillow [ˈpɪləʊ] *n.* 枕头

household [ˈhaʊshəʊld] *adj.* 家庭的

parental [pəˈrentl] *adj.* 有关父母的

present [prɪˈzent] *v.* 送

stock market 股市

Alzheimer's disease 阿尔兹海默症

run errand 跑腿

boisterous [ˈbɔɪstərəs] *adj.* 热闹的，充满活动的

bouquet [buːˈkeɪ] *n.* 花束

appointment [əˈpɔɪntmənt] *n.* 约会

 极品佳句背诵

1. We helped each other acknowledge the cycles of life and that the joys counter the sorrows.
   我们相互安慰，明白了生命的轮回，悲喜的交替。

2. I guess our love lasts because it is comfortable.
   我猜想我们的爱情能够长久是因为双方都很感到很惬意。

3. We've experienced too much that has contributed to our growth and wisdom, taking its toll on our bodies, and created our memories.
   我们一起经历了太多。这些经历使我们成长，使我们更加睿智；虽然我们的身体在其中衰老，但这些经历也构成了我们的回忆。

First Love
初恋

带着问题去阅读

1. 你曾经的初恋是什么样的？

2. 青年时代你是否疯狂的无怨无悔的爱过一个人？

3. 你如何对待一份无比美好但注定没有结果的恋爱？

美文欣赏

译文

1　I remember the way the light touched her hair. She turned her head, and our eyes met a momentary awareness in that raucous fifth-grade classroom. I felt as though I'd been struck a blow under the heart. Thus began my first love affair.

2　Her name was Rachel, and I mooned my way through grade and high school, stricken at the mere sight of her, tongue-tied in her presence. Does anyone, anymore, linger in the shadows of evening, drawn by the pale light of a window-her window-like some hapless summer

1　我还能回想起在五年级教室里喧哗的那一刻，柔和的灯光倾泻在她的秀发上，她转过脸来，我们瞬间四目相对。刹那间，我的心灵深处仿佛遭受重击。我的初恋开始了。

2　她的名字叫雷切尔，正是这个名字使我虚度了整个中学时光。只要一看到她的身影我就会心慌意乱，在她面前说话也变的结结巴巴。直到现在我还在想，是否还有人在月光下独自徘徊在她的窗前，透

insect? That delirious swooning, asexual but urgent and obsessive, that made me awkward and my voice crack is like some impossible dream now. I know I was so afflicted, but I cannot actually believe what memory insists I did, which was to suffer, exquisitely.

3 I would catch sight of her, walking down an aisle of trees or from school, and I'd become paralyzed. She always seemed so poised, so self-possessed. At home, I'd relieve each encounter, writhing at the thought of my inadequacies. Even so, as we entered our teens, I sensed her affectionate tolerance for me.

4 "Going steady" implied a maturity we still lacked. Her Orthodox Jewish upbringing and my own Catholic scruples imposed a celibate grace that made even kissing a distant prospect, however fervently desired. I managed to hold her once at a dance - chaperoned, of course. Our embrace made her giggle, a sound so trusting that I hated myself for what I'd been thinking.

过窗户的昏暗灯光看那拉长了的影子，就像夏夜里的飞虫一样可怜呢？我对她无任何生理上的渴求但却痴狂，着迷地爱着她，那种极度兴奋的情绪使我简直都要神魂颠倒了。我变得行为越来越拙笨，声音发哑，现在想来就像是一场不可思议的梦幻一样。这种情感使我长期焦灼，我简直难以相信记忆怎么会如此长久地痛苦而又美丽地折磨着我。太美妙了！

3 当我看到她在林荫道路散步或者从学校里走出来时，我痴迷的已经到了难以自拔的境地。而她看上去总是那样神情自若而又怡然。回到家里，我总是用爱她是不应该的这种理由来安慰自己以减轻痛苦。甚至，当我们都进入青年时代，我还能隐隐地感到她的柔情仍痛苦地煎熬着我。

4 "成为关系确定的伴侣"，意味着我们还缺乏成年人的那种沉稳心态。她是在信奉东正教的犹太人家中长大的，而我家则信奉天主教，这就使得我憧憬美好而遥远的未来。不管怎样我是那样狂热地渴望着。记得在一次舞会上，我以护花使者的身份试着去拥

5 At any rate, my love for Rachel remained unrequited. We graduated from high school, she went on to college, and I joined the Army. When World War II engulfed us, I was sent overseas. For a time we corresponded, and her letters were the highlight of those grinding, endless years. Once she sent me a snapshot of herself in a bathing suit, which drove me to the wildest of fantasies. I mentioned the possibility of marriage in my next letter, and almost immediately her replies became less frequent, less personal.

6 The first thing I did when I returned to the States was to call on Rachel. Her mother answered the door. Rachel no longer lived there. She had married a medical student she'd met in college. "I thought she wrote you," her mother said.

7 Her "Dear John" letter finally caught up with me while I was awaiting discharge. She gently explained the impossibility of a marriage between us. Looking back on it, I must have recovered rather quickly, although for the first few months I believed I didn't want to live. Like Rachel, I found

抱她，这使她幸福地笑出了声，这笑声消除了我所有的疑虑。而我也对自己以前的犹豫不决的想法懊悔不已。

5 无论如何我都没想到我对雷切尔的爱毫无结果。我们中学毕业后，她上了大学，我却应征入伍。当二战席卷而来的时候，我被派遣到国外。在开始的一段时间里，我们彼此鸿雁传情，她的信件成了我那段艰苦而又漫长岁月中生命里最精彩的部分。曾有一次，她给我寄去了一张身着泳装的照片，使得我对她的爱痴狂得简直想入非非了。在接下来的信件中我提出了结婚的请求，但是她的回信却渐渐稀少且缺乏激情。

6 我回国后第一件事就是要见雷切尔。她母亲打开房门告诉我雷切尔早已不在这住了。她与大学里的一位学医的同学结婚了。她母亲说"我想，我女儿写信告诉你吧。"

7 在我退役前我接到了她的那封"绝交信"。信中她娓娓道来我们之间不能结合的原因。回首往事，我又很快找到了当时的感觉。虽然在最初的几个月里我简直不想活在这个世上了。但在以后的生活

someone else, whom I learned to love with a deep and permanent commitment that has lasted to this day.

8　Then recently, after an interval of more than 40 years, I heard from Rachel again. Her husband had died. She was passing through town and had learned of my whereabouts through a mutual friend. We agreed to meet.

9　I felt both curious and excited. In the last few years, I hadn't thought about her, and her sudden call one morning had taken me aback. The actual sight of her was a shock. This white-haired matron at the restaurant table was the Rachel of my dreams and desires, the supple mermaid of that snapshot?

10　Yet time had given us a common reference and respect. We talked as old friends, and quickly discovered we were both grandparents.

11　"Do you remember this?" She handed me a slip of worn paper. It was a poem I'd written her while still in school. I examined the crude meter and pallid rhymes. Watching my face, she snatched

里，我也像雷切尔那样找到了自己的人生伴侣，我们彼此永久又深深地爱着，同甘共苦直到今天。

8　直到现在，在中断 40 多年之后，我又收到了雷切尔的来信。信中说她的丈夫已经去世。她是在路过小镇时，从昔日的一位共好友那里得知我的下落的。我们都同意再见一面。

9　当时的感觉真是又好奇又激动。因为在过去的岁月里我没有想起过她，只是一日清晨，她的一个电话又把我带回尘封的往事。餐桌面前的她令我非常吃惊，驻足在我面前的是一位白发苍苍的老妇人，难道这就是我日思夜想，梦寐以求的雷切尔吗？难道这就是相片上身着泳装，令人赏心悦目的美人鱼吗？

10　时间的流逝使我们共同回首往事，探求往日的生活。我们就像老朋友那样愉快地交谈着。很快我们就发现彼此都是做爷爷奶奶的人了。

11　"你还记得这个吗？"她递给我一张发黄的纸条，上面是我中学时代为雷切尔做的一首诗，我又重新浏览了那拙劣的韵律和呆板的韵脚。她望

the poem from me and returned it to her purse, as though fearful I was going to destroy it.

12 I told her about the snapshot, how I'd carried it all through the war.

13 "It wouldn't have worked out, you know," she said.

14 "How can you be sure?" I countered. "Ah, Colleen, it might have been grand indeed - my Irish conscience and your Jewish guilt!"

15 Our laughter startled people at a nearby table. During the time left to us, our glances were furtive, oblique. I think that what we saw in each other repudiated what we'd once been to ourselves, we immortals.

16 Before I put her into a taxi, she turned to me. "I just wanted to see you once more. To tell you something." Her eyes met mine. "I wanted to thank you for having loved me as you did." We kissed, and she left.

17 Time soon passed, as everything must, and presently I was able to stand and start for home.

着我，又把纸条抽回放到皮包里。好像怕我把它撕掉了一样。

12 我也告诉她我对那张美人鱼似的照片的感受以及在整个战争中我是如何把它带在身边的。

13 "你知道的，那又有什么用呢？"她说。

14 "你怎么知道呢？"我反驳道。"啊，柯林，那也许是我一生中的伟大壮举。因为我有爱尔兰人的良知，我不想让你有做犹太人的那种罪恶感的。"

15 我们的笑声惊动了邻桌的人，接下来我们的目光躲躲闪闪，游离不定。我们以前拥有的彼此凝视的时刻的那种感觉已经消失了，那一刻成了永恒的风景。

16 当我把她送入出租车之前，她转过身来，"我想再看你一眼，告诉你一件事。"我们又一次凝视。"谢谢你曾经如此真挚地爱过我。"我们互相吻着，之后，她便消失在我的视野里了。

17 万事都有终结，时间转瞬即逝。现在，我可以站起身来动身回家了。

阅读无障碍

momentary [ˈməʊməntrɪ] *adj.* 瞬间的

raucous [ˈrɔːkəs] *adj.* 喧闹的

delirious [dɪˈlɪrɪəs] *adj.* 非常激动的

swoon [swuːn] *v.* 痴迷，痴狂

asexual [eɪˈseksjʊəl] *adj.* 无性欲的，非性的

inadequacy [ɪnˈædɪkwəsɪ] *n.* 不足，不充分

scruple [ˈskruːpl] *n.* 顾忌，顾虑

celibate [ˈselɪbət] *adj.* 独身的，禁欲的

unrequited [ˌʌnrɪˈkwaɪtɪd] *adj.* 无报答的，无回报的

engulf [ɪnˈɡʌlf] *v.* 卷入，席卷

grinding [ˈɡraɪndɪŋ] *adj.* 刺耳的；令

人难以忍受的

commitment [kəˈmɪtm(ə)nt] *n.* 承诺，保证

matron [ˈmeɪtrən] *n.* 已婚老妇人

pallid [ˈpælɪd] *adj.* 苍白的，病态的

snatch [snætʃ] *v.* 夺取，抓住

grand [ɡrænd] *adj.* 重大的，最重要的

conscience [ˈkɒnʃəns] *n.* 良心，道德心

furtive [ˈfɜːtɪv] *adj.* 偷偷摸摸的

oblique [əˈbliːk] *adj.* 间接的，暗中的

immortal [ɪˈmɔːtl] *n.* 永恒不朽的人物

🐰 极品佳句背诵

1. I would catch sight of her, walking down an aisle of trees or from school, and I'd become paralyzed.
   当我看到她在林荫道路散步或者从学校里走出来时，我痴迷的已经到了难以自拔的境地。

2. This white-haired matron at the restaurant table was the Rachel of my dreams and desires, the supple mermaid of that snapshot?
   餐桌面前的她令我非常吃惊，驻足在我面前的是一位白发苍苍的老妇人，难道这就是我日思夜想，梦寐以求的雷切尔吗？难道这就是相片上身着泳装，令人赏心悦目的美人鱼吗？

3. I think that what we saw in each other repudiated what we'd once been to ourselves, we immortals.
   我们以前拥有的彼此凝视的时刻的那种感觉已经消失了，那一刻成了永恒的风景了。

Love Unspoken
无言的爱

带着问题去阅读

1. 爱真的要大声讲出来吗？

2. 你爱种玫瑰花吗？

3. 你怎么看待自己寡言少语的另一半呢？

 美文欣赏

 译文

1 When it comes to flowery speech or emotional expression, my husband, Dave, is a man of few words. That was one of the first things I learned about him when we married thirty-one years ago.

2 One of the next things I discovered is that Dave has little use for rosebushes. He had no second thoughts about yanking out mature plants to widen the driveway when we purchased our home. To him, roses represent hours of pruning and spraying, mulching and fertilizing. As far as he's concerned, a lawn mower and hedge trimmers are all you need for the perfect garden.

1 对于华丽的辞藻和富有感情的表达而言，我的丈夫大卫是一个少言寡语的人。这是三十年前结婚时我对他最初了解。

2 接着我发现，他很少关注玫瑰丛。当我们购置完房子的时候，他毫不犹豫地拔除了茂盛的植物来拓宽车道。对他而言，玫瑰代表着要花费数个小时去修剪和喷灌，盖膜和施肥。在他看来，一个割草机和树枝修剪机便足以建造一个完美的花园。

184

3 On the other hand, I treasure my roses. I consider every minute of their care well worth the beautiful, fragrant results.

4 One winter, I spent several evenings drooling over rose catalogs and planning a small garden. In the spring, I ordered several English varieties of self-rooted plants. I removed an area of sod, worked and reworked the ground, and planted the foot-long starts. During the heat of summer, I watered them daily. In my mind, I saw the fruits of my labor: masses of color and fragrance perfuming the air just outside my kitchen window.

5 But as it sometimes does, life spun us around and redirected our attention. In the fall, I began to have pain in my lower abdomen. At first I passed it off as nothing serious. But instead of getting better, the pain intensified. I went to see my doctor. He ordered tests; when the results came back, he asked to see me in his office right away. He also requested that Dave come with me.

6 Our worst fears became reality: colon cancer. I'd need surgery immediately. After a short recovery period, I'd undergo a six-month course of chemotherapy.

7 We cried... and prayed... and cried some more. We had one week to inform our family and friends. Then, trusting God

3 但是，我视我的玫瑰为珍宝。我把玫瑰的美丽和芳香作为我对它们每分每秒细心照顾的回报，这是值得的。

4 一个冬天，我花了几个晚上的时间去修剪玫瑰的垂枝，捣腾出了一个小花园。在春天，我预订了好几个英国品种的自根植物。我腾出了一块草皮，勤勤恳恳的耕作那块地。在炎热的夏季，我每天要给它们浇水。在我心里，我看到了自己的劳动成果：厨房的窗外万紫千红，空气中弥漫着芳香的气息。

5 但是就像往常那样，生活在我们周围旋转，然后突然调转了我们的注意力。在秋天，我的腹部下方开始感到疼痛。起初我并没有太在意。但不见任何好转，疼痛越来越强烈。我去看了医生。他给我安排了检查；当结果出来的时候，他叫我立刻去他的办公室。同时也要求大卫陪我一起去。

6 最糟糕的事情发生了：结肠癌。我需要立刻手术。在短期的恢复之后，我将接受六个月的化疗。

7 我们哭着……祈祷着……然后哭的更厉害了。我们有一个星期的时间去通知家

and my doctors, I entered the hospital.

8 One month later, as I lay on the sofa still recuperating from surgery, Dave and I watched the TV weather forecast. It promised bitter cold temperatures and possible snow.

9 "Oh," I moaned to myself, "I never did get the roses mulched."

10 Dave just sat and watched the end of the forecast. Then, always the practical, on-top-of-things handyman, he said, "I'd better go winterize the outside faucets." He bundled up and headed toward the garage.

11 Fifteen minutes later, I hobbled to the kitchen for a glass of water. What I saw from the window brought tears to my eyes. There was Dave, bending over the roses, carefully heaping mulch around every plant.

12 I smiled and watched as my quiet husband "said" I love you. You know, sometimes words aren't needed at all.

人和朋友。然后，听命于上帝和医生，我住进了医院。

8 一个月后，我还处于术后恢复期，躺在沙发上，大卫和我都在看天气预报。天气预报说会持续低温天气，也可能会有大雪。

9 "哦，"我对我自己说到，"我还从没给玫瑰盖保护膜呢。"

10 大卫只是坐着，一直看到天气预报结束。然后是例行的杂活，他说，"我最好去为外面的水龙头做御寒准备。"他捆好工具朝车库走去。

11 十五分钟过后，我一瘸一拐的走向厨房想要拿杯水。当我看到窗外的那一幕时，热泪盈眶。那是大卫，他正弯着腰，一心一意的为每一株玫瑰盖保护膜。

12 我微笑着看着安静的丈夫，说"我爱你"。你知道，有时候，并不需要太多的言语。

阅读无障碍

flowery ['flaʊərɪ] *adj.* 辞藻华丽的
emotional [ɪ'məʊʃənəl] *adj.* 富有感情的

rosebush ['rəʊzbʊʃ] *n.* 玫瑰丛
second thought 仔细思考
driveway ['draɪvweɪ] *n.* 车道

purchase ['pɜ:tʃəs] v. 购买

prune [pru:n] v. 修建

fertilize ['fɜ:tɪlaɪz] v. 施肥

trimmer ['trɪmə] n. 平整器

water ['wɔ:tə] v. 浇花

abdomen ['æbdəmən] n. 腹部

right away 马上

colon cancer 结肠癌

chemotherapy [ˌki:mə(ʊ)'θerəpɪ] n. 化疗

recuperate [rɪ'kju:pəreɪt] v. 恢复

weather forecast 天气预报

mulch [mʌltʃ] v. 给……护根

faucet ['fɔ:sɪt] n. 水龙头

garage ['gærɑ:ʒ] n. 车库

hobble ['hɒbəl] v. 跛行

极品佳句背诵

1. On the other hand, I treasure my roses. I consider every minute of their care well worth the beautiful, fragrant results.

   但是，我视我的玫瑰为珍宝。我把玫瑰的美丽和芳香作为我对它们每分每秒细心照顾的回报，这是值得的。

2. In my mind, I saw the fruits of my labor: masses of color and fragrance perfuming the air just outside my kitchen window.

   在我心里，我看到了自己的劳动成果：厨房的窗外万紫千红，空气中弥漫着芳香的气息。

3. You know, sometimes words aren't needed at all.

   你知道，有时候，并不需要太多的言语。

The Blessed Dress
幸运的结婚礼服

带着问题去阅读

1. 婚礼当中一件漂亮的礼服真的很重要吗？
2. 缘分到底会怎样导演我们的爱情？
3. 你心中白马王子的标准又是什么呢？

美文欣赏

译文

1　I got an engagement ring for Christmas. My boyfriend and I had been dating for almost a year and both felt the time was right to join our lives together in holy matrimony.

2　The month of January was spent planning our perfect Alabama June wedding. My mother, two sisters and I went to Huntsville, the closest town with a selection of bridal shops, to buy the gown that would play the leading role on my special occasion.

3　We had a wonderful time just being together and sharing silly jokes, but the day

1　圣诞节的时候我戴上了订婚戒指。我和男友交往快一年了，我们都认为是时候携手步入神圣的婚姻殿堂了。

2　整个一月我都忙于计划我们将于六月份在阿拉巴马州举行的完美的婚礼。我和母亲，连同两个姐姐前往最近的城市汉斯维尔的一些新娘服装店去挑选结婚礼服，它们可是我婚礼中的主角呢。

3　我们母女四个高高兴兴，相互开着玩笑。但是到

soon turned serious by afternoon: still no sign of the dress of my dreams. Both sisters were ready to give up and try another day in another town, but I coerced them into one more boutique.

4 I had a good feeling as we entered the quaint little shop filled with the scent of fresh flowers. The elderly clerk showed us several beautiful gowns in my size and price range, but none were right. As I opened the door to leave, the desperate shop owner announced she had one more dress in the back that was expensive and not even my size, but perhaps I might want to look at it anyway. When she brought it out, I squealed in delight.

5 This was it!

6 I rushed to the dressing room and slipped it on. Even though it was at least two sizes too large and more costly than I had anticipated, I talked Mom into buying it. The shop was so small it didn't offer alterations, but my excitement assured me I would be able to get it resized in my hometown.

7 Excitement wasn't enough. On Monday morning, my world crumbled when the local sewing shop informed me the dress simply could not be altered because of numerous hand-sewn pearls

了下午我们就再也高兴不起来了：依然没发现我中意的礼服。两个姐姐都已经准备就此打道回府，改天再到其它的城镇去买，但我迫使她们陪我再多看一家时装店。

4 当我们走进这家花香四溢、古色古香的小店时，我感觉棒极了。上了年纪的店员让我们看了几件适合我穿的漂亮的礼服，价格也都在我的预算之内，但都不是我想要的。正当我推开门准备离开时，孤注一掷的老板娘喊道，在后面库里还有一件礼服，这件礼服很贵，而且不是我穿的码，但是也许我还是想看一眼。当她拿出来时，我高兴的叫了出来。

5 就是这件了！

6 我冲进试衣间迫切的穿上礼服。尽管它至少要大上两个码，价格也比我预想的要贵很多，我仍然说服母亲买下了它。这家店很小，不提供连改衣服的服务，但是在激动之余，我确信能在家乡把它改好。

7 然而激动是无济于事的。礼拜一早上，当我们那儿的裁缝店告诉我礼服上手工缝纫的珠子和饰片太多因而没法改动时，我傻眼了。我打电话

and sequins on the bodice. I called the boutique for suggestions but only got their answering machine.

8　A friend gave me the number of a lady across town who worked at home doing alterations. I was desperate and willing to try anything, so I decided to give her a call.

9　When I arrived at her modest white house on the outskirts of town, she carefully inspected my dress and asked me to try it on. She put a handful of pins into the shoulders and sides of my gown and told me to pick it up in two days. She was the answer to my prayers.

10　When the time came to pick it up, however, I grew skeptical. How could I have been so foolish as to just leave a $1,200 wedding dress in the hands of someone I barely knew? What if she made a mess out of it? I had no idea if she could even sew on a button.

11　Thank goodness my fears were all for naught. The dress still looked exactly the same, but it now fit as if it had been made especially for me. I thanked the cheerful lady and paid her modest fee.

12　One small problem solved just in time for a bigger one to emerge. On Valentine's Day, my fiancé called.

给那家服装店寻求建议，听到的却只是机器的自动应答。

8　一个朋友给我镇上一个裁缝的电话，这个裁缝在家里做活。在绝望之余，我愿意进行任何尝试。于是我决定给她打个电话。

9　当我赶到她那位于城镇郊区的简陋的白色房子里时，她仔细的察看了我的礼服，并让我穿上。她用别针将礼服的肩膀处和两侧别上，然后告诉我两天后来取衣服。她正是我祈祷的福音。

10　该去取衣服了，然而我却忐忑不安起来。我怎么这么愚蠢，将一件价值1200美元的礼服交给一个一点儿也不了解的人呢？如果她改坏了怎么办？我甚至不知道她会不会缝扣子。

11　谢天谢地，我的担心都是多余的。礼服仍跟以前一样，不过现在很合身，仿佛它是为我量身定造的一样。谢过那个高兴的女裁缝，我付给了她合理的工钱。

12　然而这只解决了一个小问题，更大的问题还在后面。情人节那天，未婚夫打来电话。

13 "Sandy, I've come to the decision that I'm not ready to get married," he announced, none too gently. "I want to travel and experience life for a few years before settling down."

14 He apologized for the inconvenience of leaving all the wedding cancellations to me and then quickly left town.

15 My world turned upside down. I was angry and heartbroken and had no idea how to recover. But days flew into weeks and weeks blended into months. I survived.

16 One day in the fall of the same year, while standing in line at the supermarket, I heard someone calling my name. I turned around to see the alterations lady. She politely inquired about my wedding, and was shocked to discover it had been called off, but agreed it was probably for the best.

17 I thanked her again for adjusting my wedding gown, and assured her it was safely bagged and awaiting the day I would wear it down the aisle on the arm of my real "Mister Right". With a sparkle in her eye, she began telling me about her single son, Tim. Even though I wasn't interested in dating again, I let her talk me into meeting him.

18 I did have my summer wedding

13 "桑迪，我决定了，我还没有做好结婚的准备，"他宣布，语气一点也不温柔。"在成家之前，我要花几年时间到各处走走，体验体验生活。"

14 他对把取消婚礼的所有麻烦留给我表示歉意，然后很快离开了镇子。

15 我的世界一片混乱。我愤怒，心碎，不知道怎样撑过去。然而随着日子一天天，一月月流走，我熬过来了。

16 那年秋季的一天，在超市排队结账的时候，我听见有人叫我的名字。一扭头，看到那个女裁缝。她很有礼貌的问起我的婚礼，得知婚礼被取消了她十分吃惊，但随后她认为这也许并非坏事。

17 我再一次感谢她为我修改了我的结婚礼服，并向她保证，礼服被我安全的放了起来，并期待着穿上它挽着我真正的"白马王子"走上红地毯的一天。她眼睛里闪过亮光，开始跟我谈起她的单身儿子蒂姆。尽管我对约会不再感兴趣，还是听任她给我安排跟她儿子的约会。

18 我的夏季婚礼最终成

after all, only a year later. And I did get to wear the dress of my dreams - standing beside Tim, the man I have shared the last eighteen years of my life with, whom I would never have met without that special wedding gown.

为现实，只不过是一年以后。站在蒂姆身旁，我终于穿上了梦中的结婚礼服。在随后的十八年里，我们相亲相爱，相濡以沫。如果不是因为这件特殊的礼服，我们永远不会相遇。

阅读无障碍

engagement [ɪn'geɪdʒmənt] n. 订婚

matrimony ['mætrɪmənɪ] n. 婚姻

bridal ['braɪdl] n. 新娘

gown [gaun] n. 礼服

the leading role 主角

give up 放弃

boutique [bu:'ti:k] n. 时装店

quaint [kweɪnt] adj. 古色古香的

scent [sent] n. 气味

in delight 喜悦

anticipate [æn'tɪsɪpeɪt] v. 期待

alteration [ɔ:ltə'reɪʃ(ə)n] n. 修改

give a call 打电话

pick up 取回

prayer ['preə] n. 祈祷

skeptical ['skeptɪkəl] adj. 怀疑的

make a mess 弄乱

settle down 安定下来

call off 取消

sparkle ['spɑ:kəl] v. 闪烁

极品佳句背诵

1. On Monday morning, my world crumbled when the local sewing shop informed me the dress simply could not be altered because of numerous hand-sewn pearls and sequins on the bodice.

礼拜一早上，当我们那儿的裁缝店告诉我礼服上手工缝纫的珠子和饰片太多因而没法改动时，我傻眼了。

2. One small problem solved just in time for a bigger one to emerge.

然而这只解决了一个小问题，更大的问题还在后面。

3. I thanked her again for adjusting my wedding gown, and assured her it was safely bagged and awaiting the day I would wear it down the aisle on the arm of my real "Mister Right.

我再一次感谢她为我修改了我的结婚礼服，并向她保证，礼服被我安全的放了起来，期待着穿上它挽着我真正的"白马王子"走上红地毯的一天。

Destiny
前生注定

带着问题去阅读

1. 你认为爱情是命中注定的吗？
2. 你相信缘分吗？
3. 你怎么看待前世今生的说法？

美文欣赏

 译文

1 I went to a convention, with a group of friends. One of the people there was my best friend Cher she brought Juan with her. We were all staying in the dorm and Cher introduced me to Juan. I was at 21 at the time and I was rooming with my mom. Juan was very attractive, and I felt as if I knew him when I first met him. It was so strange that feeling I had and later on discovered he also had that feeling.

2 We became fast friends and we discovered we lived in the same town and stranger than we lived in same apartment

1 一天我和一群朋友去参加一个会议，我最好的朋友切尔将胡安带了过来。我们在寝室闲聊时，切尔把我介绍给胡安认识，那时我 21 岁，还和母亲住在一起。胡安英俊迷人，初次见面我便觉得他似曾相识。后来我才知道，他在初次见面时也有这种似曾相识的感觉，这真是一件奇怪的事情。

2 我们很快就成了好友，发现我们住在同一个小镇，更让我惊讶的是，我们住在同一

complex. The convention was over and we all went back home. Before I dropped my mother off she said," Kate, you know that Juan is a bit older than you so be careful." I love my mother very much, but I told her, "Mom since I'm 21 which is of legal age, it really doesn't matter how old Juan is. Especially since we are just friends." My mother looked at me in that way that all mothers have a way of doing.

3 Of course Juan was waiting for me, since I told him I had just bought a new computer and was having trouble putting all the doodads in their proper place. We had a very nice evening. I fixed dinner and we were talking getting to know each other. I asked if he wanted to go to the store with me to develop some old film that I had bought at an auction. He just smiled and said "no need to make a trip to the store since I can develop film at my department." I laughed, and said "a man of many talents huh?" I told him "Really I can take it to the store since you were so kind as to help put my computer together". That is when he said "Kate I know we just met, but I feel like I've known you all of my life. Do you believe in destiny? " I just stared at him for quite a few minutes. Of all the lame pickup lines I heard this one really touched my soul. Finally I said, "Juan from the first day we met at the convention,

个社区里。会议结束了，我们都回家了。下车前，母亲对我说："凯特，胡安可比你大，你要小心留意些。"我非常爱我的母亲，但我却说："妈妈，我已经21岁了，早已成人了，我并不在乎胡安的年龄，更何况我们只是朋友。"母亲以一种天底下所有母亲都会有的反应看着我。

3 当然，胡安正在等着我，因为我和他说我买了一台新电脑，但我总组装不好。我亲自准备了晚餐，我们聊着，慢慢的了解了对方，那一晚我们过的非常愉快。我问他能否顺便陪我到照相馆，冲洗我在拍卖会上买的一些老胶卷。他微笑的对我说："不用去照相馆，在我家就能帮你洗照片。"我笑道："你这么多才多艺啊？"我对他说："算了，我可以自己把胶卷带到照相馆去，已经很感谢你帮我把电脑组装好了。"就在那时他说："凯特，我知道我们才刚刚认识，但是我总觉得我们早已相识，你相信运气吗？"我盯着他好几分钟，在所有这些无说服力的话语中这句话触动了我的内心深处，最后我说："胡安，我们第一次在会议上

I had this nagging feeling that I also had known you all of my life." "I was afraid to sound like a big stupid, and I didn't want to scare you away before we had a chance to get to know each other." "Really Kate I don't think you could run me off with just that." He said with a twinkle in his eyes we both started laughing." Now about this film," I said. "I'm not sure what you will find on it, if anything. I just bought it on a whim and the price was right." I said smiling. He said, "Well, if you want, you can come to the apartment with me and watch me develop it and make sure that I'm very careful with it." With a twinkle in his eyes, "I promise I will be a gentleman and not do anything that you don't want me to." He said jokingly. So we went back to his department and I put some coffee for us. We went into his darkroom. I was much infested in the darkroom since I had never seen one before. I was walking around being very careful not to touch anything and admiring his photos that he took and developed, he was really an extraordinary photographer which he pointed out that it was just one of his hobbies. Like I said a man of many talents. "Kate come over here and I will show you how the negatives become the pictures."

4 "Does that mean there is something on them?" I asked with excitement. He

见面，这种感觉就不断困扰着我，我觉得我们仿佛已经认识了一辈子。""我怕你笑话我傻，怕吓跑你，这样的话，我们就没有机会认识对方了。""凯特，你不会把我吓走的。"他冲我眨眨眼。我们都笑了。"至于这个胶卷，"我说道，"不知道这些胶卷照的是什么，我只是心血来潮买了它的，而且价格也不贵。"他微笑着说："如果你能来我家，就可以看到我是怎样冲洗这些胶卷的了，我会很小心的。"他眼里充满着期待望着我。"我保证我一定会像一个绅士一样，不会勉强做你不想做的事。"他开玩笑的说。我们一起来到他家，我冲了些咖啡。他进了暗室。我对他的暗室充满了兴趣，因为之前从未见识过。我非常小心的在他的暗室走动，不敢碰任何东西，我惊叹那些他自拍自洗的那些照片，他简直就是一名非常优秀的摄影师，他却说摄影只是他的一项业余爱好。像我说的那样他简直就是一个天才。"凯特，快过来看，看看我是怎样把底片冲洗成照片的。"

4 "胶卷里真的有东西吗？"我激动的问。他开始洗

started to work his magic with the pictures and when they started developing we both look at each other with astonishment right in front of our eyes we were staring at a pictures of us, but we were dressed strangely. My hair was piled upon my head and had quite a serene look on my face. I was dressed in a white lace dress that the collar went up to my neck, and in the middle of that was a cameo, he was standing beside me with his hands on my shoulders, quite dashing in his coat and tie, and we both looked so much in the love. Then the next picture was us in the same outfit but him sitting and me sitting besides him at an angle with his hands around my waist. I was speechless how could this be, I was wondering, since I know I had only met him like a week ago. He just smiled and said: "All I can say is that it's destiny."

起了照片。照片冲好后，我们都惊诧不已的看着对方，我们盯着眼前的照片，上面是我们俩。只是，照片中，我们两个人服饰比较怪异：我的头发盘在了头顶，表情是那么的安静祥和。我身穿立领白色的蕾丝长裙，长裙中间点缀着宝石。他站在我旁边，手搭在我的肩上。他穿着外套，系着领带，很帅的样子，我们看起来就像是一对深爱的恋人。下一张照片中，我们的服饰都是一样的，只是这一次我们都坐着，他揽住我的腰，我斜靠在他的身边。怎么可能会这样呢，我惊讶的说不出话来，我们认识了才一周啊。他微笑的看着我说："我想这就是前生注定。"

阅读无障碍

convention[kən'venʃ(ə)n] n. 会议
attractive [ə'træktɪv] adj. 吸引人的，有魅力的
apartment[ə'pɑːtm(ə)nt] n. 公寓，房间
legal ['liːg(ə)l] adj. 法定的
doodad ['duːdæd] n. 小玩意
fix [fɪks] v. 准备
auction ['ɔːkʃ(ə)n] n. 拍卖
develop film 冲洗底片，冲洗胶卷

talent ['tælənt] n. 才能
touch [tʌtʃ] v. 触动
nagging ['nægɪŋ] adj. 使人不得安宁的
scare [skeə] v. 惊吓
twinkle ['twɪŋk(ə)l] n. 闪烁，发亮
darkroom ['dɑːkruːm] v.（冲洗底片的）暗房，暗室
admire [əd'maɪə] v. 钦佩，赞赏
hobby ['hɒbɪ] n. 业余爱好

astonishment [ə'stɒnɪʃmənt] *n.* 惊讶

serene [sɪ'riːn] *adj.* 平静的

dashing ['dæʃɪŋ] *adj.* 时髦的，华丽的

outfit ['aʊtfɪt] *n.* 设备，用具

 极品佳句背诵

1. It was so strange that feeling I had and later on discovered he also had that feeling.

   后来知道，他在初次见面时也有这种似曾相识的感觉是如此的奇怪。

2. That is when he said: "Kate I know we just met, but I feel like I've known you all of my life. Do you believe in destiny?"

   就在那时他说："凯特，我知道我们才刚刚认识，但是我总觉得我们早已相识，你相信命运吗？"

3. He just smiled and said: "All I can say is that it's destiny."

   他微笑的看着我说："我想告诉你，这就是前生注定。"

An Ingenious Love Letter
一封绝妙的情书

带着问题去阅读

1. 父亲有反对过你的初恋吗?
2. 你的男朋友有给你写过一封绝妙的情书吗?
3. 当你收到一封别样的情书时, 你能读懂各种滋味吗?

美文欣赏

 译文

1 There once lived a lad who was deeply in love with a girl, but disliked by the girl's father, who didn't want to see any further development of their love. The lad was eager to write to the girl, yet he was quite sure that the father would read it first. So he wrote such a letter to the girl:

2 My love for you I once expressed

3 no longer lasts, instead, my distaste for you

4 is growing with each passing day. Next time I see you,

5 I even won't like that look yours.

6 I'll do nothing but

---

1 一个小伙子非常爱一位姑娘, 但姑娘的父亲却不喜欢他, 也不让他们的爱情发展下去。小伙子很想给姑娘写封情书, 然而他知道姑娘的父亲会先看。于是他给姑娘写了这样一封信:

2 我对你表达过的爱

3 已经消逝。我对你的厌恶

4 与日俱增。当我看到你时

5 我甚至不喜欢你的那副样子。

6 我想做的一件事就是

7 look away from you. You can never expect I'll

8 marry you. The last chat we had

9 was so dull and dry that you shouldn't think it made me eager to see you again.

10 If we get married, I firmly believe I'll

11 live a hard life, I can never

12 live happily with you, I'll devote myself

13 but not

14 to you. No one else is more

15 harsh and selfish and least

16 solicitous and considerate than you.

17 I sincerely want to let you know

18 what I said is true. Please do me a favor by

19 ending our relations and refrain from

20 writing me a reply. Your letter is always full of

21 things which displease me. You have no

22 sincere care for me. So long! Please believe

23 I don't love you any longer. Don't

7 把目光移往别处，我永远不会

8 和你结婚。我们的最近一次谈话

9 枯燥乏味，因此无法使我渴望再与你想见。

10 假如我们结婚，我深信我将

11 生活得非常艰难，我也无法

12 愉快地和你生活在一起，我要把我的心

13 奉献出来，但决不是

14 奉献给你。没有人能比你更

15 苛求和自私，也没有人比你更不会.

16 关心我帮助我。

17 我真的希望你明白，

18 我讲的是真话，请你助我一臂之力

19 结束我们之间的关系，别试图

20 答复此信，你的信充满着

21 让我反感生厌的内容.

22 对我的真诚关心。再见，请相信

23 我不再喜欢你了，请

think

24 I still have a love of you!

25 Having read the letter, the father felt relieved and gave it to his daughter with a light heart. The girl also felt quite pleased after she read it carefully, her lad still had a deep love for her. Do you know why? In fact, she felt very sad when she read the letter for the first time. But she read it for a few more times and , at last, she found the key – only every other line should be read, that is the first line, the third, the fifth … and so on to the end.

你不要以为

24 我仍然爱着你!

25 姑娘的父亲看了这封信以后，非常高兴地把信给了姑娘。姑娘仔仔细细看完信后也非常快乐，小伙子依然爱着她。你知道她为什么高兴吗？其实，她初读时非常忧伤，但她怎么也不相信那是他的真心话，于是她又默读了几遍，终于，她弄懂了这封信的关键——只能一、三、五行连着读，如此类推，直到信的结尾。

阅读无障碍

be in love with sb. 爱上某人

dislike [dɪsˈlaɪk] v. 不喜欢

development [dɪˈveləpmənt] n. 发展

lad [læd] n. 小伙子

eager to 急着做某事

express [ɪkˈspres] v. 表达

expect [ɪkˈspekt] v. 期待

chat [tʃæt] n. 聊天

dull [dʌl] adj. 无聊

get married 结婚

devote [dɪˈvəʊt] v. 把…奉献给

harsh [hɑːʃ] adj. 残酷的

selfish [ˈselfɪʃ] adj. 自私的

solicitous [səˈlɪsɪtəs] adj. 关心的

considerate [kənˈsɪdərɪt] adj. 考虑周
　　到的

do sb. a favor 帮助某人

refrain [rɪˈfreɪn] v. 克制

for the first time 初次

at last 最终

key [kiː] n. 秘诀

极品佳句背诵

1. My love for you I once expressed is growing with each passing day.
   我对你表达过的爱与日俱增。

2. Please believe I still have a love of you!
   请相信我仍然爱着你!

3. The girl also felt quite pleased after she read it carefully, her lad still had a deep love for her.
   姑娘仔仔细细看完信后也非常快乐，小伙子依然爱着她。

True Love is Always Prevail All Over 真爱胜过一切

带着问题去阅读

1. 你能和自己的另一半做到"有福同享，有难同当"吗？
2. 生活中当另一半情绪低落的时候你能否谅解呢？
3. 你遭受过心理上的痛苦吗？

美文欣赏

1　True love is we stick together in "thick and thin". Especially when it's thin, when it's troublesome. Then we should really bridge over the "troubled water". That's what they say in English. But most of us fail the test, to ourselves, not to our partners. He might leave you, he might stay with you, because you're nice or not nice. But you fail yourself. You leave yourself. You leave the noblest being that you really are. So we should check up on this to our family members or whomever that is beloved and dear to us. Most of the time in critical situations, we just turn our

译文

1　真爱就是"有福同享，有难同当"特别是身陷囹圄、处境困窘时，我们更应该如俗话所说的"兵来将挡，水来土掩"，想办法克服困难。但是大部分人都不能通过这项考验并且背离了自己，而不是背离了我们的伴侣。因为不论你好或不好，你的伴侣都可能留下或是离开。是你自己通不过考验，背离了你自己，背弃了内在真正高贵的你，所以我们应该检查自己对家人或任何我们所钟爱的人的关系，通常在关

backs and that is no good.

2 Of course we have our anger, our frustrations, because our partners are not as loving as usual, or whomever that is; but he or she is in a different situation. At that time, she or he is in mental suffering. It's just as bad as or even worse than physical suffering. Physical suffering you can take a pill or you can have an injection and it stops or at least temporarily stops, and you feel the effect right away; or at least if people are in physical suffering, everyone sympathises with them.

3 But when they are in mental anguish, and we pound them more on that, and we turn our backs and become cold and indifferent, that is even crueler, even worse. That person will be swimming alone in suffering. And especially they trust us as the next of kin, the next person, the one that they think they can rely on in times of need; and then at that time, we just turn around and are snobbish, because they didn't treat us nice so we just want to revenge. That's not the time. You can revenge later, when he's in better shape. Just slap him.

4 Actually, at that time, the person is not his usual self anymore. He was probably under very great pressure that he lost his own control. It's not really lost

键的时刻我们反而背弃他们，这样做只会贻害四方。

2 当然我们也会生气、失望，因为我们的伴侣或身边的人不再像以前一样可爱，但这只是因为他（她）处境不同，精神倍受煎熬。精神痛苦和生理痛苦一样难受，有时候甚至更糟。生理的痛苦可以通过吃药或打针加以制止，至少可以暂时止痛，效果立竿见影；或者至少身体受苦时，大家都会同情她。

3 可是当有人处在心理的极度痛苦时，我们却落井下石，背弃他，变得冷漠不关心，这样更残忍、更糟糕。那个人就只能孤单地在痛苦中挣扎。尤其是他们把我们视为最亲密的人，认为在需要时可以依靠；可是通常就在这时，我们却很势利的转身离去，只是因为他们不再对我们好而我们也要抓住时机报仇。这真不是时候！你可以以后再报复，等他境况稍微好点时，然后打他一巴掌。

4 事实上，此时的他已经不再是平常的他了。可能已因巨大的压力而让他失去控制。这并不完全是失去控制，

his own control, but for example, when you are in a hurry, your talk is different. Right? "Hand me that coat! Quick! Quick! Quick!" Things like that. But normally, you would say "Honey, please, can you give me that coat." Is that not so? (Audience: Yes.) Or when you're in pain — for example stomach pain, heartache or whatever — you scream loudly; and anyone who comes to talk to you, you don't talk in the usual way anymore, because you're in pain.

5　Similarly, when you are in a mental or psychological pain, you talk also in a very grouchy way, very cross. But that is understandable. So if we — any so-called loving partner or family member — do not understand even this very least, very basic concept, then we're finished. Then we are really in a bad situation. It's not that the partner will do anything to us. Whether he does anything to us later or not, that is no problem. The problem is us. The problem is we degrade ourselves, that we make less of a being of ourselves than we should be, than we are supposed to be, or that we really are. So do not make less of a being of yourselves.

而是像当你很匆忙时，说话的语气自然会不一样，对吧？你会说："把那件外套给我，快快快！"但在平常则会说："亲爱的，能不能请你把那件外套递给我。"是不是这样？（大众回答：是。）或当你在痛苦时，例如胃痛、头痛或身体不适时——你会大叫；人家来看你时你也无法像平常那样同大家谈话，因为你正难受的不得了。

5　同样的，当你遭受精神或心理痛苦时，你的言谈自然会显得粗暴。但这是可以理解的。如果我们这些所谓的爱的伴侣或家人——不知道这最起码、最基本的观念，我们就完了。我们的处境会很糟糕。并非另一半会对我们怎样。无论对方日后有没有对我们怎样，那都不是问题。问题在于我们自己。我们贬低了自己，不配自己应有的身分。所以千万不要贬低自己。

🐱 **阅读无障碍**

troublesome ['trʌbəlsəm] *n.* 麻烦

fail [feɪl] *v.* 辜负

beloved [bɪ'lʌvd] *adj.* 心爱的

critical ['krɪtɪkəl] *adj.* 关键的

frustration [frʌs'treɪʃən] *n.* 挫折

mental ['mentl] *adj.* 精神的

physical ['fɪzɪkəl] *adj.* 身体的

injection [ɪn'dʒekʃən] *n.* 注射

at least 至少

sympathize ['sɪmpəθaɪz] *v.* 同情

anguish ['æŋgwɪʃ] *n.* 苦恼

pound on 重击

indifferent [ɪn'dɪfrənt] *adj.* 漠不关心的

kin [kɪn] *n.* 亲戚

rely on 依靠

snobbish ['snɒbɪʃ] *adj.* 势利眼的

revenge [rɪ'vendʒ] *v.* 报仇

heartache ['hɑːteɪk] *n.* 伤心

psychological [saɪkə'lɒdʒɪk(ə)l] *adj.* 心理的

egrade [dɪ'greɪd] *v.* 贬低

🐰 **极品佳句背诵**

1. True love is we stick together in "thick and thin".
   真爱就是"有福同享，有难同当"。

2. But when they are in mental anguish, and we pound them more on that, and we turn our backs and become cold and indifferent, that is even crueler, even worse.
   可是当有人处在心理的极度痛苦时，我们却落井下石，背弃他，变得冷漠不关心，这样更残忍、更糟糕。

3. And especially they trust us as the next of kin, the next person, the one that they think they can rely on in times of need.
   尤其是他们把我们视为最亲密的人，认为在需要时可以依靠。

Late at Night, Do You Turn Off Your Cell Phone?
夜深了，你关机了吗？

带着问题去阅读

1. 深夜，你的电话为谁而开呢？
2. 爱情到底需要用什么来考验？
3. 你是怎样获得自己的真爱的呢？

美文欣赏

1　Today, my friend asked me a question. At night, do you turn off your cell phone? If you don't, whom do you leave it on for?

2　I usually do not turn off my cell phone. Why? I have no idea. After reading an article, I seemed to understand a little bit: for that little bit of caring. I am now sharing this story with you.

3　The girl would turn her cell phone off and put it by her photo on the desk every night before going to bed. This habit

译文

1　今天，朋友问我一个问题，晚上你关机吗？如果没有关机，那你是为了谁呢？

2　我一向不关机，但是为什么呢？我也不知道，后来我看了一篇文章，我好像有点明白了，只为了那丝牵挂。现在我把它拿出来与大家分享。

3　女孩每天临睡会先关掉手机，然后把它放在写字台自己的相框前。自从她买

has been with her ever since she bought the phone.

4　The girl had a very close boyfriend. When they couldn't meet, they would either call or send messages to each other. They both liked this type of communication.

5　One night, the boy really missed the girl. When he called her however, the girl's cell phone was off because she was already asleep. The next day, the boy asked the girl to leave her cell phone on at night because when he needed to find her and could not, he would be worried.

6　From that day forth, the girl began a new habit. Her cell phone never shuts down at night. Because she was afraid that she might not be able to hear the phone ring in her sleep, she tried to stay very alert. As days passed, she became thinner and thinner. Slowly, a gap began to form between them.

7　The girl wanted to revive their relationship. On one night, she called the boy. However what she got was a sweet female voice: "Sorry, the subscriber you dialed is power off."

8　The girl knew that her love has just been turned off.

9　After a long time, the girl has a new love. No matter how well they got along,

了手机以后就一直保持着这个习惯。

4　女孩有个很要好的男朋友，两个人不能见面的时候，就相互打打电话或发发短信，大家都喜欢这种联络方式。

5　有一天夜里，男孩很想念女孩子，拨出了电话对方却关机了，因为女孩早已睡下。第二天，男孩希望女孩以后晚上不要关机，因为当他想念女孩的时候却找不到她心里会很不安。

6　从那以后，女孩开始养成另一种习惯——夜里从不关机。因为害怕他打来自己会因睡死而听不到，女孩夜夜都很警醒。日复一日，女孩开始便日渐消瘦。然而，慢慢地，两个人的关系出现了危机。

7　女孩很想挽回即将分手的局面。一天晚上，女孩在一个深夜里拨通了男孩的电话，回答她的却是一个甜美的女声："抱歉，您所拨打的电话已关机。"

8　于是女孩知道，她的爱情已经关机。

9　很久以后，女孩拥有了另一段爱情。无论两人相处

the girl however refused to get married. In the girl's heart, she always remembered that boy's words and the night when that phone was power off.

10 The girl still keeps the habit of leaving her cell phone on all throughout the night, but not expecting that it'll ring.

11 One night, the girl caught ill. In moment of fluster, instead of calling her parents, she dialed the new boy's cell phone. The boy was already asleep but his cell phone was still on.

12 Later, the girl asked the boy: "Why don't you turn your cell phone off at night?"

13 The boy answered: "I'm afraid that if you need anything at night and aren't able to find me, you'll worry."

14 The girl finally married the boy.

15 Later at night, do you turn off your cell phone?

的多么融洽,但女孩怎么也不肯嫁给他。在女孩心里,她永远也不会忘记前男友说过的话,还有关机的那个深夜。

10 女孩还是保持着整夜不关机的习惯,但却不再期待有铃声会响起。

11 一天夜里,女孩身染急症,慌乱之中把本想拨给父母的电话拨到了新男友那里。男孩早已睡下,但手机还开着。

12 后来,女孩问那个男孩:"为什么深夜还不关机?"

13 男孩说:"我怕夜里万一你有事却找不到我,会心慌。"

14 女孩最终嫁给了这个男孩。

15 夜深了,你的手机关了吗?

阅读无障碍

cell phone 手机

turn off 关机

article [ˈɑːtɪk(ə)l] n. 文章

message [ˈmesɪdʒ] n. 短信

communication [kəmjuːnɪˈkeɪʃ(ə)n] n. 交流

habit [ˈhæbɪt] n. 习惯

shut down 关机

alert [əˈlɜːt] adj. 警惕

gap [gæp] n. 隔阂

revive [rɪˈvaɪv] n. 恢复

subscriber [səbˈskraɪbə] n. 用户

get along 相处

refuse [rɪˈfjuːz] v. 拒绝

get marry 结婚

remember [rɪ'membə] v. 记得

ring [rɪŋ] n. 铃声

fluster ['flʌstə] n. 惊慌失措

asleep [ə'sliːp] adj. 睡着的

afraid [ə'freɪd] v. 害怕

finally ['faɪnəlɪ] adj. 最终

 极品佳句背诵

1. This habit has been with her ever since she bought the phone.
   自从她买了手机以后就一直保持着这个习惯。

2. The next day, the boy asked the girl to leave her cell phone on at night because when he needed to find her and could not, he would be worried.
   第二天，男孩希望女孩以后晚上不要关机，因为当他想念女孩的时候却找不到她心里会很不安。

3. The girl knew that her love has just been turned off.
   于是女孩知道，她的爱情已经关机。

What Love Means to Kids
孩子眼中的爱

带着问题去阅读

1. 孩子眼中的爱是简单还是深刻？
2. 你最欣赏怎样的爱？
3. 看到孩子说的这些话你会会心一笑吗？

美文欣赏

1 A group of professional people posed this question to a group of 4 to 8 year-olds: "What does love mean?" The answers they got were broader and deeper than anyone could have imagined. See what you think.

2 "When my grandmother got arthritis, she couldn't bend over and paint her toenails anymore. So my grandfather does it for her all the time, even when his hands got arthritis too. That's love." — Rebecca, age 8

3 "When someone loves you, the way they say your name is different. "You know

译文

1 一组专业人士向一群 4 到 8 岁的孩子提出了这个问题：“爱是什么？”他们给出的答案比其他人所能想像的更广泛更深刻。看看你能想到什么。

2 "当我的奶奶得了关节炎，她不能弯下腰涂指甲油，所以我的爷爷一直帮她做这件事，即使他的手也得了关节炎。这就是爱。" ——瑞贝卡，8 岁

3 "当有人爱上你时，他们呼唤你名字的方式也会不

that your name is safe in their mouth." — Billy, age 4

4 "Love is when you go out to eat and give somebody most of your French fries without making them give you any of theirs." — Chris, age 6

5 "Love is when someone hurts you. And you get so mad but you don't yell at them because you know it would hurt their feelings." — Samantha, age 6

6 "Love is what makes you smile when you're tired." — Terri, age 4

7 "Love is when my mommy makes coffee for my daddy and she takes a sip before giving it to him, to make sure the taste is OK." — Danny, age 7

8 "Love is what's in the room with you at Christmas if you stop opening presents and listen." — Bobby, age 5

9 "Love is hugging. Love is kissing. Love is saying no." — Patty, age 8

10 "When you tell someone something bad about yourself and you're scared they won't love you anymore. But then you get surprised because not only do they still love you, they love you even more." — Matthew, age 7

11 "There are two kinds of love. Our love. God's love. But God makes both

同。你知道你的名字在他们嘴里很安全。"——比利，4岁

4 "爱是当你出去吃饭时，把你大部分的薯条都给了某人，而没有让他们给你什么。"——克里斯，6岁

5 "爱是当某人伤你心时，而且你很生气，但你没有冲他大声呵责，因为你知道这会伤害他的感情。"—萨曼莎，6岁

6 "爱是当你疲倦时能让你微笑的东西"。——特里，4岁

7 "爱是当我妈妈为我爸爸煮咖啡时，在递给他之前都要尝一小口，以确定味道是否合适。"——丹尼，7岁

8 "爱是在圣诞节的时候，停下拆礼物的动作，静心聆听到的与你共处一室的气息。"——鲍比，5岁

9 "爱是拥抱，爱是亲吻，爱是说不。"——拍迪，8岁

10 "当你告诉某人你的一些坏事，并且害怕他们会不再爱你，但是你惊喜地发现他们不但还爱你，而且更爱你了。"——马修，7岁

11 "有两种爱。我们的爱。上帝的爱。但上帝赋予

kinds of them." — Jenny, age 4

12 "Love is when you tell a guy you like his shirt, then he wears it everyday." — Noelle, age 7

13 "Love is like a little old woman and a little old man who are still friends even after they know each other so well." — Tommy, age 6

14 "During my piano recital, I was on a stage and scared. I looked at all the people watching me and saw my daddy waving and smiling. He was the only one doing that. I wasn't scared anymore." — Cindy, age 8

15 "My mommy loves me more than anybody. You don't see anyone else kissing me to sleep at night." — Clare, age 5

16 "Love is when mommy sees daddy smelly and sweaty and still says he is handsomer than Robert Redford." — Chris, age 8

17 "Love is when your puppy licks your face even after you left him alone all day." — Mary Ann, age 4

18 "I know my older sister loves me because she gives me all her old clothes and has to go out and buy new ones." — Lauren, age 4

我们这两种爱。"——简妮，4岁

12 "爱是当你告诉一个男孩你喜欢他的衬衫，于是他天天穿着它。"——诺尔，7岁

13 "爱就像一位小老太太和一位小老头子，即使他们彼此非常了解但仍然是朋友。"——汤米，6岁

14 "在我的钢琴演奏会上，我站在舞台上非常害怕。我看着那些盯着我的人，发现我爸爸在向我招手和微笑，他是唯一一这么做的人，我就不再害怕了。"——辛迪，8岁

15 "我妈妈比其他人都爱我，因为你再找不到其他人会在晚上临睡前亲吻我。"——克莱尔，5岁

16 "爱是当妈妈看到爸爸满身臭汗的时候仍然说他比罗伯特·莱德福德还帅。"——克里斯，8岁

17 "爱是即使你让你的小狗孤独一整天，它还是会舔你的脸。"——玛丽安，4岁

18 "我知道我的姐姐很爱我，因为她给了我她所有的旧衣服，自己还得出去再买新的。"——劳伦，4岁

19 "When you love somebody, your *eyelashes* go up and down and little stars come out of you." — Karen, age 7

19 "当你爱上某人时，你的眼睛就会像天上的小星星一样，一闪一闪亮晶晶" ——凯伦，7 岁

20 "You really shouldn't say 'I love you' unless you mean it. But if you mean it, you should say it a lot. People *forget*." — Jessica, age 8

20 "你真的不应该说'我爱你'，除非你是真心诚意的。但要是你真心诚意的去爱一个人，你必须经常说。人们总是忘记这一点。"——杰西卡，8 岁

阅读无障碍

professional [prə'feʃənəl] *adj.* 职业的

pose [pəuz] *v.* 提出

broad [brɔ:d] *adj.* 广泛的

deep [di:p] *adj.* 深刻的

imagine [ɪ'mædʒɪn] *v.* 想像

arthritis [ɑ:'θraɪtɪs] *n.* 关节炎

toenail ['təuneɪl] *n.* 脚趾甲

grandfather ['græn(d)fɑ:ðə] *n.*（外）祖父

feeling ['fi:lɪŋ] *n.* 感情

hug [hʌg] *v.* 拥抱

surprised [sə'praɪzd] *adj.* 感到惊讶的

everyday ['evrɪdeɪ] *adj.* 每天的

recital [rɪ'saɪtəl] *n.* 独奏会

watch [wɒtʃ] *v.* 观看，注视

anymore [enɪ'mɔ:] *adv.* 不再

smelly ['smelɪ] *adj.* 发出难闻气味的

sweaty ['swetɪ] *adj.* 浑身出汗的

lick [lɪk] *v.* 舔

eyelash ['aɪlæʃ] *n.* 睫毛

forget [fə'get] *v.* 忘记

极品佳句背诵

1. Love is when someone hurts you. And you get so mad but you don't yell at them because you know it would hurt their feelings.

爱是当某人伤你的心时，而且你很生气，但你没有冲他大声呵责，因为你知道这会伤害他的感情。

2. Love is what makes you smile when you're tired.

爱是当你疲倦时能让你微笑的东西。

3. Love is when your puppy licks your face even after you left him alone all day.

爱是即使你让你的小狗孤独一整天，它还是会舔你的脸。

Of Love
论爱情

带着问题去阅读

1. 你对爱情抱有怎样的态度？
2. 你赞同作者对爱情的看法吗？
3. 爱和情一样吗？

美文欣赏

1 Love is a vine that grows into our hearts.

2 The stage is more beholding to love, than the life of man. For as to the stage, love is ever matter of comedies, and now and then of tragedies; but in life it doth much mischief; sometimes like a siren, sometimes like a fury.

3 You may observe that amongst all the great and worthy persons (whereof the memory remained, either ancient or recent) there is not one, that hath been transported

译文

1 爱是生长在我们心里的藤蔓。

2 舞台上的爱情要远比生活中的爱情美好得多。在舞台上，爱情永远都是喜剧的题材，也不时成为悲剧的内容。但在人生中，爱情时而有如美艳的妖女，时而有如复仇的女神，惹是生非，招灾致祸。

3 值得注意的是，所有古今伟大而尊贵的人物（无论是古人、今人，只要是其英名永铭于人类记忆中的），还没

to the mad degree of love: which shows that great spirits, and great business, do keep out this weak passion. You must except, nevertheless, Marcus Antonius, the half partner of the empire of Rome, and Appius Claudius, the decimvir and lawgiver; whereof the former was indeed a voluptuous man, and inordinate; but the latter was an austere and wise man: and therefore it seems (though rarely) that love can find entrance, not only into an open heart, but also into a heart well fortified, if watch be not well kept.

4 It is a strange thing, to note the excess of this passion, and how it braves the nature, and value of things, by this; that the speaking in a perpetual hyperbole, is comely in nothing but in love.

5 Neither is it merely in the phrase; for whereas it hath been well said, that the arch-flatterer, with whom all the petty flatterers have intelligence, is a man's self; certainly the lover is more. For there was never proud man thought so absurdly well of himself, as the lover doth of the person loved; and therefore it was well said, that it is impossible to love, and to be

有一个会在爱情中被诱至冲昏头脑的程度，可见伟大的人物和伟大的事业的确与这种孱弱之情毫不沾边。然而，有两个必须视为例外的事，一是曾为罗马帝国两个合伙统治者之一的马库斯·安东尼奥斯，还有就是作为十大执政官之一和拟订法典的阿皮尔斯·克劳迪亚斯。前者确是一个好色之徒，放纵无度；然而后者却是一个严肃多谋的人。所以，虽然不多见，但看起来，爱情不但会对不设防之心长驱直入，即或对严阵以待之心，也照样随进随驻，如果把守稍有松弛的话。

4 显而易见的是，看这种情欲之放纵，及其不顾事情就里和意义而肆意妄为的结果，真是触目惊心。就此而言，浮夸诡媚的词令仅仅适用于谈情说爱。

5 这不仅是在言论上如此，因为一直都有这样一个很有见地的说法，说人主要吹嘘的是自己，但情人要算例外。情人眼里出西施，再自大的人也都不会夸张至此。所以，有人很精辟地说过："人在爱情中不会聪明。"这种缺点并非只有外人可见，并非恋爱对象

wise. Neither doth this weakness appear to others only, and not to the party loved; but to the loved most of all, except the love be reciproque.

6 For it is a true rule, that love is ever rewarded, either with the reciproque, or with an inward and secret contempt.

7 By how much the more, men ought to beware of this passion, which loseth not only other things, but itself!

8 As for the other losses, the poet's relation doth well figure them: that he that preferred Helena, quitted the gifts of Juno and Pallas. For whosoever esteemeth too much of amorous affection, quitteth both riches and wisdom.

9 This passion hath his floods, in very times of weakness; which are great prosperity, and great adversity; though this latter hath been less observed: both which times kindle love, and make it more fervent, and therefore show it to be the child of folly. They do best, who if they cannot but admit love, yet make it keep quarters; and sever it wholly from their serious affairs, and actions, of life; for if it check once with business, it troubleth men's fortunes, and maketh men, that they can no ways be true to their own ends.

看不见——除非恋爱双方也在爱着对方。

6 铁定的规律是，爱情所得到的回报，从来都是要么得到回爱，要么得到对方内心隐隐地轻蔑。

7 因此，人们更应小心对待这种情欲，它不但使人失去其它的东西，连爱情自己也保不住。

8 至于其他方面的损失，诗人的诗史刻画的极好，说那个喜欢海伦的人放弃了朱诺和帕拉斯的礼物。凡是沉迷于爱情的人就会丢弃财富和智慧。

9 每当人处于脆弱状态时，即最亨通和最受挫时，这种情欲就泛滥成灾（虽然人在最受挫时也有此问题是一直较少人注意的）。这两种状态都在引燃爱火并使其热烈，因此可见，爱情是愚昧之子。但有些人处理得极好，当他们非爱不可的时候，就予以节制，并使之与其重大任务和人生主旨彻底分离，因为爱情一旦掺和到正事上，就会破坏人的运气，使人再也无法持守自己既定的目标。

10 There is in man's nature, a secret inclination and motion, towards love of others, which if it be not spent upon some one or a few, doth naturally spread itself towards many, and maketh men become humane and charitable; as it is seen sometime in friars.

11 Nuptial love maketh mankind; friendly love perfecteth it; but wanton love corrupteth, and embaseth it.

10 人本性中有一种深藏的主动爱人的倾向和动机，若无具体对象得以倾注，它便会撒向大众，并使人变得仁厚而慈善，正如有时在天主教修道士身上所见到的情形那样。

11 夫妻之爱，使人类繁衍；朋友之爱，给人以帮助。荒淫纵欲的爱，却只会让人堕落自我毁灭！

阅读无障碍

behold [bɪˈhəʊld] *adj.* 欣赏的
siren [ˈsaɪrən] *n.* 性感妖女
fury [ˈfjʊərɪ] *n.* 复仇女神
amongst [əˈmʌŋst] *prep.* 相互间，彼此
keep out 远离
passion [ˈpæʃən] *n.* 强烈的感情
perpetual [pəˈpetʃʊəl] *adj.* 永久的
hyperbole [haɪˈpɜːbəlɪ] *n.* 夸张法
merely [ˈmɪəlɪ] *adv.* 仅仅
contempt [kənˈtempt] *n.* 轻视，轻蔑
beware [bɪˈweə] *v.* 谨防

amorous [ˈæmərəs] *adj.* 表示爱情的
adversity [ədˈvɜːsɪtɪ] *n.* 逆境
inclination [ɪnkləˈneɪʃən] *n.* 爱好、倾向
motion [ˈməʊʃən] *n.* 手势、动作
humane [hjuːˈmeɪn] *adj.* 仁爱的
charitable [ˈtʃærɪtəbl] *adj.* 行善的
mankind [mænˈkaɪnd] *n.* 人类
perfect [ˈpɜːfɪkt] *v.* 使完美
wanton [ˈwɒntən] *adj.* 蛮横的

极品佳句背诵

1. For as to the stage, love is ever matter of comedies, and now and then of tragedies; but in life it doth much mischief; sometimes like a siren, sometimes like a fury.
   在舞台上，爱情永远都是喜剧的题材，也不时成为悲剧的内容。但在

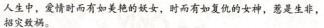

人生中，爱情时而有如美艳的妖女，时而有如复仇的女神，惹是生非，招灾致祸。

2. For it is a true rule, that love is ever rewarded, either with the reciproque, or with an inward and secret contempt.

铁定的规律是，爱情所得到的回报，从来都是要么得到回爱，要么得到对方内心隐隐地轻蔑。

3. Nuptial love maketh mankind; friendly love perfecteth it; but wanton love corrupteth, and embaseth it.

夫妻之爱，使人类繁衍；朋友之爱，给人以帮助。荒淫纵欲的爱，却只会让人堕落自我毁灭！

My One and Only
我的惟一

带着问题去阅读

1. 你曾经暗恋过一个人吗？
2. 你和你的初恋是怎么认识的？
3. 有没有一个人在你心目中留下了永恒的记忆？

美文欣赏

1 It was all started when I was in high school; I still remember my love one. I am not sure if it is puppy love or first love, but I know deep inside my heart that I still remember him.

2 At first we were bus mate and schoolmate too. We still didn't know each other before, but later on when I was still in front of him in the bus, he used to talk and tease me, which makes me angry with him. I used to say that I hate him but later on... I only eat my words. One day when

译文

1 所有的一切都始于我的高中时代，直到现在我仍记得我爱的那个他。我不能确定那是孩子间不成熟的恋情，还是我的初恋，但我知道在我的内心深处，我始终无法忘却他。

2 一开始，我们只是同乘一辆车的车友，同学。之前，我们互不相识。但是，后来，在公共汽车上，我坐在他的前面，他经常拿话题取笑我，这使我极为恼怒。我常说我痛恨他，但是后来我食言

my best friends wanted to see what I wrote in my diary, I was reading it in the bus and without noticing the guy whom I hate was sitting back of me with his buddies. He was peeping and reading the things what I wrote in the diary. I looked sharply at him and put the book down, then my friend who was in front of me that she was read what wrote there love is BOG, BOG, BOG in my heart. He was hearing it and suddenly without my knowledge he stood and snatched the diary from me! Whew! What he did was to read the book so loudly where everything was written there about love! Goodness! I was so shocked that I was screaming just to get it back. I couldn't believe it, because he was the most intelligent student in my school and he was the representative of our school too. Then after the bus dropped me to my house there felt that I was so flushing hotly that my checks were red! There, I realized that I have a crush on him!

3 Sports date came, and he was the champion for C group boys for running. Whew! Wow! I was really amazed when he runs, because he always comes 1st in running and he runs like a wind. That day I felt more feelings for him. I used to write him always in my diary, but mostly he always went to another because of interschool quiz.

了。一天，我的好朋友想看看我平时都写了些什么，我在汽车上读起我本子上写的东西。当然，我不知道我非常痛恨的那个男孩和他的一群兄弟就坐在我的后面。他偷看我写的内容，当时，我用犀利地眼神看着他，赶快把本子放下。这时，坐在我前面的好朋友对我说她读完我写的东西，她说在我心中把爱情比作"泥潭"。那个男孩听到这些话，突然站起身来把我的本子抢走了。天呀，他大声地朗读着我所写的内容，本子上写的内容全都是关于爱情的！我尖叫着把我的东西抢回来，我真的不敢相信，因为他是全校最聪明的学生，是我们学校的学生代表。汽车停下后，我赶忙奔到家中，我害羞地直发热，脸颊也变得通红！那时我意识到我有些迷恋他。

3 体育竞赛的时刻到来了，他获得了 C 组男生的冠军！他经常赢得赛跑比赛冠军，我很惊叹他的跑步速度，风驰电掣。那天，我对他又多了一些感觉。我还会常在日记里写到他，但他经常不在学校，因为他经常参加一些校际竞赛。

4 I cried that time, because I was missing him so much, that I wish one day he'll like me too. Then one day I heard he likes me! My god, I nearly faint! Rumors spread that in the bus we always fights for simple things like teasing, because I used to call him NUTCRACKER which makes him so mad at me, and I always teased him for his pimples and about his using FACIAL cleanser which made my whole bus mates burst out laughing, and he was blushing, and then one fine day the rumors spread that we both are loving each other! Whenever we cross our paths we just look each other casually, but my hearts beats fast because he looks at me so intensely which makes my hearts tremble. I used to be always so naughty that time. One day I decided to ask my friend to write a love letter in language of German I loved, since we both are different nation.

5 My friend wrote it, and in the bus I asked him to read the letter for me. He read it and explained what was written, and I know the last word written there was just I love you, but he told me that the last words means "I love you" which makes me blushed!

6 One day, I heard that he likes another girl which makes my heart break! In the bus, I used to make him jealous

4 有一次，因为太想念他，我哭了起来，我真的希望有那么一天他会喜欢我。一天，当我听别人说他喜欢我时，我几乎晕过去了。以前，大家常说我俩总为一些小事，比如相互讥讽而在汽车上大动干戈。我常常叫他"坚果钳"，这使他气愤不已，我常常取笑他因为脸上的粉刺而用洗面奶，这使得全车的人听后都捧腹大笑，他简直就是羞红了脸。突然有一天，却传出我们彼此喜欢对方！不论什么时候穿过街头，我们也只是偶尔地相互看看。我的心在他热烈的目光下跳得很快，那时，我很调皮，有一天，我决定让我的朋友用我喜欢的德语写一封情书，因为，我们俩不是来自一个国家。

5 我的朋友写好了这封情书了。在车上，我让他给我念，他边读边给我解释情书的内容，我知道情书上最后写的是"我爱你"。他念到那儿时，告诉我，那几个字的意思是"我爱你"。这句话使我的脸颊绯红！

6 一天，听别人说，他喜欢了别的女孩，我的心都快碎了。在车上，我故意和别

of me by saying that I have a boyfriend. I made it, and he was jealous! Then examination came. I was really broken-heart when I saw him waiting for a girl in the gate! I cried, because of his caring for dating girl. Five days before the exam came, he told me in the bus that he's going to his country! My god! I can't believe it. He's leaving me! The last day in the school and in the bus, I took a picture of him in my own camera! And when he went down in the bus I told bye… and then I still can't believe that he's gone.

7 To tell you we both are in the same bus, same school, we both are born on the same year. That was HAMLET! By Shakespeare I was the dancer, and he's Hamlet. I can never forget my one, my only one. He dreamed about me so many times! He even included the poem A KISS IN THE RAIN in his dream and we both composed a poem for each other, I composed a poem for him ONLY YOU, and he composed a poem for me SHE IS MINE. I still can't forget the happy unforgettable moments once we shared! Oh, nostalgia…

人说我已经有了男朋友，故意让他嫉妒，我成功了，他真的是极为嫉妒。考试的日子来临了，我看到他在门口正等着和一个女孩约会。我哭了，因为他开始在意别的女孩了。

考试前的五天，在车上，他告诉我他要回国了，我几乎不相信自己的耳朵。最后一天，在校园里、在车上，我用自己的相机给他拍了好多照片。他乘上了回国的汽车，我向他挥手告别，我不敢相信他离开了我。

7 我们以前坐同一班汽车，我们在同一所学校读书，我们同年出生，简直就是莎士比亚笔下的《哈姆雷特》，我便是那个舞女，他就是哈姆雷特。我永远无法忘记我心爱的人，我的唯一。他甚至在梦中梦到《雨中吻》这首诗，我们彼此都给对方写了一首情诗，我为他写了《你是唯一》，他为我写了《她是我的》。我仍然无法忘记我们一起度过的愉快的、令人难忘的时光！怀旧的思绪啊……

阅读无障碍

schoolmate['sku:lmeɪt] *n.* 同学，校友

tease [ti:z] *v.* 取笑，戏弄

guy [gaɪ] *n.* 家伙

buddy ['bʌdɪ] *n.* 伙伴，好朋友

peep [pi:p] *v.* 窥视，偷看

snatch [snætʃ] *v.* 抢夺，抢走

intelligent [ɪn'telɪdʒ(ə)nt] *adj.* 聪明的

flush [flʌʃ] *v.*(脸) 发红

crush [krʌʃ] *v.* 迷恋

amazed [ə'meɪzd] *adj.* 吃惊的，惊奇的

quiz [kwɪz] *n.* 知识竞赛

mad [mæd] *adj.* 疯狂的

pimple ['pɪmp(ə)l] *n.* 粉刺，小脓包

naughty ['nɔ:tɪ] *adj.* 淘气的，顽皮的

jealous ['dʒeləs] *adj.* 嫉妒的

Shakespeare ['ʃekspɪr] 莎士比亚（英国剧作家）

compose [kəm'pəuz] *v.* 写诗

poem ['pəʊɪm] *n.* 诗

unforgettable [ʌnfə'getəb(ə)l] *adj.* 难忘的

nostalgia [nɒ'stældʒə] *n.* 怀旧之情

极品佳句背诵

1. I am not sure if it is puppy love or first love, but I know deep inside my heart that I still remember him.

   我不能确定那是孩子间不成熟的恋情，还是我的初恋，但我知道在我的内心深处，我始终无法忘却他。

2. He even included the poem A KISS IN THE RAIN in his dream and we both composed a poem for each other, I composed a poem for him ONLY YOU, and he composed a poem for me SHE IS MINE.

   他甚至在梦中梦到《雨中吻》这首诗，我们彼此都给对方写了一首情诗，我为他写了《你是唯一》，他为我写了《她是我的》。

3. I still can't forget the happy unforgettable moments once we shared!

   我仍然无法忘记我们一起度过的愉快的、令人难忘的时光！

Say Your Love Bravely
勇敢说出你的爱

带着问题去阅读

1. 如果你是那位男孩的话你会怎样做?
2. 如果你是那位女孩的话你又会怎样做?
3. 你能勇敢说出你的爱吗?

美文欣赏

译文

1 There was once a guy who suffered from cancer, a cancer that can't be cured. He was 18 years old and he could die anytime. All his life, he was stuck in his house being taken cared by his mother. He never went outside but he was sick of staying home and wanted to go out for once. So he asked his mother and she gave him permission.

2 He walked down his block and found a lot of stores. He passed a CD store and looked through the front door for a second as he walked. He stopped and

1 曾经有一个男孩得了一种无法治愈的癌症。年仅18岁的他随时都可能因为病发死去。从小到大,他被困在家中,由母亲照顾。他厌倦了大门不出的生活,他想走出家门一次。他征求了母亲的意见,母亲同意了。

2 他沿着他们的街区走着,沿路有许多商店。当他路过一家CD店时他朝它的前门望了一下。他停了下来,并重

went back to look into the store. He saw a beautiful girl about his age and he knew it was *love at first sight*. He opened the door and walked in, not looking at anything else but her. He walked closer and closer until he was finally at the front desk where she sat.

3 She looked up and asked, "Can I help you?"

4 She smiled and he thought it was the most beautiful smile he has ever seen before and wanted to kiss her right there.

5 He said, "Uh... Yeah... Umm... I would like to buy a CD."

6 He picked one out and gave her money for it.

7 "Would you like me to wrap it for you?" she asked, smiling her *cute* smile again.

8 He *nodded* and she went to the back. She came back with the *wrapped* CD and gave it to him. He took it and walked out of the store.

9 He went home and *from then on*, he went to that store every day and bought a CD, and she wrapped it for him. He took the CD home and put it in his *closet*. He was still too shy to ask her out and he really wanted to but he couldn't. His mother found out about this and told him to just ask her. So the next day, he took all

新走回去朝商店里看了看。他看见一个漂亮的、年纪和他相仿的女孩，他明白他遇到了传说中的一见钟情。他打开门走了进去，眼中只有那个女孩。他一点一点走近她，最终走到了她所坐的桌子前。

3 她抬头看了看，问道："我能为你做什么？"

4 她笑了笑，男孩觉得这是他所看到过的最美丽的笑容，让他都想立刻亲吻这个女孩。

5 他说，"嗯……嗯……我想买一张CD。"

6 他随手取出一张CD并且把钱付给了女孩。

7 "需要我把它包起来吗？"女孩问道，再次露出了她那可爱的笑容。

8 男孩点了点头，女孩向后储藏室走去，然后她拿着已经包好的CD出来递给了男孩。男孩拿着CD走出了商店。

9 他回了家，从那以后他每天都去那家商店买一张CD，并且每次女孩都帮他包好。他把CD带回家放在他的壁橱里。他一直不敢约女孩出来，他真的很想，但是他不敢。他的母亲知道这件事情后鼓励他去约那个女孩。第二

his courage and went to the store as usual. He bought a CD like he did every day and once again she went to the back of the store and came back with it wrapped. He took it and when she wasn't looking, he left his phone number on the desk and ran out...

10 RRRRRING!!!

11 One day the phone rang, and the mother picked it up and said, "Hello?"

12 It was the girl!!! The mother started to cry and said, "You don't know? He passed away yesterday..."

13 The line was quiet except for the cries of the boy's mother. Later in the day, the mother went into the boy's room because she wanted to remember him. She thought she would start by looking at his clothes. So she opened the closet.

14 She was face to face with piles and piles and piles of unopened CDs. She was surprised to find all these CDs and she picked one up and sat down on the bed and she started to open one. Inside, there was a CD and as she took it out of the wrapper, out fell a piece of paper. The mother picked it up and started to read it. It said: Hi... I think U R really cute. Do u wanna go out

天，他鼓足了勇气，像往常一样去了那家商店。他像平常那样买了一张 CD，女孩还是同样走到商店的后储藏室，然后拿着已经包裹好的 CD 回来。他接过 CD，趁她不注意时将自己的电话号码放在柜台上，然后跑了出去……

10 叮铃铃！！！

11 有一天电话响了，男孩的母亲接起了电话并问道："你找谁？"

12 是那个女孩！！！男孩的母亲哭着说道："难道你不知道吗？他昨天已经去世了……"

13 电话两端安静了，只留下男孩母亲的哭泣声。那天晚些时候，男孩的母亲走进了男孩的房间因为她很想念她的儿子。她想应该从儿子生前穿过的衣服开始，于是她打开了儿子的衣橱。

14 她看到了一堆又一堆没有打开的 CD。发现这些 CD 她很吃惊，就拿起一张坐到男孩的床上打开了它，里面有一张 CD，当她把 CD 从包装纸里取出来时，一张纸条掉了出来。男孩的母亲捡起了那张纸条。上面写着：你好……我觉得你的很可爱。你想和

with me? Love, Jocelyn.

15 The mother was deeply moved and opened another CD...

16 Again there was a piece of paper. It said: Hi... I think U R really cute. Do u wanna go out with me? Love, Jocelyn.

17 Love is... when you've had a huge fight but then decide to put aside your egos, hold hands and say, "I Love You."

我约会吗？爱你的，约瑟琳。

15 男孩的母亲被深深地感动了，她打开了另外一张CD……

16 同样有一张纸条在里面。上面写着：你好……我觉得你真的很可爱。你想和我约会吗？爱你的，约瑟琳。

17 爱是……当你经历一番激烈的思想斗争之后最终决定放下你的自尊心，握紧双手，勇敢说出："我爱你。"

阅读无障碍

suffer ['sʌfə] v. 患，受折磨

cure [kjʊə] v. 治愈

sick of 厌倦

for once 一次

permission [pəˈmɪʃ(ə)n] n. 同意，许可，允许

a lot of 许多的

love at first sight 一见钟情

cute [kjuːt] adj. 可爱的

nod [nɒd] v. 点头

wrap [ræp] v. 包

from then on 从那时起

closet ['klɒzɪt] n. 壁橱

as usual 像往常一样

once again 再次

face to face 面对着

surprised [səˈpraɪzd] adj. 感到惊讶的

wrapper ['ræpə] n. 包装纸

deeply ['diːplɪ] adv. 深刻地；浓浓地；

a piece of 一张，一片

put aside 放下

极品佳句背诵

1. He saw a beautiful girl about his age and he knew it was love at first sight.
   他看见一个漂亮的、年纪和他相仿的女孩，他明白他遇到了传说中的一见钟情。

2. She smiled and he thought it was the most beautiful smile he has ever seen before and wanted to kiss her right there.

    她笑了笑，男孩觉得这是他所看到过的最美丽的笑容，让他都想立刻亲吻这个女孩。

3. Love is... when you've had a huge fight but then decide to put aside your egos, hold hands and say, "I Love You."

    爱是……当你经历一番激烈的思想斗争之后最终决定放下你的自尊心，握紧双手，勇敢说出："我爱你。"

Love Is Just a Thread
爱只是一根线

带着问题去阅读

1. 你对"爱情就像是生活中被子里的一根线"怎么看？
2. 你认为什么是真爱？
3. 你父母之间是什么样的爱？

1　Sometimes I really doubt whether there is love between my parents.

2　Every day they are very busy trying to earn money in order to pay the high tuition for my brother and me.

3　They don't act in the romantic ways that I read in books or I see on TV. In their opinion, "I love you" is too luxurious for them to say. Sending flowers to each other on Valentine's Day is even more out of the question.

4　Finally my father has a bad temper. When he's very tired from the hard work, it is easy for him to lose his temper.

1　有时候，我真的怀疑父母之间是否有真爱。

2　他们天天忙于赚钱，为我和弟弟支付高昂的学费。

3　他们从未像我在书中读到，或在电视中看到的那样互诉衷肠。他们认为"我爱你"太奢侈，很难说出口。更不用说在情人节送花这样的事了。

4　我父亲的脾气非常坏。经过一天的劳累之后，他经常会发脾气。

5 One day, my mother was sewing a quilt. I silently sat down beside her and looked at her.

6 "Mom, I have a question to ask you," I said after a while.

7 "What?" she replied, still doing her work.

8 "Is there love between you and dad?" I asked her in a very low voice.

9 My mother stopped her work and raised her head with surprise in her eyes. She didn't answer immediately. Then she bowed her head and continued to sew the quilt.

10 I was very worried because I thought I had hurt her.

11 I was in a great embarrassment and I didn't know what I should do. But at last I heard my mother say the following words:

12 "Susan," she said thoughtfully, "Look at this thread. Sometimes it appears, but most of it disappears in the quilt. The thread really makes the quilt strong and durable. If life is a quilt, then love should be a thread. It can hardly be seen anywhere or anytime, but it's really there. Love is inside."

13 I listened carefully but I couldn't understand her until the next spring.

14 At that time, my father suddenly

5 一天，母亲正在缝被子，我静静地坐在她旁边看着她。

6 过了一会，我说："妈妈，我想问你一个问题。"

7 "什么问题？"她一边继续缝着，一边回答道。

8 我低声地问道："你和爸爸之间有没有爱情啊？"

9 母亲突然停下了手中的活，满眼诧异地抬起头。她没有立即作答。然后低下头，继续缝被子。

10 我担心伤害了她。

11 我非常尴尬，不知道该怎么办。不过，后来我听见母亲说：

12 "苏珊，看看这些线。有时候，你能看得见，但是大多数都隐藏在被子里。这些线使被子坚固耐用。如果生活就像一床被子，那么爱就是其中的线。你不可能随时随地看到它，但是它却实实在在地存在着。爱是内在的。"

13 我仔细地听着，却无法明白她的话，直到来年的春天。

14 那时候，我父亲得了

got sick seriously. My mother had to stay with him in the hospital for a month.

15　When they returned from the hospital, they both looked very pale. It seemed both of them had a serious illness.

16　After they were back, every day in the morning and dusk, my mother helped my father walk slowly on the country road.

17　My father had never been so gentle. It seemed they were the most harmonious couple. Along the country road, there were many beautiful flowers, green grass and trees. The sun gently glistened through the leaves.

18　All of these made up the most beautiful picture in the world.

19　The doctor had said my father would recover in two months. But after two months he still couldn't walk by himself. All of us were worried about him.

20　"Dad, how are you feeling now?" I asked him one day.

21　"Susan, don't worry about me." he said gently. "To tell you the truth, I just like walking with your mom. I like this kind of life." Reading his eyes, I know he loves my mother deeply.

22　Once I thought love meant flowers, gifts and sweet kisses. But from this experience, I understand that love is

重病。母亲在医院里待了一个月。

15　当他们从医院回来的时候，都显得非常苍白。就像他们都得了一场重病一样。

16　他们回来之后，每天的清晨或黄昏，母亲都会搀扶着父亲在乡村的小路上漫步。

17　父亲从未如此温和过。他们就像是天作之合。在小路旁边，有许多美丽的野花、绿草和树木。阳光穿过树叶的缝隙，温柔地照射在地面上。

18　这一切形成了一幅世间最美好的画面。

19　医生说父亲将在两个月后康复。但是两个月之后，他仍然无法独立行走。我们都很为他担心。

20　有一天，我问他：“爸爸，你感觉怎么样？”

21　他温和地说：“苏珊，不用为我担心。跟你说吧，我喜欢与你妈妈一块散步的感觉。我喜欢这种生活。”从他的眼神里，我看得出他对母亲的爱之深刻。

22　我曾经认为爱情就是鲜花、礼物和甜蜜的亲吻。但是从那一刻起，我明白了，爱

just a thread in the quilt of our life. Love is inside, making life strong and warm.

情就像是生活中被子里的一根线。爱情就在里面，使生活变得坚固而温暖。

 阅读无障碍

tuition [tjuːˈɪʃən] *n.* 学费

romantic [rəʊˈmæntɪk] *adj.* 浪漫的

luxurious [lʌɡˈʒʊərɪəs] *adj.* 奢侈的

out of the question 毫无可能的

temper [ˈtempə] *n.* 脾气

lose one's temper 发脾气

sew [səʊ] *v.* 缝

quilt [kwɪlt] *n.* 被子

bow [baʊ] *v.* 低头

embarrassment [ɪmˈbærəsmənt] *n.* 尴尬

thoughtfully [ˈθɔːtfəlɪ] *adv.* 深思地

thread [θred] *n.* 线

durable [ˈdjʊərəbl] *adj.* 持久的

pale [peɪl] *adj.* 无力的

dusk [dʌsk] *n.* 黄昏

gentle [ˈdʒentl] *adj.* 温和的

harmonious [hɑːˈməʊnɪəs] *adj.* 和谐的

glisten [ˈɡlɪsn] *v.* 闪光

recover [rɪˈkʌvə] *v.* 复原

mean [miːn] *v.* 意思是

极品佳句背诵

1. If life is a quilt, then love should be a thread. It can hardly be seen anywhere or anytime, but it's really there. Love is inside.
   如果生活就像一床被子，那么爱就是其中的线。你不可能随时随地看到它，但是它却实实在在地存在着。爱是内在的。

2. Along the country road, there were many beautiful flowers, green grass and trees. The sun gently glistened through the leaves.
   在小路旁边，有许多美丽的野花、绿草和树木。阳光穿过树叶的缝隙，温柔地照射在地面上。

3. Love is just a thread in the quilt of our life. Love is inside, making life strong and warm.
   爱情就像是生活中被子里的一根线。爱情就在里面，使生活变得坚固而温暖。

The Last Relationship
曾经的一段恋情

带着问题去阅读

1. 你与你的另一半是怎么相识的？
2. 你和你的另一半经常吵架吗？
3. 当你们吵架后都是怎么解决的？

1 I remember the first time we met; you were so cute as can be and then we started to play fight then you sat on me.

2 You started to throw popcorn while I was going down the stairs and I came back to beat you up while you lay there.

3 I saw you again on Valentine's Day when I was a little shy, and didn't know to say.

4 I remember the first time I asked you to come to my house with your brother; at first you didn't want to because of my mother, father, and brother.

1 记得我们初次相遇时，你是那么的可爱。我们一起玩打仗，之后，你骑在我的身上。

2 看到我从楼梯走下你开始扔着爆米花，后来你躺在地上，我转身回去打了你。

3 再次见到你是在情人节的那天，我害羞得不知说什么。

4 记着第一次我邀请你和你的弟弟来我家做客，你不愿来，因为怕见我的父母和弟弟。

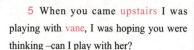

5 When you came upstairs I was playing with vane, I was hoping you were thinking –can I play with her?

6 While you were sitting on my couch changing channels on my TV, I was staring at you hoping you wouldn't catch me. Then we became all cool and started to play fight, you bit me and I bit you , and then we held each other a little tight.

7 Then I remember our first kiss; you were sitting on the chair I was in front of you and stood there.

8 But the moment had to last and you had to go and in my mind I was saying, "no, he can't go!"

9 Then on March the 3rd you asked me to be your girl and I replied yes and we became a couple; I was hoping there would be no trouble.

10 I always remember on a Sunday night you surprised me and said," I LOVE YOU." I asked you over and over and said don't play. I replied to you and said ,"I love you too always."

11 Then two month past, you said you wanted to leave so I said don't worry just stay calm. So later on, we were going our way, but sometimes we had our bad days.

5 你上楼时，我正在玩风信旗。我真希望你是这样想的：我能和你一起玩风信旗吧？

6 你坐在沙发上，调换着电视频道，我款款深情地望着你，却希望不要接触到你的目光。然后，我们冷静下来一起嬉戏打仗，你打我一下，我打你一下，我们彼此的心在慢慢靠近。

7 记得我们初吻的情景，你坐在椅子上，我站在你面前。

8 但是，时间无法停驻，你要走了，我在心里默念道："别，不要走。"

9 然后，3月3日那天，你请求我要我成为你的女朋友，我答应了你，很快我们成为出双入对的情侣。我希望我们的感情从此能一帆风顺。

10 那个星期天的晚上让我铭记终身。你对我说："我爱你。"我问了你千万次，并对你说不要和我开玩笑。最后，我对你答道："我爱你一辈子！"

11 两个月后，你说你想离开。我对你说不要担心，保持冷静。之后，我们又在一起了，但是我们会常常发生一些

12 It was about our 4th month we had planned a day so we went out, but we had a big argument and didn't know what to say.

13 Then the date finally came. You called to me a bitch, so I got up and walked away. I walked away and stood behind a wall then I just thought "God please don't let this relationship fall."

14 As a tear dropped from my eye, you walked by and said, "baby I'm sorry, please don't cry."

15 So finally we went home and you kissed me and I told you to go.

16 You made new friends and went out and do you know I sat there pissed, mad, and a kind of blue.

17 So then I finally told you, you don't need me and I don't need you.

18 So you said let's just take a break 1 month, 2 months then I felt like it went away.

19 Then after a while you called me that you miss me, you love me and you want me.

20 We talked for a while, I was being cold then you asked me again and I explained myself and then said no.

小口角，那些日子过得不大愉快。

12 第四个月的某一天，我们计划一起出去，但也就是那一天，我们吵得很厉害，彼此都不想说话。

13 那一天终于来临了。你骂我泼妇，我气愤地站起来转头走开。我站在一面墙后，祈祷："上帝呀，不要让我们的关系破裂。"

14 我的眼泪慢慢滑下，你走过来对我说，"宝贝，我错了，别哭了！"

15 最终，我俩一起回到家中，你亲吻了我，我对你下了逐客令。

16 你交了新朋友，并与我们一起出去玩，可你不知道我有多生气，我有多恼怒，我有多伤心。

17 最后，我对你说，你不需要我，我也不需要你了。

18 你只是说让我们暂时先分开吧，一个月，两个月过去了，我感觉爱已走远

19 一段时间后，你打电话对我说你想念我，你爱我，你需要我。

20 我态度冰冷地和你聊了一会儿，你又让我回到你身边，我解释说一切都不再可能了。

21 So after that I wrote about a guy who stole my heart away as we said goodbye, he went his way and I went mine and here I am today.

21 在那之后，我写到就是这个我与之分手的男孩偷走了我的心，我们分道扬镳，他走他的路，我走我的路；如今，我仍旧好好地生活着。

阅读无障碍

cute [kjuːt] *adj.* 可爱的
popcorn [ˈpɒpkɔːn] *n.* 爆米花
lie [laɪ] *v.* 躺
Valentine's Day 情人节
upstairs [ˌʌpˈsteəz] *adv.* 上楼，往楼上
vane [veɪn] *n.* 风信旗
channel [ˈtʃænl] *n.* 频道
stare [steə(r)] *v.* 凝视，盯着看
tight [taɪt] *adv.* 紧密地
couple [ˈkʌpl] *n.* 对，双，情侣

calm [kɑːm] *adj.* 平静的，镇定的
argument [ˈɑːgjumənt] *n.* 争论，争吵
date [deɪt] *n.* 约会
bitch [bɪtʃ] *n.* 坏女人＜俚＞婊子
relationship [rɪˈleɪʃnʃɪp] *n.* 关系
drop [drɒp] *v.* 落下，滴
pissed [pɪst] *adj.* 恼火的，厌烦的
mad [mæd] *adj.* 愤怒的，生气的
blue [bluː] *adj.* 沮丧的，忧郁的
break [breɪk] *n.* 中断，间断

极品佳句背诵

1. While you were sitting on my couch changing channels on my TV, I was staring at you hoping you wouldn't catch me.
   你坐在沙发上，调换着电视频道，我款款深情地望着你，却希望不要接触到你的目光。

2. Then we became all cool and started to play fight, you bit me and I bit you, and then we held each other a little tight.
   然后，我们冷静下来一起嬉戏打仗，你打我一下，我打你一下，我们彼此的心在慢慢靠近。

3. So after that I wrote about a guy who stole my heart away as we said goodbye, he went his way and I went mine and here I am today.
   在那之后，我写到就是这个我与之分手的男孩偷走了我的心，我们分道扬镳，他走他的路，我走我的路；如今，我仍旧好好地生活着。

Keeping the Passion of Love Alive 保持爱的激情

美文欣赏

译文

1　Young love is a flame; very pretty, often very hot and fierce, but still only light and flickering. The love of the older and disciplined heart is as coals, deep burning, unquenchable.

2　——Henry Ward Beecher, American clergyman

3　Imagine that you've decided to build a fire, perhaps while you're camping, or at home in your fireplace. You carefully choose the logs, the kindling, and after lighting a match to start the fire, you watch

1　年轻的爱是一团火焰；它美丽，时常伴随着炽热与激烈，但这种情感依然仅仅是昙花一现。成熟的爱与约束的心就像木炭，无法消除并且可以持久燃烧。

2　——亨利·沃德·比彻 美国牧师

3　想象一下你已经决定要生火，或许是在露营期间或者在家里的壁炉里，你仔细的挑选圆木和引火柴并且在点燃一根火柴开始生火后你会一直

over it until you're sure the fire is burning strongly and steadily. Then you sit back and enjoy the comforting warmth, the delightful play of the flames, the magical light. You don't need to be as vigilant about keeping the fire blazing, since it has enough fuel for now. But at some point, when you notice it's getting a little colder, or the light is growing dim, you realize that the fire needs your attention again. And so you rouse yourself from whatever you've been doing and add more wood, or adjust the position of the logs so that, once more, the flames can rise high.

4 Even if you've neglected the fire for a while, even if it appears to have died out, you see that the embers still radiate a deep, orange glow that can only be created by hours of extreme heat. The embers are deceptive, and they contain great power within their quiet light. Although by themselves they produce no flames, they can ignite a newly added piece of wood in seconds, suddenly rekindling the full force of the fire, transforming the dormant coals into a roaring blaze.

5 We can learn a lot about the passion between two lovers by thinking about what we intuitively know about building and maintaining a fire. When you first meet someone and fall in love, you carefully

照看着直到确定火已经强烈稳定地燃烧。然后你会坐下来享受那舒适的温暖，令人愉悦的火焰和神奇的火光。因为暂时已有足够的燃料，你不必警醒的来保持火的燃烧。但是，在某一时刻当你注意到周围变冷了，火光变弱时，你意识到你需要再次照看一下燃烧着的火。因此你放下正在做的任何事情去添加更多的木头或者调整圆木的位置，这样火焰就能够再次旺盛起来。

4 尽管火已经被你忽视了一段时间，尽管它看起来将要熄灭，你会看到燃烧的灰烬仍在发出深橙色的火光，这种火光只有在数小时极热的情况下才会产生。燃烧的灰烬具有欺骗性，它们微弱的火光内蕴含着强大的能量。尽管灰烬自身无法产生火焰，它们能够在短时间内再次引燃新添加进来的木头，并且引发火的最大威力，把静止的煤炭转换成咆哮的火焰。

5 通过思考我们直观上了解关于如何生火和保持其燃烧这一过程，我们能够了解到很多关于情侣之间爱的激情和与之类似的东西。当你一开

court and seduce him or her, adding the right amount of intimacy, the perfect amount of commitment until the fire of passion flares up between your hearts and your bodies. For awhile, this blaze burns brightly on its own and you grow accustomed to the joy it brings into your life. How lucky we are, you tell yourself, to have such a passionate relationship!

6 But one day, you realize there is less light, less heat between you and your mate, and that, in fact, it's been that way for some time. You don't feel the same intense degree of physical attraction, the same desire to unite, the same stimulation you once felt with each other. The passion is gone, you may conclude. I guess I've fallen out of love. This relationship is over.

7 How many people ask themselves, at this critical point in a love affair, if the fire of passion has died down simply because no one has been tending it, because no one has added the fuel necessary to keep it burning? How many people walk away from the smoking embers of their marriage, and make certain that the fire has died out, without noticing that the coals of love still contain enough

始遇到一个人并和他或她相爱时，你会仔细地向对方献殷勤，引诱对方，适当地提高你们之间的亲密度，许下完美的承诺，直到你们身心都燃起了激情之火。一段时间内，激情之火明亮地燃烧，你们逐渐习惯了激情之火带给你们生活带来的快乐。你们告诉自己，你们是如此的幸运能够拥有一个充满激情的爱人。

6 但是有一天你意识到你和恋人之间的激情变冷淡了。事实上，爱的激情在一段时间内本就是会变冷淡的。你感受不到与曾经相同的彼此强烈的身体吸引力，彼此相结合的欲望，彼此在一起时所感受到的兴奋。你会断定你们之间的激情消失了，你已经不爱对方了，你们之间的情侣关系结束了。

7 有多少人在爱的激情这方面问过自己，激情之火熄灭是否仅仅是因为没人照看它，没人添加燃料来保持其燃烧。有多少人在婚姻关系变得冷淡后就离婚了，他们确定激情之火已经熄灭，而没有注意到他们爱的燃料仍拥有足够的热量，如果他们再添次加燃料爱的余烬能够再次

heat to reignite into flames, if only they are given a chance?

8　Respect the fire of passion, the fire of love. Understand that to stay alive, it needs to be honored, to be cared for, to be tended as diligently as you would tend a fire you had built in the wilderness to help keep you warm and safe from harm. Feed the fire of your love with kindness, communication, appreciation and gratitude, and it will always blaze strong and brightly for you.

9　Barbara De Angelis, Ph.D.

点燃激情之火。

8　尊重激情之火，爱情之火。理解要保持爱的激情之火燃烧，你应该尊重它，关爱它，照顾它就像你照看在野外为取暖和保持安全而生起的火一样的勤勉。添加善良，沟通，欣赏和感激到你们的爱情之火中，你们的爱情之火将会燃烧的更加激烈和明亮。

9　芭芭拉.安吉丽思，博士

阅读无障碍

Pretty ['prɪtɪ] n. 漂亮的，优美的

fierce [fɪəs] adj. 凶猛的，猛烈的

flickering ['flɪkərɪŋ] adj. 闪烁的，忽隐忽现的

log [lɒg] n. 圆木

kindling ['kɪndlɪŋ] n. 引火柴

magical ['mædʒɪk(ə)l] adj. 神奇的

vigilant ['vɪdʒɪl(ə)nt] adj. 警惕的，警醒的

at some point 在某一时刻

dim [dɪm] adj. 暗淡的，昏暗的

die out 熄灭，消失

radiate ['reɪdɪeɪt] v. 辐射，流露

ember ['embə] n. 灰烬，余烬

deceptive [dɪ'septɪv] adj. 迷惑的，欺诈的

ignite [ɪg'naɪt] v. 点燃，燃烧

dormant ['dɔːm(ə)nt] adj. 静止的，休眠的

intuitively [ɪn'tjuːɪtɪvlɪ] adv. 直观地，直觉地

court [kɔːt] v. 求爱，向…献殷勤

seduce [sɪ'djuːs] v. 引诱，诱惑

awhile [ə'waɪl] adv. 一会儿，片刻

intense [ɪn'tens] adj. 强烈的，激烈的

极品佳句背诵

1. Young love is a flame; very pretty, often very hot and fierce, but still only light and flickering. The love of the older and disciplined heart is as coals, deep burning, unquenchable.

   年轻的爱是一团火焰；它美丽，时常伴随着炽热与激烈，但这种情感依然仅仅是昙花一现。成熟的爱与约束的心就像木炭，无法消除并且可以持久燃烧。

2. Understand that to stay alive, it needs to be honored, to be cared for, to be tended as diligently as you would tend a fire you had built in the wilderness to help keep you warm and safe from harm.

   理解要保持爱的激情之火燃烧，你应该尊重它，关爱它，照顾它就像你照看在野外为取暖和保持安全而生起的火一样的勤勉。

3. Feed the fire of your love with kindness, communication, appreciation and gratitude, and it will always blaze strong and brightly for you.

   添加善良，沟通，欣赏和感激到你们的爱情之火中，你们的爱情之火将会燃烧的更加激烈和明亮。